CHINA'S CHRISTIAN MARTYRS

CHINA'S CHRISTIAN MARTYRS

Paul Hattaway

MONARCH
BOOKS

Oxford, UK & Grand Rapids, Michigan

First published in the UK in 2007 by Monarch Books
(a publishing imprint of Lion Hudson plc),
Mayfield House, 256 Banbury Road, Oxford OX2 7DH.
Tel: +44 (0)1865 302750 Fax: +44 (0)1865 302757
Email: monarch@lionhudson.com
www.lionhudson.com

ISBN: 978-1-85424-762-9 (UK)
ISBN: 978-0-8254-6127-9 (USA)

Distributed by:
UK: Marston Book Services Ltd, PO Box 269,
Abingdon, Oxon OX14 4YN;
USA: Kregel Publications, PO Box 2607,
Grand Rapids, Michigan 49501

The text paper used in this book has been made from wood
independently certified as having come from sustainable forests.

British Library Cataloguing Data
A catalogue record for this book is available from
the British Library.

Printed and bound in Malta by Gutenberg Press.

DEDICATION

Dedicated to the thousands of China martyrs whose stories have never been recorded here on earth and to those who even today take part in the fellowship of Christ's sufferings. All glory be to the risen Jesus Christ, who is not only worth living for, but also worth dying for.

CHRISTIAN SOLIDARITY WORLDWIDE

Christian Solidarity Worldwide is a human rights charity which specialises in religious freedom, works on behalf of those persecuted for their Christian beliefs and promotes religious liberty for all.

CSW's guiding principle comes from Proverbs 31:8.

Speak up for those who cannot speak for themselves, for the rights of all that are destitute. Speak up and judge fairly; defend the rights of the poor and needy.

CSW's advocacy team is active in lobbying the UK and EU parliaments, the governments of the EU, the US government and administration and the UN, bringing human rights and religious freedom issues onto the political agenda of the international community. Countries of particular concern include Burma, India, China, North Korea, Colombia, Eritrea, Cuba, Pakistan, Nigeria, Indonesia, Iran and Somalia. CSW's Advocacy Officers travel to these areas to assess persecution climates firsthand, meet with government officials and international partners and speak to former prisoners and victims of religious persecution. Findings are then compiled into briefings and reports which are used for lobbying purposes.

CSW also works hard to raise awareness of religious persecution among Christians in the UK. The charity's team of speakers travels around the country encouraging UK Christians to stand in solidarity with persecuted Christians all over the world.

CSW also produces a number of publications, including **Response** magazine, which aims to inform supporters about our work and inspire them to take action by writing to their MP, MEP and other key decision makers. The magazine is also combined with CSW's prayer diary, equipping supporters to pray for the persecuted on a daily basis.

While CSW is primarily an advocacy charity, we are also committed to providing practical and immediate help to those who need it. This may be on an individual basis, providing a small amount of money to a victim of religious violence, or to local partner organisations facing threats of violence on a daily basis for their work.

Above all, Christian Solidarity Worldwide is a voice for the voiceless, serving those who are unable to worship freely, and who face discrimination, torture, deprivation, homelessness, imprisonment and even death as a result of their faith.

Christian Solidarity Worldwide
PO Box 99
New Malden
Surrey
KT3 3YF
Email: admin@csw.org.uk

Martyrs for the Lord – a Chinese house church song

From the time the church was birthed on the day of Pentecost
The followers of the Lord have willingly sacrificed themselves
Tens of thousands have died that the gospel might prosper
As such they have obtained the crown of life

Chorus:
To be a martyr for the Lord, to be a martyr for the Lord
I am willing to die gloriously for the Lord

Those apostles who loved the Lord to the end
Willingly followed the Lord down the path of suffering
John was exiled to the lonely isle of Patmos
Stephen was stoned to death by an angry crowd

Matthew was stabbed to death in Persia by a mob
Mark died as horses pulled his two legs apart
Doctor Luke was cruelly hanged
Peter, Philip and Simon were crucified on a cross

Bartholomew was skinned alive by the heathen
Thomas died in India as five horses pulled his body apart
The apostle James was beheaded by King Herod
Little James was cut in half by a sharp saw

James the brother of the Lord was stoned to death
Judas was tied to a pillar and shot by arrows
Matthias had his head cut off in Jerusalem
Paul was a martyr under Emperor Nero

I am willing to take up the cross and go forward
To follow the apostles down the road of sacrifice
That tens of thousands of precious souls can be saved
I am willing to leave all and be a martyr for the Lord.

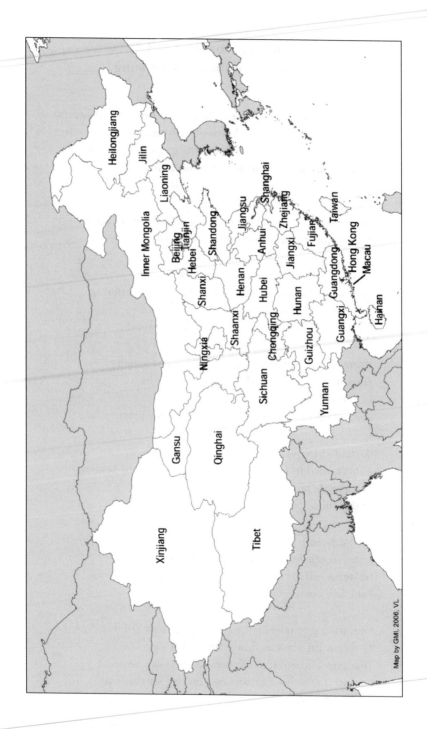

CONTENTS

Preface by Moses Xie   11

Forewords by Brother Yun and Tom White   12

A Biblical View of Persecution by Glenn Penner   17

Introduction   22

PART ONE: The First Thousand Years

1. 845 to 1599 – The Earliest Beginnings   29
2. 1600s – A Century of Catholic Carnage   39
3. 1700s – The Bitter-Sweet Century   50
4. The Great Religious Incident   58
5. Slaughter in South China   64
6. China's First Protestant Martyrs   77
7. Trouble in Guangxi and Guizhou   87
8. The Tianjin Massacre   101
9. Murderous Monks in Tibet   111
10. The Gutian Massacre   125
11. Storm Clouds on the Horizon   132

PART TWO: The Boxer Rebellion of 1900

12. Prelude to the Summer of Slaughter   143
13. Beijing   148
14. The Tongzhou Massacre   162
15. Hebei Province   168
16. The Zhujiahe Massacre of 3,000 Catholics   182
17. Little Anna Wang and Her Family   186
18. The Yanshan Slaughter   190
19. The Baoding Massacre   196
20. The Terrible Escape   211
21. Manchuria   221
22. Blind Chang   227

23. Zhejiang — 234
24. Inner Mongolia — 240
25. Shanxi — 247
26. The Taiyuan Massacre — 256
27. Shouyang — 271
28. Trouble at the Great Wall — 276
29. Taigu — 283
30. Peter Ogren – The Man Who Wouldn't Die — 293
31. Letters of Faith and Courage — 297

PART THREE: Bandits and Communists

32. 1901 to 1948 – Martyrs of the Bandit Years — 309
33. Bloodbath in Xi'an — 319
34. Alphonso Argento – The Last Boxer Martyr — 325
35. Trouble Among the Tribes — 329
36. Caught in the Crossfire — 343
37. 1925 to 1953 – The Early Years of Communism — 356
38. The Father and Son Martyrs — 366
39. Sadhu Sundar Singh — 373
40. In the Land of Mohammed — 378
41. John and Betty Stam — 388
42. Eric Liddell – Olympic Champion and Martyr — 397
43. Massacres in North China — 402
44. Thirty-Three Trappist Monks — 409
45. Bill Wallace — 416
46. Martyrs Among the A-Hmao — 423
47. 1954 to 1982 – Behind the Iron Curtain — 430
48. Zhu Yiming — 438
49. Molly O'Sullivan — 442
50. Watchman Nee — 450
51. Old Tactics in New China — 456
52. Lilies Among Thorns — 465
53. House Church Martyrs of the 1990s — 471
54. Martyrs of the New Millennium — 480
55. Into the Future — 487

PREFACE

Over many years and from one generation to another, the followers of Christ in China have set their hearts to be the witnesses of Christ to the nation. Many have paid a great price for their ministry, and the brutal persecutions they have suffered for their faith have been unimaginable.

The Bible commands all believers to "Go into all the world and preach the good news to all creation" (Mark 16:15). Many missionaries from around the world responded to this command in the past, traveling to China and proclaiming the Word of God. They blessed the land with their message of new life in Christ, and also suffered greatly when the darkness tried to counter God's light. Their faithful service in spite of great hardship was a beautiful example for Chinese believers to serve God throughout China and around the world.

China today still urgently needs more servants and workers to take the gospel throughout the land. God is looking for people who will stand up and declare, "Lord, here am I. Please send me!" The day of our Lord is near. May our hearts be encouraged by the testimonies of China's Christian martyrs! May the Lord raise up more and more testimonies that would glorify His name from our generation, from the next generation, and forever more!

Lord, You are the victorious King. Blessed are those who follow you to the end!

A humble servant of Christ,
Moses Xie (a Chinese house church leader who spent 23 years in prison for the Gospel).

FOREWORDS

Like the apostle Luke, the author of this book is a faithful servant called by the Lord. This God-fearing man is a devout prayer warrior who studies the Bible carefully and walks in the ways of the Lord.

Paul Hattaway was stirred by the Holy Spirit to record the testimonies of hundreds of Christian martyrs since the gospel first reached China during the Tang Dynasty (635 AD). Those martyrs, who spilled their blood on China's soil, are like Abel, of whom it is written "By faith he still speaks, even though he is dead" (Hebrews 11:4).

I believe those Christian martyrs understood that the blood Jesus Christ shed on the cross is able to save China. They believed that the gospel is able to transform China into a nation filled with disciples who love the Lord, a nation that overflows with heaven's blessings. By faith, those martyrs operated with great zeal to spread the Good News. Because of their sacrifices and willingness to lay down their lives they have produced a fruitful harvest for the kingdom of God, for Jesus said: "Unless a kernel of wheat falls to the ground and dies, it remains only a single seed. But if it dies, it produces many seeds" (John 12:24).

The testimonies of China's martyrs and their steadfast faith have touched the hearts of many Christians. I remember in the early 1980s – when Chinese house churches were undergoing severe persecution and many of our co-workers were arrested and imprisoned – our favourite songs at the time were "Be the Lord's witness to the ends of the earth" and "Martyrs for the Lord". When we sang "To be a martyr for the

Lord, to be a martyr for the Lord", everyone would cry out, "Lord, send me to preach the gospel! I am willing to follow you! I am willing to preach and be a martyr to glorify your name." Praise the Lord! God's time is now, and China is experiencing a rich harvest that has grown out of the ground watered by the tears and blood of those martyrs.

I believe this book is not only a gift to the people of China, but that God will use it to inspire Christians of this generation everywhere to imitate their examples and obey God's call, to serve with a willing heart, even to lay down our lives, so that the Great Commission might be completed and the gospel reach everyone who has yet to know Jesus, the risen Saviour. Hallelujah! I believe this gospel of salvation will be preached to the ends of the earth, even back to Jerusalem, until the blessed return of our Lord. Amen.

A servant of God,
Brother Yun (author of *The Heavenly Man*)

*   *   *

"For this cause I was born, and for this cause I have come into the world, that I should bear witness to the truth...."

—The words of Jesus to Pontius Pilate as recorded in John 18:37, before He was crucified.

China has been plagued with a history of warlords and worldviews that have dominated and deceived the hearts and minds of its people for centuries. The existence of such philosophies and false religions as animism, ancestor worship, Buddhism, Confucianism and atheism have been threatened when confronted by those who bear witness to the Truth—Jesus Christ.

Many of these witnesses have been rewarded with the crown of martyrdom.

As we read about martyrs throughout China's history, we realize they would never have been killed if they had just kept their mouths shut; or, as many like to say today, "If they kept their faith a private matter." If we had the opportunity to sit down with them, how would we advise them? Would we say, "Hide your Bible... Don't worship together... Don't tell your relatives you have become a Christian... It's too dangerous to go to China..."? Or would we say as the apostle Paul wrote to the Thessalonians: "We are bound to thank God always for you, brethren,...so that we ourselves boast of you among the churches of God for your patience and faith in all your persecutions and tribulations that you endure,...that you may be counted worthy of the kingdom of God, for which you also suffer" (2 Thessalonians 1:3-5)?

More than a century ago, missionaries packed their few belongings in a casket, knowing they may never return to their country of birth. They could not let the threat of death keep them from taking the chance of letting even one soul perish in the eternal flames of hell. And for those Chinese nationals who turned to Christ, they could not help but speak of the One who delivered them from the darkness of atheism, ancestor worship, animism and Buddhism. They had entered a new world...a new kingdom...one that is unshakable and will never end.

As we consider the political and cultural laws that have governed China throughout its history, we realize these brave believers who bear witness to His truth are unauthorized "lawbreakers." Jesus' Great Commission and the Book of Acts clearly state that God's "law of evangelism" pre-empts any law made by man.

In China's Christian Martyrs, you will read about such "law breakers" as Adrien Zhu Liguan, who was exiled outside the

Great Wall of China and died in 1785; Peter Wu Guosheng, whose last words while being executed in 1814 were, "Heaven, heaven, my true home!"; and missionary Mildred Clarke, who wrote to her family before she was brutally cut to pieces, "I long to live a poured-out life unto Him among these Chinese, and to enter into the fellowship of His sufferings for souls, who poured out His life unto death for us."

Chinese pastor Watchman Nee, who spent 20 years in prison and perished there, understood the urgency of a poured-out life. He wrote: "The Lord longs to find a way to bless the world through those who belong to Him. Brokenness is the way of blessing, the way of fragrance, the way of fruitfulness, but it is also a patch sprinkled with blood. Yes, there is blood from many wounds. When we offer ourselves to the Lord to be at His service, we cannot afford to be lenient, to spare ourselves. We must allow the Lord utterly to crack our outward man, so that He may find a way for His out-working."

The fruit of this brokenness sprinkled with blood is evident in China today, as the number of men and women who come to Christ every ten days can fill an entire stadium. China's communist government has tried to stop this outworking of God by implementing laws and restrictions to control the number of converts and even the distribution of Bibles and gospel literature. But believers have not waited to ask permission from the government to do what Jesus commanded almost 2,000 years ago: "Go and make disciples of all the nations" (Matthew 28:19). They have only asked for prayer and for the tools to evangelize, to witness to the truth of Jesus Christ amidst the darkness.

It is this Truth that has proven indestructible throughout China's history: An emperor couldn't eliminate God from China in the ninth century. Fanatical Muslims couldn't decapitate Him in the 1300s. The Boxers couldn't murder Him in 1900. And Mao couldn't march Him out of China in 1949. His

Body is moving forward, adding numbers to its masses every day.

In *China's Christian Martyrs*, Paul Hattaway carefully and masterfully details this anthology of China's martyrs from the first recorded arrival of missionaries in AD 635. You will be sobered, saddened and perhaps even angered at times as you read about those who allowed their lives to be sprinkled with blood for the sake of proclaiming the truth. And you will celebrate as you read of their relentless courage to stand for Jesus in the face of imprisonment, torture and death, knowing the promise of heaven awaited them.

We need the testimonies of these dear brothers and sisters, as their poured-out lives sprinkled with blood encourage us to stand for Jesus in a world that denies the existence of God—our ultimate Truth—and even hates the notion of this reality. As we enter into fellowship with these saints who are wearing a martyrs crown, may we be willing to bear witness to the truth and face the consequences for doing so, that we may be counted worthy of the kingdom of God (2 Thessalonians 1:5).

—Dr. Tom White has served as the Executive Director of The Voice of the Martyrs in the U.S. since 1991. He was given a 24-year prison sentence in Cuba for gospel activity.

A BIBLICAL VIEW OF
PERSECUTION

When seeking to understand the scriptural teaching of persecution, it is important to understand, first of all, that the New Testament is not overly concerned to answer the question of suffering in general (i.e. suffering due to living in a fallen world). This is assumed. Rather, most of the passages dealing with suffering in the New Testament have to do with suffering because of *righteousness*. As I have studied many of the classic books on suffering, it is noticeable that this is hardly ever stressed. This is to be expected, I suppose, since Christians in the West have little or no experience with persecution per se.

Because the biblical texts on persecution cannot readily be applied to a setting where there is little or no persecution, the tendency seems to be for preachers to misapply these passages to situations of general physical, psychological and spiritual suffering. This misapplication has subsequently been turned around upon the text itself. Hence, the application influences the interpretation, resulting in the typical Bible student in the West never even suspecting that the texts that deal with pain and suffering might be dealing with suffering for righteousness' sake rather than suffering because of sin.

There is a clear scriptural link between persecution and discipleship. There can be no discipleship without persecution; to follow Christ is to join him in a cross-carrying journey of reconciling the world to the Father. That this journey is set in the context of conflict, self-sacrifice and suffering is alluded to as early as Genesis 3:15 when the Lord affirms that Satan's judgement, accomplished through human instrumentality, will bring deliverance to the offspring of the woman, but it will take place in a process of bruising and pain. The deliverance will come through the crushing of the serpent's head, but in the process the heel that crushes the serpent will be bruised. This truth is illustrated in the very next chapter when the first murder takes place following an act of worship, as Cain's sacrifice is rejected by God while his brother's is accepted. In jealousy (a common reason given in Scripture for persecution), Cain kills his brother. It is obvious that the New Testament views Abel's murder as much more than the result of sibling rivalry or a family squabble that got out of control. Jesus clearly saw Abel's death as an act of martyrdom (Matthew 23:35), as does the apostle John (1 John 3:12). John explains that Abel's death was because Cain's acts were evil and Abel's were righteous. Abel's death is clearly set in a context of martyrdom, a result of the conflict between the world and those who belong to God (1 John 3:13).

Persecution is hardly an exclusively New Testament phenomenon. Numerous passages refer to the suffering inflicted on the people of God throughout the historical narratives. It is likely that the psalms of lamentation address the issue of the suffering of God's people more clearly than any other portion of Scripture (including the New Testament). The thrust of Job is how the man of God suffers not because of sin but because of righteousness and the call to trust God in the face of such a paradox. This train of thought is amplified by the call of the prophets to look ahead to the Day of the Lord, believing that history is under the control of an Almighty God who, from the foundation of the world, has set his plans in motion of reconciling the world to himself.

All of this comes into focus with the coming of Jesus Christ, the revelation of the triune God. Through Christ, we see, among other things, that sacrificial love is in the very nature of God. To suffer and die to accomplish his purposes was not to be unexpected; he could not be God and do anything but. Weakness, suffering and sacrifice are God's *modus operandi*. This is how God accomplishes his work: not through strength or compulsion but through love and invitation.

In the process, the Servant of God suffers and dies, as do those who follow him. This is to be expected; this is God's way of reconciling the world to himself. A cross-centred gospel requires cross-carrying messengers. When Jesus declared, "If anyone would come after me, let him deny himself and take up his cross and follow me" (Matthew 16:24), we need to take his words much more literally than we are accustomed to doing. The demand of Jesus on his followers is to tread the path of martyrdom. He was about to send his disciples out as sheep among wolves and he had told them that they would likely die in the process of carrying out their ministry. In order to build his church (Matthew 16:18), his death was necessary, as he points out in verse 21. This is the foundation. Without Christ's death there is no redeemed community. But just as Christ's cross was needed to establish his church, our crosses are needed to build his church. Both are needed. There is no better way to put it than to follow the lead of the Romanian church leader Josef Ton who coined the phrase: "Christ's cross was for propitiation. Our cross is for propagation." To be called to follow Christ was to receive a call to suffer (e.g. Acts 9:16; 14:22; 1 Thessalonians 3:3; 1 Peter 2:21; 3:9, 17).

It was this understanding that sacrifice, suffering and even death were the normal cost of discipleship that fuelled the evangelistic efforts of the first-century church. They did not expect to experience all of the blessing of heaven in this world. They knew that by their faithfulness, even unto death, they were storing up rewards in heaven. Contrary to our belief that it is a blessing not to be persecuted, they knew that it was the persecuted who are blessed (Matthew 5:10–12). Rather than following our example of thanking God for the privilege of not suffering for him, they thanked God for the honour of suffering for his sake (Acts 5:41). They knew that in order to bring life to others, they must die; to see others experience peace with God, they would have to suffer the violence of the world; to bring the love of God to a dying world, they would have to face the hatred of those whom they were seeking to reach. It is in this context that they described spiritual warfare; not freedom over bad habits or psychological problems, but the brutal reality of witnessing to the faithfulness of God in the face of suffering, sacrifice and death. It was only in this context that the purposes of God would be accomplished.

This is also the reality of persecution today. We continue the task of taking the gospel to the ends of the earth, knowing that he goes with us and that we do not suffer alone. In all of our afflictions, he is afflicted, and just as Jesus demanded of Saul of Tarsus, so he asks of today's persecutors, "Why do you persecute me?" The knowledge that nothing can separate us from Christ's love (Romans 8:35), that the Spirit prays for us when we can only groan in agony (Romans 8:26–27) and gives us his words in the face of our accusers (Matthew 10:19–20), provides the help that the disciples of Jesus require to remain faithful witnesses. God has provided all that is necessary for the disciple to stand firm. Yes, there may be fear, but by God's grace, it need not control us. Yes, there may be terrible suffering, but suffering is not the worst thing that can happen to the child of God; disobedience to the Father is.

As you read the testimonies of these courageous brothers and sisters in the pages that follow, it is worthwhile to reflect on the words of Peter: "For it is commendable if a man bears up under the pain of unjust suffering because he is conscious of God" (1 Peter 2:19). In these words, Peter defines grace as suffering due to one's faithfulness to God. As we read the accounts of those who have suffered for the sake of Christ, we might be justified in saying that from the world's perspective, those who endure persecution are heroic, but from God's perspective they are recipients of grace. Peter stresses that enduring suffering is evidence that God is at work in one's life. There is no glory for the sufferer. No hero worship. No merit for those who are able to endure hardship, no boasting of one's achievements. It is evidence of God's grace. It is all a work of God, from beginning to end. When people can suffer horrible persecution and endure, it is evidence that God has been at work. Is it any wonder that near the end of this epistle, written especially to instruct persecuted believers to stand firm in their faith, the apostle writes, "And the God of all grace, who called you to his eternal glory in Christ, after you have suffered a little while, will himself restore you and make you strong, firm and steadfast" (1 Peter 5:10).

Glenn Penner

*   *   *

Glenn Penner has served the persecuted church with The Voice of the Martyrs in Canada since 1997, increasingly in a teaching ministry focusing on the biblical theology of persecution. In 2006 he was appointed CEO of VOM Canada. He is the chairman of the Religious Liberty Commission of the Evangelical Fellowship of Canada and serves on the academic board of the International Institute for Religious Freedom. Glenn is the author of *In the Shadow of the Cross: A Biblical Theology of Persecution and Discipleship* and a visiting professor at Oklahoma Wesleyan University.

INTRODUCTION

When the history of the Martyr Church of China is written, it
will be a beautiful record of suffering for His Name!

Frank Simcox, martyred in 1900

In *Safely Home* – a gripping novel by Randy Alcorn about the
persecution of a Christian family in China – the main Chinese
character of the story is a pastor named Li Quan who ends up
being martyred for his faith. During his life Li Quan had often
expressed the wish that he could write a book about those who
have died for Christ in China, but for one reason or another he
never had the opportunity to complete it. He had been inspired
by the testimonies of Christians slaughtered during the Boxer
Rebellion of 1900, and wished he could have had the opportunity of meeting them and recording their stories in full. After
his death Li Quan meets the King of heaven, who tells him,

> "I have much for you to do. You will go to the great hall of litera-
> ture. There is a book you started writing. I want you to finish it."
> "A book?"
> "Yes ... The book you started in the dark world survived the
> transition to this one. The rest of the story needs to be told, and
> many need to read it. You can interview the Boxer martyrs now.
> And there are an unlimited number of fascinating subjects for
> your future books. Now you can write it with clarity you caught
> only glimpses of in the Shadowlands."

In a real sense all work a person does in this life is but a pale
imitation of the beautiful reality of heaven. The world's most
skilled artists can never match the majesty God displays in

creation, while even an intimate time of Christian prayer and worship is just a pale reflection compared to what is in store when we see our Lord face to face. As the apostle Paul wrote, "No eye has seen, no ear has heard, no mind has conceived what God has prepared for those who love him" (1 Corinthians 2:9). Often to us martyrdom appears a wasteful tragedy, but the perspective from heaven will seem very different. The psalmist declared, "Precious in the sight of the Lord is the death of his saints" (Psalm 116:15).

In this book I have been privileged to compile the testimonies of many Christian martyrs throughout Chinese history, from various Christian creeds. Some readers may feel uncomfortable to see Protestants, Catholics, Orthodox and others all presented together, but I am including them all in the belief that in heaven all that counts is faith in Jesus Christ. When martyrs' crowns are handed out there is not one line for Protestants and another for Catholics! To focus only on one particular creed would deprive readers of the chance to learn and appreciate the faith and commitment of so many followers of Christ down through the ages. It should be sobering to many Protestants to consider that Christianity had been in China 1,172 years before the first Protestant missionary arrived. Likewise, Catholics would do well to consider the sacrifice of thousands of Protestants who have laid down their lives for the Lord Jesus Christ.

I am often asked why the Chinese church has experienced such wonderful revival for so many years, whereas in many other parts of the world the spiritual climate seems barren. I believe one of the main reasons for the present harvest in China is that the once-hard soil has been moistened by the blood of many martyrs throughout history. Since the first recorded martyrdoms in 845 AD, as many as 250,000 Christians have been killed in China for their faith. Since 1900 the church in China has experienced more martyrdoms than the church in all other nations combined.

The Chinese Christians have learned to walk on the path of the cross. They have learned that there is a cross not only for Jesus, but also a cross for all of his true followers. While many in the West love to quote "positive" promises from the Bible, the Chinese have discovered the meaning of other promises, such as "Everyone who wants to live a godly life in Christ Jesus will be persecuted" (2 Timothy 3:12); "I am sending you out like sheep among wolves" (Matthew 10:16); and "If they persecuted me, they will persecute you also" (John 15:20).

Through many decades of perseverance and suffering the Chinese church emerged through the suffering of the cross to the place of resurrection power. Broken and humble vessels have seen God move mightily in recent decades, and tens of millions of hungry people have repented and come into the kingdom of God.

As Glenn Penner skilfully points out in his essay "A Biblical View of Persecution", suffering and martyrdom are not meant to be the experiences of a few marginalized Christians in nations controlled by wicked governments. Suffering is part of the call for every Christian, irrespective of the era he or she lives in, location, or environment. In many parts of the world, however, a deceptive heresy has crept into the church that places people and their needs at the centre, and God at the peripheral. People are falsely taught that God's greatest desire is for their happiness. We are not on this earth to pursue our own happiness, health and prosperity. We are here only for the glory of the Almighty God. He requires a full commitment to his cause, regardless of the kind of life we receive in return. Such radical faith can produce in us the same kind of triumphant resolve as Job, who declared, "Though he slay me, yet will I hope in him" (Job 13:15).

There is an interesting story in an ancient Chinese book

about a man named Bian He who lived some 500 years before Christ. One day Bian He found a large stone which was actually an unpolished piece of jade. He presented it to the emperor. The emperor saw nothing but a large stone, thought he was being tricked, and ordered Bian He's left foot to be chopped off. Bian He later sent the same present to the next emperor, who also saw only a stone and ordered his right foot to be chopped off. When a third emperor came to the throne, Bian He held his jade in his arms outside the emperor's palace and wept three days and three nights. The emperor sent someone to investigate, then ordered the stone to be polished. Only then did they discover a beautiful jade inside it.

One day China (and many other nations) will discover that the Christians they torture, whom they suppose to be ignorant lumps of worthless stone, are actually the polished jewels sent by God to bring his kingdom.

As you read *China's Christian Martyrs* my heartfelt desire and prayer is that you will not simply read it as an account of suffering and slaughter, for if that is all you glean from these pages then I will have failed. The story of China's martyrs is far more than the ugly and barbaric facts that accompany their deaths, for each martyrdom is also a story of beauty, of faith and perseverance, and of ultimate victory. It would have been easy for many of China's Christian martyrs to save their lives by indicating to their tormentors that they were willing to recant, but they did not take that option, for they were convinced of the eternal life Jesus had promised to all who endure to the end. Like the early church, the Chinese martyrs were "looking forward to the city with foundations, whose architect and builder is God" (Hebrews 11:10).

My hope is that every Christian who reads this book will be better equipped as a soldier for Jesus Christ, esteeming those things of eternal significance while learning to cling less tightly to the things of this earth. Like China's martyrs, may God "Teach us to number our days aright, that we may gain a heart of wisdom" (Psalm 90:12).

Paul Hattaway

PART ONE

The First
Thousand Years

CHAPTER 1

845 TO 1599 – THE EARLIEST BEGINNINGS

The first Nestorian persecution

Although anecdotal evidence suggests the gospel may have first come to China just a few decades after the death and resurrection of Christ, the first firm evidence of Christianity in China dates from 635 AD. In that year Nestorian missionaries from Central Asia and the Middle East travelled down the Silk Road into China, bringing the gospel with them. The "Nestorian Stone", a large tablet unearthed in Shaanxi Province, provides details of these earliest days of Chinese Christianity.

By 638 the first church was built at Chang'an, and 21 Persian monks had commenced work in China. Over the next two centuries the Nestorians enjoyed great freedom to preach the gospel throughout China, and soon Christian communities were established from northwest Xinjiang as far as the southeast China coast, thousands of miles away. At the beginning the Nestorians enjoyed the favour of the rulers of the day. Emperor Taizong welcomed them to China, and good relations continued after his death in 649. He was succeeded as emperor by his son Gaozu, who built monasteries for the Nestorians in many locations. Things started to go wrong for the young emperor when he took one of his deceased father's concubines into his own ménage. The concubine, Wu Hou, schemed her way to the top, eventually overthrowing the empress and seizing the position for herself. The new queen

A fresco of a Nestorian worshipper, found in Xinjiang
and now housed in Berlin Museum

dominated the government and gradually turned the state against the Christians. The emperor died in 683. Within seven years Wu Hou had seized full control of the country and adopted Buddhism as the state religion. Persecution against the Nestorians began. Mobs destroyed churches, but the Nestorians struggled on for more than 150 years until everything came to an abrupt halt.

In 845 the emperor issued an edict ordering all religious clergy to leave the monasteries and enter secular work. Although Buddhism suffered the most, more than 2,000 Christian monks and nuns were forced to abandon their spiritual vocation, which dealt a deathblow to the fledgling church in China at the time. After the persecution of 845 the Nestorian enterprise in China faltered remarkably quickly. A Muslim traveller, Sulayman, visited the southern city of Guangzhou in 878 and reported that 120,000 people "including Muslims, Jews, Christians and Zoroastrians" had been slaughtered. A later Arab who travelled through China in 987 reported that Christianity was extinct and the church had been completely obliterated.

A Syriac book dating from the thirteenth century, found in the Imperial Library in Beijing, talks about how Christianity was introduced into China by the Nestorians and commemorates "the martyrs of China". Although more details from the first Nestorian persecution have been lost in the sands of time, there seems little doubt that many Christians were persecuted to death. For the first time the Chinese church went "underground". For almost 400 years little evidence of its existence was seen. By the time Marco Polo arrived in China in the thirteenth century Nestorian Christianity had resurrected in a number of locations and appeared to be thriving.

1320 – China's first Catholic martyrs

A sketch of the influential John of
Montecorvino

The Catholic missionary enterprise in China commenced
when John of Montecorvino arrived in the late thirteenth century. In 1299 he constructed a magnificent church building in
Beijing, and by 1305 he counted 6,000 converts.

In those days a journey from Europe to the Orient could
take up to two years, and was so dangerous on both sea and

land that it was a miracle for anyone to make it to China alive. A letter from André de Pérouse broke the sad news that four Franciscans who tried to join the Beijing mission were killed en route. The four Catholic martyrs were Thomas de Tolentino, James of Padua, Pierre de Sienna and Demetrius of Tiflis (now Tblisi in Georgia). On the way to China their ship was blown to Salcetti, an island off the coast of India that was inhabited by fanatical Muslims.

The governor of the region seized the four Franciscans and asked what they thought about Mohammed. Their response infuriated the governor, who threatened to kill them unless they would denounce Christ and embrace Islam. When they refused to do so, the four Christians were de-robed and tied to posts in the blazing sun. While they baked under the hot sun they sang praises to God in one voice, thanking him that they had been counted worthy to suffer for his name. This only served to further infuriate the persecutors, who subjected the four Christians to horrible tortures before murdering them.

James of Padua had his head split open by a sword; the aged Thomas de Tolentino had a sword plunged into his back as another man cut his throat. Pierre de Sienna was beheaded and Demetrius of Tiflis, after receiving several wounds, was also executed.

The story of China's first four Catholic martyrs should have ended in this remote place then, but some years later, when Oderic of Friuli travelled to India, he found that the murderous governor had received a vivid dream of the four Franciscans surrounding his bed, brandishing swords of fire. The terrified governor cried for mercy and immediately set free a number of Christians he had taken captive. He issued a public edict making it illegal, under pain of death, for anyone to insult Jesus Christ or his followers. Oderic noted that the new law resulted in a great number of Muslims and Hindus converting to Christ.

Oderic, who arrived in China around 1322, decided to honour the four martyrs by gathering up their remains and carrying them to China. And so, in this most bizarre manner, the bones of China's first Catholic martyrs were buried on Chinese soil in the city of Hangzhou. The four Franciscans were the firstfruits of many thousands of Chinese Catholics who have followed their footsteps into martyrdom in the nearly 700 years since.

The Ili massacre of 1342

One of the earliest Catholic missions in China flourished in the most unlikely place – the frontier town of Ili Bâliq (now known as Yining) in a remote region of northwest China. In the fourteenth century Ili was considered beyond the extent of Chinese civilization. Thousands of criminals (and persecuted Christians) were banished there to serve the rest of their lives in exile.

The Catholics managed to establish a thriving work in this remote and needy place. The bishop of Ili was Richard of Burgundy, France. He handpicked some mature brothers from his order to join him in the remote work. Among them were Francis and Raymond Ruffa, two priests from Alexandria in Egypt; three laymen: Peter Martel from the French town of Narbonne, Lawrence of Alexandria and Matthew Escandel from Hungary; and a black man known as John of India. These Christians were pioneer evangelists in the true sense of the word. They travelled around the sparsely populated region on camel and horseback, stayed in the tents of Mongol nomads, and succeeded in winning many families to Jesus Christ.

Soon after the Franciscans arrived, the prince of Ili fell ill.

Francis of Alexandria had some experience as a surgeon, and he succeeded not only in helping the prince recover, but also in winning the confidence and favour of the prince and his father, the khan. For several years the missionaries were granted freedom to preach the gospel anywhere within the realm, but this came to an abrupt end in June 1342 when the khan was poisoned by one of the princes who was a fanatical Muslim. The murderer usurped the throne and immediately issued an edict ordering all Christians to renounce Jesus Christ and embrace Islam. Failure to do so would result in death. The Christians, however, courageously took no notice of the tyrant's threats and continued to meet together for worship.

At the time there were seven missionaries serving at Ili. They were arrested, chained together, and made to stand before a furious Muslim mob which abused the missionaries and struck them on the head with whips and sticks. Battered and bloodied, the disciples of Christ refused to deny their faith. The enraged crowd responded by cutting off their noses and ears. Realizing they were drawing near to the gate of heaven, the seven men cried out to Jesus in the midst of the cruel tortures, and to their last breath continued to preach the gospel to the Muslims who were killing them. Seeing that nothing could change the missionaries, the mob finally cut their heads off.

The local Christians – who included ethnic Uygurs, Kazaks, Mongols, Russians and Han Chinese – refused to flee from their homes. They were thrown into prison and tortured with barbaric cruelty. Many Ili Christians died as martyrs. Those who survived the torment were eventually released after the tyrant ruler was overthrown and put to death by a Mongol chief. Despite being deprived of leadership and direction, the church in Ili survived against all odds. Remarkably, the gospel was still being preached in this remote outpost 400 years later.

1368 – The Second Nestorian Persecution

The remnant of Nestorian Christianity that survived the persecutions of 845 was barely discernable for almost four centuries, but gradually the hidden root of Christianity resurfaced again. The Mongols, led by Genghis Khan, broke through the Great Wall in 1213. They swept all opposition before them, establishing the largest kingdom the world has ever seen, stretching from Southeast Asia to Eastern Europe. By 1271 they had conquered all of China and established the Yuan Dynasty. By the time Marco Polo arrived in China in the late thirteenth century the political atmosphere was accepting of the Nestorians and churches once again flourished in the open. Polo wrote about Nestorian churches in many parts of China. In 1330 Nestorians had risen to such prominence that some even held high positions under the emperor in Beijing. Tragically, the religious freedom the Nestorians enjoyed came at a cost to their spiritual life. Gradually their light dimmed, and their moral demise caused them to be a stench to those they sought to reach.

In 1368 the Mongol Empire fractured from internal strife and the Yuan Dynasty came crashing down. For more than a century the Chinese had been oppressed by the Mongols, and when a chance for revenge presented itself there was no holding back. Hundreds of thousands of Mongols were slaughtered throughout the nation. Christians were also targeted because of their connection to the Mongol leaders. What exactly happened in the second Nestorian persecution following the overthrow of the Yuan Dynasty is not clear. Some historians believe thousands of Christians were slaughtered in the chaos,

The Da Qin pagoda in Shaanxi Province is a Nestorian Christian
pagoda dating from the eighth century

while others believe the church simply withered away without the support of the Mongols.

What is known is that the Nestorian church disappeared from China, leaving almost no trace of its existence. The disappearance of Christianity was so complete that when missionaries returned two centuries later they seemed to be completely unaware that there had ever been Christians there before them.

CHAPTER 2

1600s – A CENTURY OF CATHOLIC CARNAGE

The White Lotus Society persecution

A series of persecutions against the Catholic church in China during the 17th century resulted in the deaths of hundreds of Christians.

The White Lotus Society was a secret Buddhist sect that first appeared in the late thirteenth century. They encouraged worship of the Eternal Mother, who they believed would one day gather all her children together into one family at the start of a thousand years of peace. During the Yuan Dynasty (1271–1368) the White Lotus Society was prominent in instigating dissent against the hated Mongol leaders, which ultimately led to the downfall of the Yuan. Their successors, the Ming Dynasty, also fell out of favour with the White Lotus Society, who progressively became less of a Buddhist sect and more a collection of gangsters. By the 1610s the government was besieged by uprisings across the country, most of which were organized by the White Lotus Society.

When Beijing came directly under threat from the insurgents the emperor realized it was time to crush the rebellious sect. Orders were distributed throughout the provinces, giving local officials authority to arrest the leaders of the sect and to crush them mercilessly. The enemies of the gospel saw an opportunity to persecute Christians. One leading government official, Shen Que, displayed much animosity against the Jesuits. This evil man composed a "thunderous manifesto" against secret societies, which was distributed throughout the whole empire, encouraging the arrest and torture of all who would not denounce their faith in the Lord of heaven.

During 1616 and 1617 churches were demolished throughout the nation and thousands of Catholics were seized and hauled off to prison. Most were cruelly tortured and forced to confess to imaginary crimes. A number of Chinese Catholics died from the afflictions. Some foreign missionaries also perished, including an old priest named André whose body was so badly mangled that he expired as he knelt on the courtroom floor.

At Nanjing the edict against the Jesuits arrived at midnight on 30 August 1616. Two missionaries, Alphonse Vagnoni and Alvarō Semedo, nervously waited inside the Jesuit mission. Within a few hours three Chinese officials arrived. Soldiers occupied the buildings, and the missionaries were told that orders had been received to expel them from China. Semedo was gravely ill at the time, and so was allowed to remain in bed with an armed guard at the door, while Vagnoni was carried into the city through crowds of hostile people who hurled insults at him.

The Chinese believers in Nanjing soon heard about the arrests. Showing no fear, they rushed to the mission compound to protest. One believer named John Yao was particularly bold. He marched at the head of the procession, holding aloft a placard that declared he was a Christian. In a loud voice he proclaimed, "I come to die, to shed my blood with my spiritual fathers!" The officials immediately took him at his word. They bound his hands behind his back, fastened a chain around his neck, and dragged him to court.

When the wicked official, Shen Que, learned that the ill priest Semedo had been left behind in the mission house he flew into a rage and punished the soldiers for not fully carrying out his orders. The next day more Catholics were rounded up. Sebastian Fernandez joined Vagnoni and Semedo in prison where they were subjected to barbaric torture. Their beards were torn from their faces and they were punched and kicked until their entire bodies resembled a large bruise from head to toe.

When the three missionaries were finally made to appear before the God-hating Shen Que, Sebastian Fernandez began to share his faith with the court. Shen could not bear to listen, and ordered that the prisoner be beaten with 20 more strokes. It was reported that blood gushed out of Fernandez "like water from pipes", sprinkling the feet of the judge.

The three priests were sent back to prison where for three months they were frightfully tortured, with chains fastened around their necks and ankles the entire time. Nobody was allowed to visit the faithful trio, and whenever the Chinese believers tried to bring food or other gifts the goods were stolen by the prison guards. Finally the missionaries were so weakened and malnourished that they passed into eternity, their bodies unable to bear another day on this earth.

In the aftermath of this persecution all foreign missionaries were obliged to leave China, but many remained secretly, dwelling in remote mountains or thick forests. Some made their home in cemeteries, living among the tombs. Incredibly, some missionaries survived more than 20 years in China before being detected, having been protected by local Christians.

Two Chinese Catholic brothers, Sebastian Zhong Mingren and Zhong Mingli, were imprisoned at Nanjing and punished with 70 strokes each. After this cruel torture, which left them half dead, they were sent into exile. In March 1617 Zhong Mingren was sentenced to render manual labour as a stone mason in a location where the Great Wall was being reinforced, while Zhong Mingli was compelled to drag ropes hauling the imperial vessels along the banks of the Grand Canal, a task usually performed by oxen and horses. Sebastian Zhong Mingren escaped when a heroic Christian, known only as Matthew, offered to take his place. He in turn was later released. Zhong Mingli never saw his family again, and is believed to have died while still serving his sentence.

Tibet's first martyrs

Antonio de Andrade

Born in Portugal in 1581, Antonio de Andrade is one of the greatest pioneer missionaries in history, and is credited as being the first Westerner ever to step foot inside Tibet. Andrade entered the Jesuit order at the age of 16 and three years later was sent to the Portuguese colony of Goa in south India to complete his training. The zealous missionary decided to join a group of pilgrims travelling to Tibet. He left in March 1624, disguised as a Hindu pilgrim, and finally arrived in the western Tibetan kingdom of Guge after months of fighting over high Himalayan passes and battling local officials who desired to keep Andrade out of their land. On one occasion he waded through waist-high snow. He wrote, "Once when I tried to hold something, a bone came out of one of my fingers, but I was not aware of it till I saw the blood on my hand; while our feet were so swelled and numbed, that if a hot iron had touched them we should not have felt it."

After arriving at Guge the Portuguese priest impressed the king and queen, who gave him permission to return and establish a mission. When Antonio de Andrade's report of his journey through Kashmir, Ladakh, and into Tibet made its way back to Europe, most people thought it was a work of fiction, or a scurrilous account of exaggeration and lies. Tibet had appeared as an empty space on maps at the time. Many years later travellers proved the accuracy of Andrade's account.

Andrade returned to Zaburang in 1625 with four co-workers. They made good progress in acquiring the local Tibetan dialect, and they were soon able to preach. On one occasion as Andrade spoke on the torments of hell, the king and queen wept silently. The king was so interested in the missionaries' work that on 12 April 1626 he personally laid the cornerstone of the first church in Tibet. The king paid for all the construction costs and often came into the church to pray and ask the missionaries deep questions.

All signs for a flourishing work in Tibet were positive, until the mission came to an abrupt end when Buddhist lamas, alarmed at the king's interest in Christianity, incited a revolution and overthrew the royal family. Antonio de Andrade was recalled to India in 1629. The following year the revolution ravaged the Tibet mission, and Andrade found all efforts to re-enter Tibet and continue the work were blocked. The Tibetan Christians were singled out for retribution. They were either sold into slavery or sent into exile, while the church and missionaries' houses were demolished. Andrade suddenly died while attempting to return to Tibet in 1634. Some accounts say he was poisoned by an enemy, while others blame the Muslims for the Portuguese missionary's death. Although he died in India, Andrade's heart and soul were among the Tibetan people that he loved so dearly.

The missionaries continued with efforts to re-establish their work. Seven workers were sent to Tibet in 1635, but three fell sick on the way and two more died from the extremities of the trip. Just two made it alive. In 1642 there was just one Jesuit missionary, Manuel Marques, remaining in Zaburang. He was attacked and badly injured, and is believed to have died in prison. A Christian remnant remained in the Zaburang region until the work was finally abandoned in 1650. Andrade's journals were rediscovered in Calcutta in the 19th century. They captured the imagination of author James Hilton, whose novels depicting Shangri-La owed much to the Portuguese martyr's accounts from 300 years earlier.

1648 – Francisco de Capillas

Francisco de Capillas

Born at Palencia, Spain, Francisco de Capillas longed to see God's kingdom established in the far-flung corners of the world. In February 1632, aged just 24, he set sail for the Philippines where he served in the Dominican mission. After a decade in the Philippines, Capillas transferred to Fujian Province in southeast China in 1642. What little has been written about Capillas indicates he was a man of deep compassion and humility. One of his fellow priests said he visited the sick in hospital every day, expressing the love of Christ and feeding those who could not feed themselves.

An anti-Christian riot broke out on 13 November 1647 and a number of Chinese believers were seriously injured. As soon as he heard this, the Spaniard set out to help them. As he hurried along a path Capillas was captured by a group of soldiers and thrown into prison. Despite his dire surroundings, Capillas radiated great joy from the Lord. He wrote, "I am not concerned about getting out of here because here I know I am doing the will of God. They do not let me stay up at night to pray, so I pray in bed before dawn. I live here in great joy without any worry, knowing that I am here because of Jesus Christ."

On 16 January 1648 Capillas was taken out of his prison cell and decapitated. Two months later local Christians lovingly buried his remains.

1650 – General Sung

Catholic work commenced in Manchuria (now the three northeast provinces of Liaoning, Jilin and Heilongjiang) in 1620. As the Manchu Dynasty extended their rule throughout China, numerous handpicked Manchu magistrates and military leaders were placed over different regions. The territory of Liaodong was placed under the leadership of General Sung, a man of deep Christian conviction. The soldiers under Sung's command respected him, but when the government in Beijing failed to send money to pay the soldiers' wages unrest rose in the ranks. Other officials sent bribes to Beijing in order to secure the release of funds, but General Sung refused to contemplate such an action, as bribery went directly against his Christian convictions. Sung wrote to the government, explaining that his army was falling into a state of insubordination, but he received no reply from the overstretched officials. The coffers were empty, and paying General Sung's men was not high on the list of their priorities. The patience of the soldiers under Sung's command finally ran out. In desperation they raided a town, pillaging food, money and possessions. By this act of violence the soldiers knew they had destroyed their leader, and the only chance for his safety was if Sung openly declared his opposition to the emperor. The soldiers promised to support Sung in this endeavour, and vowed to never lay down their arms until he became the emperor.

Being a Christian, General Sung could not reconcile treason with his principles. He strongly rebuked his soldiers for their devious plan. News of the mutiny soon reached the palace in Beijing. The emperor immediately summoned General Sung to appear before him. Sung's men strongly urged their beloved leader not to go, but the Christian general listened only to the voice of his conscience. He was condemned to death and swiftly executed with his faith and integrity untarnished.

The Jesuit persecution of 1665

Adam Schall, a Jesuit priest, arrived in China in 1619 at the age of just 28. His skills in geography, map-making, mathematics and astronomy soon caught the attention of the Chinese leaders. Schall was a brilliant man, yet he considered his knowledge merely a tool by which God could use him to reach many with the gospel.

Trouble for the Jesuits started in 1664 after two

missionaries published an article that portrayed Christianity as superior to the Chinese religions. The article antagonized every Chinese who read it. On 20 April 1664 Schall suffered a stroke and was barely able to move or speak. On 15 September of that year, Schall and his Christian colleagues were charged with treachery, accused of preaching an abominable religion and teaching false astronomical methods. Schall was arrested with several missionaries and a number of Chinese Christians associated with the Institute of Astronomy. The men were brought before a court in Beijing. Schall's condition was pathetic. A mat was positioned on the floor for him to lie on, bound with chains. After a lengthy trial the prisoners were handed over to the Minister of Justice for sentencing. The decision shocked the devout men. Adam Schall was condemned to death by strangulation, and the others were to be beaten and then sent into exile. Three judges later changed the method of Schall's death from strangulation to the cruellest method of death known to the Chinese, when the victim was slowly cut to pieces with a sharp sword while each wound was cauterized with a red hot iron to prevent too quick a death through loss of blood.

For the next two months Schall contemplated the gruesome death he was faced with, when a series of remarkable events occurred in Beijing that spared his life. On 13 April a comet appeared in the sky. Then at eleven o'clock in the morning of 16 April, at the exact time the emperor was to have signed Schall's death warrant, a large earthquake struck the city. The emperor ran out of his palace in terror. Aftershocks continued for the next two days, while the sun was obscured by the great amount of dust that had been thrown into the atmosphere by the earthquake. The comet and earthquake were taken as signs that heaven was unhappy with the imperial decision against the Christians. An amnesty was declared and Schall's death sentence commuted, although he remained

Emperor Kangxi, who ruled China for 60 years from 1662 to 1722

chained up. Then on 29 April a huge fire gutted more than 40 rooms in the palace. Some people claimed they had seen a fireball descend from heaven. All the inhabitants of Beijing were terrified and believed the God of the Christians was displaying his wrath and upholding the cause of his servants.

Adam Schall was released and allowed to return to his home, but five Chinese Christians from the Institute of

Astronomy were beheaded, and 30 missionaries who had taken up residence in Beijing were banished to southern China. One of the martyrs was Li Zubai – the leading Chinese astronomer of his generation. Baptized in 1622, Li was executed along with four Chinese Christian co-workers, namely Song Hecheng, Song Fa, Zhu Guangxian and Liu Youtai.

Adam Schall finally died on 15 August 1665 at the age of 74, having given 47 years of his life to the Lord's service in China. Some say the broken heart Schall suffered after the murders of his five Chinese friends was the main cause of his death, his broken body being just a contributing factor.

CHAPTER 3 1700s – THE BITTER-SWEET CENTURY

18th-century Christians were subjected to brutal forms
of torture and confinement.

Overall, the 1700s was a bitter-sweet century for Christians in China, ranging from times of great freedom and official favour to times of intense persecution and martyrdom.

Emperor Kangxi (reigned 1662–1722) is remembered as one of China's greatest rulers. He issued an edict tolerating Christianity in 1692, but the goodwill did not extend to his son Yongzheng (r. 1723–1735), who outlawed Christianity as a "perverse and sinister sect". In the early 1700s the Franciscans dominated Catholic work in much of China. Some missionaries were even given influential positions as advisors to the emperor. When Yongzheng ascended the throne in 1724 he issued an edict against Christianity and expelled most of the missionaries. Despite the risks a number of the missionaries secretly re-entered China in disguise to visit their flocks and baptize new believers.

One incident to shake the Catholic Church was known as the "Sunu Case" of 1724. It began as a political persecution, but ended up being a case of religious martyrdom. Sunu was a member of the royal family who tried to crown Emperor Kangxi's eighth son, Yun Yi, after his father's death. This angered the crown prince Yongzheng, and undoubtedly contributed to his edict against Christianity. During the second year of his reign Yongzheng sentenced the entire Sunu family to exile at Xining, the present-day capital of Qinghai Province. Sunu's sons Sunijing, Shunichen, Leishihong, Wunichen and Mu'erchen were all baptized Christians. Leishihong and Wunichen preached with enthusiasm after arriving in Xining. The governor reported to Yongzheng that the brothers had violated his ban on Christianity by preaching and raising money for the construction of a church. Yongzheng summoned both of them back to Beijing and executed them. Sunu was blamed and persecuted, and died shortly afterwards. His other family members were scattered throughout China and many were brutally tortured.

The Spanish Dominican martyrs

A new and more ferocious crackdown against Christians occurred from 1746 to 1748. Church buildings were destroyed and hundreds of Chinese Catholics were martyred. The coastal province of Fujian was the location of several pitiless martyrdoms of Spanish Dominican missionaries. The Dominicans had established 37 churches throughout the province, and the authorities were eager to crush their successful work. Fourteen Chinese believers who were found guilty of harbouring the Dominicans were also executed. Hundreds of Christians were arrested and cruelly treated in prison, and many young girls were sexually abused because of their faith.

Pedro Martyr Sanz was one of the Spanish missionaries who hid in Fujian when the persecution of 1724 commenced. After six years in hiding, during which time he continued to serve the flourishing Christian community, Sanz was appointed bishop of Fujian. For many years Sanz hid in Christians' homes, secretly ministering to them. The Chinese authorities presumed he and several other missionaries had fled China, but when rumours started to abound that the priests were in hiding, a large manhunt was launched to flush them out. At that stage Sanz and the other foreigners decided to surrender, believing it was not worth endangering the lives of their protectors. This act of surrender did nothing to lessen the punishment against Sanz. He was cruelly tortured and

Pedro Martyr Sanz

sentenced to death. In prison at Fuzhou, Sanz found out about his pending execution in a letter from a Chinese priest, who wrote: "Your Excellency will soon be crowned with the palm of martyrdom. We cannot hold back our tears. But now we ask your blessing and intercession before God."

After reading the letter in his prison cell, Sanz prostrated himself on the ground and recommitted himself to Jesus Christ. For three days he prayed in order to prepare his soul to meet the Lord. On 26 May 1747 an executioner's sword separated Sanz' head from his body, and the Spaniard's spirit ascended to heaven. During his time in prison Pedro Martyr Sanz had converted many Chinese prisoners and guards, including the executioner who was given the task of beheading him. Sanz' peace and joy in the face of death proved a powerful witness.

When the edict against Christianity was issued, Joachim Royo was travelling around the provinces of Jiangxi and Zhejiang. He was the only foreign missionary in those places and so was easily detectable. Local believers helped the

Joachim Royo

Spaniard evade the authorities. Royo hid during the day and ministered at night, often sleeping in caves, tombs and grave-yards.

Royo was discovered in July 1746 and sent to prison at Fuzhou. For the next two years he remained behind bars. Other prisoners reported he spent most of his time in prayer and in preaching the gospel to his cellmates and guards. His face had a glow to it which reflected the beauty and holiness of Jesus Christ.

Joachim Royo was finally put to death by suffocation on 17 October 1748. He was 57 years old. The men charged with executing him declared, "He received us with joy. We felt a deep remorse about being forced to carry out the order for his execution, because we revered him as a very good and inno-cent man. He constantly preached to us about the Christian religion and in prison we always saw him praying to God with a joyful countenance. Oh, he was indeed a holy man."

Juan Alcober joined the Dominican order when he was just thirteen, and commenced his ministry in Asia at the age of 33. Chinese believers courageously sheltered Alcober in

Juan Alcober

their homes, moving him about from one place to another to evade detection. On one occasion soldiers were closing in on a village where Alcober was hiding, so an ingenious plan was devised to place him inside a coffin and stage a mock funeral. The "mourners" carried the coffin to safety right through the lines of the unsuspecting soldiers. On another occasion Alcober was disguised as a water-seller, which enabled him to travel from village to village encouraging the believers. Troops came to the place where he was hiding, so he climbed into a tree. As the night wore on, Alcober realized he would need to spend the whole night in the tree. When the missionary quietly said his evening prayer he was surprised to hear someone else praying. His friend Francis Serrano was hiding on a different limb in the same tree!

Finally Alcober was discovered and was sent to prison in Fuzhou where he was tortured mercilessly. As Alcober awaited his execution he wrote, "*Expectantes beatam spem et adventum gloriae magni Dei*" (Awaiting the blessed hope and the coming glory of our Mighty God).

For more than two years this humble Spanish priest was detained, until his sentence of death by strangulation was carried out on 28 October 1748. He died alongside his compatriot Francis Diaz. The executioner later described the martyrdoms of Alcober and Diaz: "I called two guards and my brother to help me carry it out. As we approached them, we saw them praying. They urged us to follow the law of God. We tied a rope around their necks and began to spin them around until they strangled to death. They died praying, welcoming death peacefully."

Francis Diaz was the "baby" of the four Spanish Dominican martyrs. He was aged just 35 at the time of his death, yet had already spent twelve years in Asia as a missionary. Even as a child Diaz had told his father he wanted to preach the gospel in China. When Diaz first arrived in Fujian he found the mission in turmoil because the government was

Francis Diaz

hunting for Christians, seeking to put them to death. Not being fluent in the language, he was forced to rely on the help of local believers to survive. His fellow Dominican Francis Serrano often spent time with the new recruit. Serrano gave Diaz permission to leave China if he wanted, but Diaz chose to remain regardless of the consequences.

In 1746 Francis Diaz was finally captured and thrown into prison. On 28 October 1748 he was taken outside the prison and suffocated to death. Some brave Christians risked arrest by coming to retrieve his remains so they could give him a proper burial.

Born in Granada, Spain, in 1691, Francis Serrano joined the Dominican order in his hometown and was considered a holy and virtuous man. In 1725 he departed Spain for the Philippines, and a short time later was reassigned to work in China's Fujian Province where he was highly respected as a pastor.

Serrano's success in hiding from the authorities finally ended in June 1746. He was arrested and taken to the Fuzhou Prison, where he was interrogated and tortured for the next

Francis Serrano

28 months. One of his ears was permanently damaged from the beatings he endured. The interrogators were desperate to obtain the names of key Chinese Catholics who had protected Serrano, but he refused to give them any of the information they desired. In those days when a criminal was sentenced to death he was branded across his face. Serrano wrote, "Our hearts exulted. We were branded as slaves of Jesus Christ. Since our great Lord accepts us, these heads of ours are no longer ours any more, but the Lord's. He can take them whenever he wishes."

On the night of 28 October 1748 Francis Serrano was put to death by suffocation. He had lived his 57 years to the full, and had spent 23 of those preaching the gospel in China.

CHAPTER 4

THE GREAT RELIGIOUS INCIDENT

One of the cruel ways 18th-century Chinese Christians
were tortured by their captors

The year 1784 witnessed the start of a particularly severe persecution against Christians, which is remembered in Chinese history as *Da Jiao'an* ("The Great Religious Incident"). Muslim revolts in Shaanxi had made the government suspicious of all religious activity. Emperor Qianlong ordered the destruction of churches and the arrest of all European and Chinese priests. Believers were ordered to denounce Christ or face severe consequences. In the months following the edict dozens of missionaries and priests were arrested and sent to Beijing, where they were cast into prison.

By Chinese New Year so many Catholics had been arrested that the prisons in Beijing were overcrowded. To solve the problem the officials brought them to trial sooner than planned, executing many of them immediately. The first group of 53 Christians was summoned to appear before the tribunal. Before the trials were completed ten out of the 53 prisoners died from the filthy conditions and lack of food. Thirty Chinese catechists (those who instructed and prepared new converts for baptism) were sentenced to perpetual slavery, and banished beyond the Great Wall to the inhospitable realms of the barbarian tribes. Six European and four Chinese priests died in prison, including the 33-year-old Italian Atto Biagini who perished after suffering persistent attacks of dysentery.

The second set of trials concluded without the passing of any death sentences, but missionaries Giovanni da Sassari, Giuseppe Mattei, Giovanni Battista da Mandello, Antonio Luigi Landi, Giacomo Ferretti and Manuel Gonsalvez were sent to prison for the rest of their lives. These men were new arrivals in China. After risking their lives on the long sea journey from Europe to the Orient, they were arrested while on their way from Macau to their appointed mission in north China. They spent the remainder of their lives rotting in a Chinese prison, chained and manacled to the wall.

Five Chinese Catholics – Philip Liu Kaidi, his friend and servant Dominic Chang, Simon Liu, Xue Chenglin and Thomas Liu Renjie – were condemned to perpetual slavery in the backwater town of Ili in northern Xinjiang, at the time considered the furthermost extremity of civilization. Prisoners sent to Ili had the words *Wai Xian* branded on their foreheads, meaning "beyond the frontiers". Before departing for the cross-country journey Xue and Chang were beaten with 100 blows each. The 33-year-old Philip Liu Kaidi was worn out by the hardships and died during the journey. Many other Chinese laymen who had assisted the missionaries in their travels were also sent into slavery. Hundreds of others received beatings and a range of other severe tortures.

As their investigations progressed the government became aware that dozens more missionaries were in China than they had originally thought. Reports came in from each province telling of numbers of foreigners arrested. Most had been living and ministering secretly in China with even local officials unaware of their existence. In April 1785 a delegation from Shandong Province arrived in the capital with five Catholics in chains. Crescenziano Cavalli, Adrian Zhu Xingyi, Li Song and Shao Heng were dispatched into exile at Ili and never heard of again. Sichuan Province yielded four missionaries who arrived in chains at Beijing on 28 April.

Francesco Magni and Antonio Sacconi were two Italian martyrs of the 1784–85 persecution. Magni was the bishop of Shaanxi until Sacconi succeeded him in 1777. In December 1784 the officials in the far north of Shanxi arrested a group of Christians and held them in prison under horrific conditions. Some of the believers, under duress, provided the names of several missionaries – including the bishop – who had been hiding in Shanxi for years.

When the persecution commenced Magni was captured first, and Sacconi heard that the government had arrested a group of Chinese believers in order to lure him out of hiding. He decided to give himself up, and presented himself at the governor's residence the day before Christmas 1784. The bishop, who spoke fluent Chinese, explained that it was only his love for the Chinese people that had prompted him to leave his native country and come to China to teach the way of salvation. The officials came to see the situation in its true light and removed the heavy chains that Sacconi, Magni and some of the prisoners had worn for months. The governor explained that he did not have the power to release the men, however, as the order for their arrest had come from the emperor in Beijing, and to disobey his orders would result in his own death. The two bishops were sent on the long over-land journey to Beijing for trial. After weeks of travelling over bumpy roads, confined inside cages like wild animals and jeered at and reviled by crowds at each town along the way, Magni and Sacconi arrived at the nation's capital and were thrown into a filthy prison along with 51 other Catholic leaders from around the country. The two Italians were among ten prisoners who died from the dire conditions.

One of the better-known martyrs from the Great Religious Incident was Francesco della Torre. Born in 1732 in Genoa, Italy, della Torre held a vital job as procurator of the Sacred Congregation of Propaganda for China and Indo-China (today's Vietnam, Laos and Cambodia). Della Torre had official permission to live in China and be in charge of foreigners' mail, and so was legally protected as long as this status remained in place. The Guangdong Province officials wanted to prosecute della Torre, but did not dare to do so until they received permission from the imperial court in Beijing.

In January 1785 Beijing undertook steps to have della Torre arrested. The emperor revoked his official status, and in the next few weeks "evidence" against the Italian came flooding in from the provinces, resulting in a warrant being issued for his arrest. The court discovered that dozens of missionaries had stayed at his home before embarking for inland provinces.

During numerous court appearances della Torre refused to betray a single missionary. On 23 January 1785 the Italian was bound and sent on the long journey north to Beijing. He arrived in the nation's capital after an arduous ten-week journey. Within weeks he was a dying man. On 29 April his body expired. The faithful Francesco della Torre had endured to the end.

Frenchmen Etienne Devaut and Joseph Delpon were among the earliest China martyrs of the Paris Foreign Missionary Society. Devaut had been working in Sichuan Province for nine years when the storm of persecution broke in 1785. Devaut was arrested and imprisoned at Chengdu before being cruelly transferred to Beijing for trial, travelling for months across terrible roads while confined inside a cage. The torturous journey ruined Devaut's health and he died in prison on 3 July. Joseph Delpon realized there was no point trying to hide, so he voluntarily surrendered to the authorities. Reaching Beijing barely alive, Delpon expired on 8 July 1785, aged just 31. Another French missionary, Paul Souviron, died in prison in Guangdong Province while the authorities debated what to do with him. Two of his travelling companions were banished to Xinjiang where they were enslaved for the rest of their lives.

In late 1785 the remaining missionaries were released from prison on condition that they leave China immediately. Most decided to leave, with the plan of secretly returning to China as soon as possible.

When the dust settled on the persecution of 1784–85, hundreds of believers in Christ had been martyred or condemned to slavery for the rest of their lives. The trials in Beijing had featured only those foreign missionaries and the

Chinese who had helped them. More severe punishment was meted out to believers in the provinces.

The Catholic Church in China flourished in the years following the Great Religious Incident. The threat of severe persecution had done nothing to hamper the growth of Christianity. The emperor and his advisors believed that once the missionaries were removed the church would collapse. They were wrong. Many stories were told of the courage and commitment of believers throughout the nation, including one old man who, while being cruelly tortured, encouraged his persecutors to be even harsher with him because for many years he had longed to experience the fellowship of sharing in Christ's sufferings.

CHAPTER 5 SLAUGHTER IN
SOUTH CHINA

Many Christians in China were tortured like these
condemned criminals.

Since their arrival in south China centuries earlier, Catholic
missionaries had established strong works among both the
Han Chinese and ethnic minority communities. By the 19th
century the government was wary of the burgeoning
Christian population and decided to systematically destroy
the church by removing the shepherds and scattering the
sheep.

The 19th century again saw much hostility towards
Catholics throughout China, with hundreds being killed for
their faith in Christ. In 1807 the Protestant Robert Morrison
arrived in China, and for the first time since the demise of the
Nestorians several hundred years earlier, Catholics had to
share this massive land with other representatives of Christ,

although for the first several decades Protestants remained small in number and influence compared to the Catholics.

From the 1820s onwards there was a large number of martyrdoms in the border region between south China and north Vietnam. The situation was greatly exacerbated after the start of French military action in 1847. The French seized control of Vietnam, Laos and Cambodia – a region they collectively called Indo-China – and had plans to expand their colonial influence deep into China. The Chinese struck back hard. Almost all of the missionaries in the area at the time were members of the Paris Foreign Missionary Society. They were viewed as spies and agents of the French government, and their converts were considered traitors. The result was a bloodbath. When an angry mob drove one particular missionary out of a city they cried after him: "You burned our palace, you killed our emperor, you sell poison to our people, and now you come professing to teach us virtue!"

Some of the worst persecution occurred in Guizhou Province, which had long been considered the most impoverished in China. In 1814 Peter Wu Guosheng lived among a community of 600 believers at Longping. He was a hard worker, and saved enough money to open a large hotel,

Peter Wu Guosheng

through which weary travellers from faraway places regularly passed. One day two Catholics named Xu and Leng stayed at the hotel. They saw that Wu had a warm and outgoing personality, and one night when a full moon was in the sky they led Wu to a relationship with the Creator of the universe, using the stars and moon to illustrate their message. Wu, like Peter in the Bible, enthusiastically followed after Christ straightaway. He destroyed all the idols in his house and compelled the guests staying in his hotel to accept Jesus Christ. Not long after his conversion to Christ, Wu brought 128 of his relatives and friends to faith!

A widespread persecution broke out in Guizhou during 1814. On 3 April of that year Wu was imprisoned and tortured in an attempt to break his spirit and cause him to denounce Christ, but he endured the cruel punishments and remained firm in his faith. Wu wrote a letter to his anguished wife from prison, exhorting her to "Be loyal to the Lord and accept his will."

In prison Peter Wu Guosheng was a great example to the other inmates. He was full of the joy of the Lord and constantly led them in songs of praise. This infuriated the guards, who one day brought a crucifix into the cell and ordered Wu to stand on it. He refused and was condemned to death. His last words before being executed on 7 November 1814 were "Heaven, heaven, my true home!"

Joseph Zhang Dapeng grew up in a non-Christian home without any knowledge of the gospel. As a young man he moved to the provincial capital Guiyang where he went into the silk business with a man named Wang. It was through Wang's oldest son that Zhang first heard the good news of Christ's salvation. He repented of his sins and put his faith in Jesus Christ. After hearing of his baptism, Zhang's two younger brothers strongly opposed him, being enraged that his association with Christianity was tarnishing their good family name.

Joseph Zhang Dapeng

Feeling he had wasted the first part of his life, the 46-year-old Joseph Zhang Dapeng was determined not to waste the remainder and was a zealous evangelist, sharing the Good News with as many people as possible. He even purchased a house on a busy city street so he could teach the Bible. In 1808 he was asked to be the principal of a Catholic school, a position which he accepted. During a persecution in 1815 Zhang went into hiding but was betrayed by his brother-in-law.

The following year he was offered the chance for freedom after his family members came to the prison and pleaded with the authorities for clemency. The authorities agreed he could gain his release upon just one condition – Zhang must first renounce his faith in Christ. He refused, preferring the death sentence instead. He was executed and buried on 2 February 1815.

Louis Dufresse was born in Lezoux, France, and departed for China as a 24-year-old. His arrival in China coincided with a time of persecution, so after spending a year studying Chinese in the Portuguese colony of Macau, Dufresse disguised himself and started the long overland journey to Sichuan Province in 1777.

Louis Dufresse

Over the years Dufresse's ministry in China was fraught with many trials and tribulations. He was arrested during the nationwide persecution of 1785 and condemned in Beijing to life imprisonment. This sentence was later commuted to exile in the Philippines, but Dufresse successfully slipped back into Sichuan in 1789. For the next decade he continued his ministry while being smuggled from one location to another by Chinese believers. After years of ministry Dufresse found the 40,000 Christians under his care to be generally shallow in faith and ignorant of many of the basic tenets of Christianity. Consequently, the now Bishop Dufresse established secret seminaries to train up Chinese leaders for the church.

Finally, after managing to survive for 38 years in China, Louis Dufresse was captured in the countryside and transferred to Chengdu. Thirty-three Chinese believers were arrested with him. Dufresse was thrown into a dungeon for several months before being hanged near the city's north gate on 14 September 1815. His executioners hung his head on the gate for three days as a warning to other Christians.

The Italian Joannes de Triora joined the Franciscan order as a teenager. After arriving in China in 1800 he encountered great success, conducting more than 7,000 baptisms during his 16 years of ministry. In 1816 he was arrested and suffered much during seven months in prison. The authorities tortured the Italian, hoping their remorseless brutality would weaken Triora's resolve and cause him to denounce Christ. On one occasion the prison guards brought a crucifix and put it on the floor, promising to release Triora and send him home to Italy if he would just place his foot on the cross. His refusal to do so made his persecutors angry with rage and they sentenced him to death. The 56-year-old Joannes de Triora was hanged at Changsha, the capital of Hunan Province, on 13 February 1816.

The following year Joseph Yuan Zaide was killed at Chengdu. Yuan had grown up in a God-fearing home, and was ordained a priest in 1795. The following year a severe persecution against the White Lotus Society was launched by the Chinese authorities, and many Catholics were caught up in it. Yuan risked his life by continuing to take care of the flock entrusted to his care. In the end he had to hide on a farm while the authorities searched for him. During this time he continued to share the gospel whenever he had an opportunity.

After more than 20 years of faithful ministry he was

Joseph Yuan Zaide

betrayed by a parishioner and imprisoned. A female member of his flock had fallen into the sin of adultery. Yuan reprimanded her publicly for her sin and lack of repentance. The woman felt deeply humiliated and looked for an opportunity to get revenge on Yuan. Learning that he was leaving on a secret mission to Hezhou, she passed the information on to the local authorities. As he was taken to the execution ground to be killed, Joseph Yuan Zaide encouraged his flock to remain faithful to Jesus Christ. He was put to death on 24 June 1817.

Paul Liu Hanzuo received a martyr's crown in another part of Sichuan Province. Because of his family's poverty, Liu was required to work from an early age. He was given the job of tending sheep, and as a consequence never had an opportunity to attend school. By the time he was 24 years old he had still not learned how to read or write. Despite these disadvantages he strongly desired to attend seminary and was allowed in on account of his impressive character.

When the persecution broke out Liu was forced to disguise himself as a merchant. He sold goods during the day and visited his church members at night. In 1818 Liu went to Dezhou where he stayed in the home of a Catholic family. A feast was approaching so he asked a new convert, who was a carpenter, if he would construct a canopy for the feast. When the canopy was finished it wasn't to the specifications they had agreed upon. The carpenter was angry at Liu's lack of appreciation. To get his revenge, the man went to the authorities and told them where Liu was. They stormed the building and arrested him. For the next five months Paul Liu Hanzuo was held in dire conditions in prison, his feet and hands chained to the wall. On 21 February 1819 he was executed by hanging and his body was buried on a mountain outside the town.

François Clet was born at Grenoble, France, in 1748. He was the tenth child of fifteen in a devoutly Catholic family.

François Clet

Clet's first ministry assignment was to teach moral theology at Annecy Seminary. During fourteen years of faithful service the students endowed Clet with the nickname, "The Walking Encyclopedia".

Because of the chaos during the French Revolution, Clet volunteered for missionary work in China. He reached the Orient in 1791, serving at the mission in Hubei Province. For the next 28 years the Frenchman ministered at great cost and personal danger because all missionary work was illegal at the time. Clet was betrayed by a false believer and was imprisoned at Wuchang, Hubei Province, in October 1819. One account lists some of the horrors the elderly French priest was subjected to:

> Wasted by disease and weak from hunger, he was finally brought before the judge. Asked if he would renounce Jesus Christ, he answered firmly, "No." The soldiers beat him until his body was one big bruise. They stuck slivers of wood under his fingernails, and burnt his flesh with live charcoal. They pulled the hair from his head, and hung him up by the thumbs for hours. Every possible torture they could think of, they used. It was of no avail. François was firm. For Christ he had lived, and, if necessary, for Christ he would die.

Clet was sentenced to death by strangulation, a punishment that was carried out on 18 February 1820 by tying the 71-year-old Frenchman to a cross and choking him. At the same time as Clet's martyrdom, 23 Chinese Christians were sentenced to lifelong banishment to regions outside the Great Wall.

Peter Liu Wenyuan was born in 1760 into a simple farming family. He grew up helping his family grow vegetables and later inherited the farm. One day in 1797, when Liu was 37, a Catholic from Wuchuan passed through Liu's village selling silk. He told Liu about Jesus Christ and the way of salvation. Liu was so convicted by the words he heard that he decided to go to Guiyang, the provincial capital, so he could learn more. His soul was like a dry sponge, soaking in every drop of information it could. Liu repented of his sins and put his faith in Christ. At his baptism he took the Christian name Peter and immediately began to share the gospel with others.

In 1800 Liu was arrested with five other believers and sent into exile in northeast China. On arrival in Manchuria he was sold as a slave to a family and for 30 years was treated worse than a dog. He bore the humiliation for God, making no complaint but remaining confident that God would later reward him for his unjust treatment. In 1830 a general

Peter Liu Wenyuan

pardon was declared for all exiled prisoners throughout China. Liu made the long journey home, only to find that after such a long absence nobody remembered him. Liu was kept from utter despair, however, by the comfort of the Holy Spirit and the promise that God would never leave or forsake his children. Finally after much effort Liu was able to locate his wife and two sons, who were now grown adults.

Four years later the authorities launched another severe persecution against Christians. This time Liu's two sons and a daughter-in-law were arrested. Having been separated from his family for so much of his life, Peter Liu Wenyuan disguised himself and succeeded in seeing his sons, whom he encouraged to be steadfast in the faith. However, a soldier recognized him and dragged him off to prison, where he was subjected to barbaric tortures. Peter Liu Wenyuan prayed constantly and sang praises to God.

Again threatened with exile, Liu refused to renounce his faith. Their threats did not trouble him; after all, he already had 30 years' experience in exile. The authorities, maddened by Liu's stubborn faith, exiled his second son and daughter-in-law to Ili in northwest China. A few months later Liu's eldest son died. Through his grief, Liu was nevertheless overjoyed that his sons had persevered for Christ. One day while in prayer, a large white cloth appeared before Liu in a vision. When he reached out to pick it up, the cloth disappeared. Liu took it as a sign that he would soon die, for in China white cloth is associated with death and mourning. Soon after, on 17 May 1834, the provincial authorities in Guiyang gave an order for Peter Liu Wenyuan's execution. When it was carried out, astonished eyewitnesses reported that a ball of fire came down from heaven and rested over his head, and an angel appeared to wipe the blood from his face and carry his soul to heaven. The following day Liu's wife came to carry his body away for burial.

One of eight children born into a peasant family at Le

Puech in southern France, Jean Gabriel Perboyre entered the Congregation of the Mission of Saint Vincent at the tender age of 16. After many years of service in France he begged and prayed for permission to "go to China, there to preach, suffer, and to die".

Perboyre had expected to go to China immediately, but the mission delayed his request due to his poor health. When Perboyre's missionary brother Louis died in China in 1835, Jean Gabriel was sent to replace him. A widespread persecution of Christians broke out in 1839 after Britain attacked China. Despite the risks, Perboyre continued to operate openly. During one meeting a believer rushed in and

A sketch depicting Jean Gabriel Perboyre's crucifixion

announced that soldiers were coming to arrest the missionary. Perboyre was in two minds whether he should flee or stay with his flock, but when all the Chinese fled he slipped into a nearby bamboo grove and obscured himself from the soldiers' view as they looted and burned the church. The next day the French missionary remained in a nearby forest along with three Chinese servants, but a false believer named Zhong Laosan betrayed their location. The soldiers immediately ran throughout the forest like ferocious wolves seeking their prey, and Perboyre was discovered. He was severely beaten, stripped of all his clothes, and dragged by the hair into the town where he appeared before the local magistrate.

Perboyre was hung by his thumbs and flogged with bamboo rods. Over the coming weeks he was questioned on numerous occasions. A local Catholic girl, Anna Gao, was brought in and the missionary was falsely accused of having had sexual relations with her. The fierce indignation with which Perboyre denied these charges was of such intensity that the magistrate ordered the girl to be removed, and he was too afraid to utter the dirty accusation again.

On another occasion Perboyre was offered a last chance of escape. All he had to do was place his foot on a stone cross and he would be released. He proclaimed, "I have never disgraced the cross of Christ in my life, and never will I bring dishonour to it now." The incensed magistrate ordered Perboyre's face to be struck 40 times with a leather belt for his act of insolence. By the end his appearance was horribly disfigured, but his integrity and witness remained intact. Perboyre was sent for trial to the city of Wuchang, along with about a dozen Chinese believers who had remained true to the faith. For nine long months Perboyre remained in a filthy prison cell, his feet fastened in a wooden vice that was attached to the wall. The consequence of this treatment was that Perboyre lost part of his foot through gangrene and one of his fingers withered away.

Still, the Chinese officials tried to force the Frenchman to give up his faith. During one interrogation they forced him to kneel on broken pottery for four hours, until his feet and legs were cut and the floor covered with blood. The most difficult experience for Perboyre was yet to come. The magistrate brought in the dozen Chinese Catholics and ordered them to spit in Perboyre's face, to beat him, and to pull out his hair. Five of the men had been persuaded to deny their faith, and they reviled the missionary with filthy insults. Perboyre's heart was pained, not for the beatings he was subjected to, but because five precious souls had abandoned the faith. Many more vicious tortures were inflicted on the battered body of Jean Gabriel Perboyre. The following account of his appearance just before death is sufficient for us to imagine the kind of savage treatment he was subjected to:

> His face was swollen to a prodigious size; his flesh was so bruised and torn by the rod and scourge that it hung in shreds around his body; enormous pieces had been torn off; all his limbs were but one wound; he no longer possessed the appearance of a man; he resembled his Divine Saviour.

Finally, on 11 September 1840 the Frenchman's sufferings came to an end when he was marched to the outskirts of Wuchang City and tied to a cross on a hill known as Red Mountain. A large crowd of onlookers watched as Perboyre was strangled with a rope. His body was buried in the same cemetery as François Clet, who had been killed 20 years earlier. The magistrate of Gucheng who had cruelly tortured Perboyre was removed from office shortly after and hanged himself in despair. The viceroy who had overseen many of the worst brutalities inflicted on the missionary was later sent into lifelong exile on account of the evil he had committed while in office.

CHAPTER 6

CHINA'S FIRST PROTESTANT MARTYRS

The Protestant missionary era in China commenced with the arrival of Robert Morrison in 1807, and the number of missionaries quickly grew until there were thousands spread across the empire by the end of the 19th century. As the size of the Protestant force grew the incidents of martyrdoms among both missionaries and their converts also increased. In addition to the victims of violent acts, there were numerous missionaries who died from disease and other hardships. At Fuzhou in Fujian Province the first Protestant missionary graveyard was opened and soon filled up with the bodies of those who had given their all for Jesus Christ.

Although the first recorded Protestant martyrdom in China occurred in 1847, many Chinese Christians had faced years of excruciating hardship and persecution from their families and communities. To most Chinese, becoming a Christian was an act of betrayal, as the general perception was that Christianity was a tool of Western imperialism. It was said, "One more Christian, one less Chinese." Sadly, this perception lingers to some degree even to the present time in China.

1847 – Walter Lowrie

The honour of being the first Protestant martyr in China belongs to the American Walter Lowrie, the son of a famous politician from Butler in Pennsylvania. Lowrie's father,

Walter Lowrie

Walter Lowrie Sr, represented Pennsylvania in the United States Senate from 1819 to 1825. On the expiration of his term he was elected secretary of the US Senate, an office he held for twelve years. He engaged in politics with the fear of God and founded the congressional prayer meetings. His eldest son John was a missionary to India, while Walter Jr volunteered for missionary work to China after graduating from Princeton Theological Seminary in November 1841.

Walter Lowrie sailed for China in January 1842, aged just 22. He could read both Hebrew and Greek, and was highly respected by his fellow missionaries for his knowledge and humble demeanour. In August 1847 Lowrie was invited to attend a mission meeting in Shanghai. During the conference a messenger arrived from Ningbo asking him to return immediately because of an emergency. Lowrie left Shanghai, crossing Hangzhou Bay in a small vessel, when a pirate ship suddenly bore down upon his boat. The pirates, armed with swords and spears, boarded and plundered everything of value. Concerned that Lowrie might testify against them, they decided to throw him overboard. Lowrie floated around in the water for some time and then sank out of sight.

Walter Lowrie was dead at the age of just 28. When his home church in Pennsylvania heard the tragic news they were shocked and full of grief. In 1850 Lowrie's father published a huge 504-page book entitled *Memoirs of the Rev. Walter M. Lowrie, Missionary to China*. Tens of thousands of copies were printed. The result was that many people recommitted their lives to Christ.

1850 – Carl Fast

In 1850 the second Protestant martyr in China perished in an incident remarkably similar to that which killed Walter Lowrie three years earlier. The career of Swedish missionary Carl Fast had barely commenced when pirates killed him in Fujian Province.

At the start of 1850 two young Swedish men – Carl Fast and Anders Elquist – arrived in Fuzhou. They were the first two Swedish missionaries sent to a foreign land, but the history of these promising young Christians was brief and tragic.

After spending much time trying to secure a permanent residence from where they could launch their mission work, Fast and Elquist were finally able to rent a home near the city wall. In October 1850 they visited a British ship that was docked at the mouth of the river to exchange money for their work. As they returned in their small boat they were suddenly attacked by Chinese pirates. Fast was seriously wounded and fell from the boat into the river. He quickly perished and his body was never recovered. Elquist, in a brave attempt to rescue his friend, jumped into the river and succeeded in reaching the shore despite having received several wounds.

Elquist wandered in the hills above the river for two days before he was rescued by a passing ship and taken back to Fuzhou. His physical wounds coupled with the mental and emotional trauma of the incident were too great for Elquist to overcome. He tried to recommence his missionary work but his health worsened. He returned to Sweden in 1852.

1861 – James Holmes and Henry Parker

James Holmes was born in Preston County, West Virginia, in 1836. He was ordained by the Southern Baptists at the age of 22, just a month after he was married. Holmes and his wife Sallie boarded the ship *Falcon* for Shanghai, arriving six months later in February 1859.

Shanghai was a bottleneck for missionaries, and the Holmes desired to work in a more needy location where the people had no exposure to the gospel. In May 1859 they conducted an exploratory trip northward into Shandong Province, finally settling in Yantai. They were joined in April 1861 by Henry Parker and his wife, who pioneered the work of the American Protestant Episcopal Church in the city.

Internal chaos was raging throughout China and conditions were unsafe as rebel groups and bandits took advantage of the unrest to murder and loot. The dreadful Taiping Rebellion brought untold suffering to millions and claimed the lives of many Catholics in the 1850s and 1860s. Protestants, though not numerous in China at the time, were largely spared because the Taiping leader Hong Xiuquan had struck up cordial relationships with a number of Protestant missionaries. For a time a number of Protestant missionaries were hopeful that the rebellion might result in a breakthrough for the gospel in China, but these hopes were soon dashed when the murderous nature of the Taiping movement was revealed. The deception Hong was under became apparent when he proclaimed himself the brother of Jesus Christ and gathered a large number of followers with claims he was on a mission from God to establish a "Heavenly Kingdom of Great Peace". In 1864 a multinational army attacked the Taiping base at Nanjing in Jiangsu Province, slaughtering the rebels and ending the movement. The false pseudo-Christian uprising had resulted in as many as 20 million deaths in China, including thousands of Christians.

Taking advantage of the Taiping chaos, a band of marauders known as the Nianfei neared Yantai in October 1861, having destroyed numerous towns and villages throughout the province. Holmes and Parker decided to go out to the rebels' camp and plead for the safety of their town. They did not return, and eight days later their bodies were found covered in wounds and burn marks. They had lost their lives while attempting to protect others.

Although she was left a widow with a young son, Sallie Holmes decided to continue the work God had called her to. She courageously served in China for 20 more years.

1861 – Che Jinguang

By the late 1850s the work of the London Missionary Society was slowly advancing in Guangdong Province. In the town of Boluo a Chinese man named Che Jinguang had worked as a keeper of the Confucian temple until well into his fifties, before becoming a Christian in 1856. Che first heard the gospel when he received literature from two travelling evangelists. He asked to be baptized, showing the evangelists his ancestral tablet which he had defaced with a chisel to prove his commitment to Christ. Che travelled to Hong Kong to gain further instruction from the missionaries. They were reluctant to baptize him, suspecting he wanted to join the church in order to secure a paid job with them. Che persisted, saying that if the missionaries would not baptize him then he would baptize himself!

Che Jinguang was the first Protestant believer in Boluo, but he was not to remain alone for long. In 1858 he returned to Hong Kong accompanied by two new believers whom he had led to Christ, followed in 1859 with two more. In 1860 Che turned up with nine new converts, and told the missionaries there were dozens more back in his village. The foreigners were astounded by the success Che was encountering, for China at the time was considered a difficult place to present the gospel and converts were generally few and far between. John Chalmers decided he should visit Boluo to see for himself what God was doing. When he arrived in the spring of 1860 he was thrilled to find many genuine believers who had gained a solid understanding of the faith through Che's teaching. Chalmers baptized 44 people.

In May 1861 an additional 40 people were received for baptism at Boluo. Plans to construct a church building were commenced. The missionaries marvelled at how "the seed of truth sown in the heart of an aged and obscure man had been watered by the grace of the Holy Spirit, and through successive years it had brought forth 30, 60, and 100-fold".

Satan and his forces set about to destroy the Boluo church. Almost all of the converts had been simple farmers from villages surrounding Boluo, and now the "high class" men from the town decided to stop the movement before it grew any larger. Encouraged by the local authorities, the men staged a riot which resulted in the martyrdom of Che Jinguang. Seized by the ruffians on 13 October 1851, Che was strung up by his arms and feet to a beam for two nights. Seeing that even torture could not make him deny Christ, the persecutors took him to the river, and while still bound, he was thrown into the water and drowned. The elderly Christian had been promoted to the glorious presence of the Heavenly Father, and entered the history books as the first recorded Chinese Protestant martyr.

1865 – Evangelist Ling

In 1865 the Methodist Episcopal Church commenced work in the town of Jian'ou in northern Fujian Province. A small house was rented from a local businessman and turned into a hall where people came to listen to the gospel being preached or to ask questions about the Bible. The missionaries recruited a Chinese evangelist from Fuzhou, Ling, to lead the work. For the first few months everything seemed promising. Dozens of interested people listened to the message of the Son of God. Many gospel booklets and tracts were sold, and Ling and his co-workers expressed excitement at the prospects for the kingdom of God in that city.

Every year Confucian students flocked to Jian'ou when examinations were held. In the summer of 1865 hundreds came in from the surrounding districts. These men were moved with hatred at the sight of a "Jesus Hall" in the middle of their town. They gathered a crowd together and demolished the church. Ling was dragged into the street and severely beaten. A short time later he died from his wounds. Ling's wife, who had been educated in Singapore, testified, "My husband was a very good, earnest and faithful man. His work is finished – he is most happy now in that beautiful, blessed home above."

The scholars of Jian'ou erected a memorial tablet among the ruins of the "Jesus Hall", with an inscription that said, "Abolish the false, keep the true." They announced that they would never again allow Christianity to gain a foothold in their city.

Satan's desire to keep the gospel out of Jian'ou failed. A man named Xia was the first convert in the town. He came from a well-educated and influential family. At his baptism he changed his name to a Chinese phrase meaning "Keep the Truth" – a bold and direct challenge to the memorial tablet that had been erected over the ruins of the Jesus Hall. Today approximately 50,000 of the 500,000 people living in Jian'ou profess Jesus Christ as Lord and Saviour.

1868 – Samuel Johnson and Wan Taiping

It is difficult enough for family and friends to cope with the news of the death of a loved one, but perhaps a much worse fate befell the families of missionary Samuel Johnson and Chinese evangelist Wan Taiping, who disappeared without a trace in the interior of China in 1868. For the next 18 years there was no news whatsoever about their fate.

Johnson had served with the British and Foreign Bible Society in Shanghai for three years, when in late 1867 he planned a monumental journey by boat into China's interior provinces, intending to distribute Christian literature along the way. Johnson was accompanied by Wan Taiping.

After leaving Shanghai, Johnson and Wan successfully made their way westward to the large river port of Zhenjiang in Jiangsu Province. From there they seemed to drop off the face of the earth. In 1886 a Scottish missionary made a journey in the general direction that Johnson and Wan were meant to have taken. When he returned to the safety of Shanghai he said that at a small town called Huailiu an old man told him, "Twenty years ago there was another foreigner here selling books. During the day a fire broke out, and burned a large part of the place. The people attributed this fire to the evil influences of the foreigner. At dead of night, a body of men went on board and killed the foreigner, his assistants, and all on board. The boat likewise was destroyed."

Finally a glimmer of light was shed on the martyrdom of two bold and zealous Christians, Samuel Johnson and Wan Taiping. They joined the ranks of those who endured to the end, and received the crown reserved for those who taste martyrdom in the service of the Lord Jesus Christ.

1869 – James Williamson

James Williamson was a British missionary serving in the large coastal city of Tianjin in northeast China. Williamson and W. B. Hodge left Tianjin by boat on the morning of 24 August 1869. Travelling south along the Grand Canal, their plan was to visit the mission outstations in Shandong Province before returning to Tianjin. By the following night the missionary duo had made it as far as the village of Chenguantun. At around midnight their boat was attacked by a band of robbers who plundered everything of value they could get their hands on. Hodge was awakened by the noise. The first thing he noticed was that Williamson was missing from the room where they had both been sleeping. Hodge attempted to escape to the shore, but the robbers beat him with the blunt edges of their swords. Despite being severely injured, he managed to make it to safety.

Staggering into the village, Hodge roused the local magistrate from his sleep. A few soldiers were sent to the boat, but the thieves had already made off with their booty. A party of soldiers was dispatched to follow them, while another group was given the task of finding out what had happened to James

Williamson. For three days no trace of him was found, until around noon on 28 August, when his body was found floating in a canal downstream from where the attack had taken place.

The Protestant Church was gaining a foothold in the hard soil of China, but even in these early decades it had come at great loss of life. These early martyrs were only the firstfruits of tens of thousands of Protestants who would be called to lay down their lives for the advancement of the gospel in the world's most populated nation.

CHAPTER 7

TROUBLE IN GUANGXI AND GUIZHOU

The two south China provinces of Guangxi and Guizhou are similar in many ways. They are poor, mountainous, and contain dozens of ethnic minority groups. A series of devastating persecutions against Christians between 1856 and 1862 resulted in many heroic martyrdoms.

Auguste Chapdelaine

Auguste Chapdelaine

Auguste Chapdelaine was born at La Rochelle-Normande, France, in 1814, the youngest of nine children. From an early age he felt the call to Christian ministry, but his parents opposed him, saying they needed him to work on the family farm instead. He obeyed their wishes until two of his brothers suddenly died. Their deaths forced Chapdelaine to urgently reconsider his life's vocation, and his parents finally approved. After a lengthy struggle Chapdelaine finally gained permission from his bishop to work overseas, and in 1852 he was sent out as a missionary to the southern Chinese province of Guangxi. Two years after arriving he had won about 200 people to Christ.

In 1856 the Frenchman visited Xilin, a small town in western Guangxi that was home to approximately 300 Christians, most of whom were members of the Miao ethnic minority group. Two soldiers were ordered to arrest Chapdelaine on 24 February. Afraid that the Christians would defend their leader, the soldiers mobilized a mob of about 100

A sketch showing Chapdelaine being bound to a stake and publicly flogged

ruffians, armed with long pikes and large knives, to assist in the attack.

Local believers heard the approaching mob and encouraged Chapdelaine to escape. He replied, "If I leave, you will suffer for it. To save you from greater harm, I must stay with you." Chapdelaine was arrested on 26 February, along with fourteen Chinese believers.

When the magistrate ordered Chapdelaine to renounce his faith, he replied, "My religion is the true religion and I cannot betray it. I have done no evil, but only persuaded people to do good and win eternal life in heaven." The magistrate was unimpressed and locked Chapdelaine up in a *cangue* – a Chinese cage for prisoners in which their heads and hands are immobilized through holes in the top and sides, causing severe pain and discomfort. Before being secured inside the torture device, Chapdelaine received 100 blows on the cheeks with a leather belt. One blow was enough to draw blood, so the cruel punishment ruined the Frenchman's face and rendered him unable to speak. He also received 300 blows on the back with a cane.

Auguste Chapdelaine tried to imitate his Saviour by enduring the punishment in silence. The torturer thought that Chapdelaine's apparent lack of pain was due to magic and ordered a dog sacrificed and the blood poured over the captive in an attempt to break whatever spell the missionary had conjured up to immunize himself from the pain. By the end of the torture Chapdelaine was almost dead, and was dragged back to the prison cell. An eyewitness said that when the Frenchman was brought back to the cell he was unable to walk, but by a miracle of God he was completely restored and seemed in perfect health a short time later. When the guards asked how he had been able to recover, Chapdelaine replied, "It is the good God who protects and blesses me." Attributing the missionary's recovery to magic powers, the magistrate secured Chapdelaine's bloodied and torn body inside a cangue for further punishment. This last torture was more than his body and mind could endure and he died during the night of 29 February 1856.

The Chinese believed a man's strength and character resided in his heart. They were so impressed by Chapdelaine's courage that after the Frenchman's death his heart was torn from his body, cut into pieces, and cooked in a frying pan. The cannibals devoured it like wild beasts. Even then the insults were not finished. The authorities decided to decapitate the martyr and hung his head on the city gate as a warning to the public not to follow Christ. Boys knocked it down with stones and it lay in the dust and mud, until being devoured by dogs. Chapdelaine no longer cared. He was safe in the arms of Jesus Christ.

Lawrence Bai Xiaomin

One of the Chinese believers who laid down their lives for the gospel with Chapdelaine was Lawrence Bai Xiaomin. Bai came from an extremely poor family, a position exacerbated when both his parents died while he was still a young boy. Bai was forced to hire himself out as a labourer in order to survive. In 1851, when he was 30, Bai moved to Guangxi where he married a local woman. Three years later the missionary Auguste Chapdelaine visited Guangxi and instructed the local Christians in the faith. Bai was strangely drawn both to the foreigner and his strange teachings. He followed him around, listening intently to every word the Frenchman said and comparing those words with the quality of his life. Bai gradually became convinced of the truth of the gospel and decided to follow Christ. Just ten days after his baptism, on 24 February 1856, a mob of 100 armed men descended on Yaoshan village to capture Chapdelaine. Bai managed to escape, but the next day he decided to return to the village to see how he could help. While he was there five or six women – wives and mothers of men who had been arrested and dragged away by the mob – were in deep distress, not knowing what they should do to secure the return of their loved ones. Bai consoled them, and agreed to help them lodge a protest with the local magistrate. The women expressed some concern for their safety, as it was the same magistrate who had ordered the arrest, but the brave new Christian assured them, "What are you afraid of? If it is necessary for us to die, let us have no fear in offering our lives for the glory of God."

Lawrence Bai Xiaomin then led the women to the magistrate's office, but instead of listening to their appeal the judge had them all chained and beaten. When the judge threatened to cut off Bai's head if he refused to abandon his belief, the young Christian answered, "You can cut off my head, and not only mine, but also those of my wife and children; but to renounce my religion, the religion of the Lord of heaven – to give up offering my humble prayers and adorations to him, oh no! I will never be guilty of such treachery! Magistrate! Cut off my head if you will, but I will never be an apostate."

This response infuriated the officials, who ordered that Bai be severely flogged and tortured. Several times he passed out from the pain. When physical force failed to affect the Christian, he was sentenced to death. He was executed outside the southern gate of the town and his remains were eaten by wild animals.

Agnes Cao Guiying

When Agnes Cao Guiying's parents died she moved to the town of Xingyi where a kind old Catholic woman allowed her to stay in her home. Agnes heard the gospel and immediately warmed to the message and hungered for a relationship with Christ.

Agnes Cao Guiying

In 1839, when she was just 18, Agnes married a local farmer. The man's family never accepted the young woman. She was frequently left nothing to eat and was treated as an outsider. Just two years after the marriage Cao's husband suddenly died. After the French missionary Chapdelaine heard about Cao he asked her to consider moving to Guangxi where there was a growing church full of women who needed help and teaching. In the winter of 1852 she journeyed to Xilin. Agnes bonded with the minority tribeswomen, and was dearly loved by all who knew her.

In 1856 Agnes was arrested with fourteen other believers. The captives were taken to a local temple where they were tortured and interrogated. Most of the local believers were soon released, but Agnes was taken and held in a filthy cell. The magistrate summoned Agnes to appear before him, and attempted to manipulate her with his questions. The corrupt man asked Agnes (who was by all accounts a beautiful woman) if she was married to Chapdelaine, insinuating an immoral connection with the missionary. She indignantly replied, "No, I am not. I did not know him until I came here." The judge tried to coerce the young Christian in every way he knew how, but her faith proved unconquerable. The magistrate had Agnes Cao Guiying locked in a cage so small that she could not stretch out. She repeatedly prayed, "Jesus, save me!" On 4 March 1856 she cried out with a loud voice, "God help me!" and breathed her last in this life.

Jerome Lu Tingmei

To the north of Guangxi lies Guizhou Province, home to dozens of tribes and fascinating cultures. A severe anti-Christian persecution in 1857 led to the martyrdom of several key Catholic leaders, including Jerome Lu Tingmei. Lu, a member of the Bouyei ethnic minority group, was trained in the Chinese classics and in Confucian philosophy and culture. Nobody would have guessed this popular young man would one day end up being put to death as a despised Christian. By the time he was 38 Lu was a wealthy man with a wife, two sons and a daughter. He joined the Qingshui religious sect, a branch of the outlawed White Lotus Society, whose adherents worshipped Buddha. In 1852 Lu borrowed some books from a Christian named Paul Yang. They had a profound impact on his heart and mind, and he realized he had made a wrong choice by joining the sect. He renounced his involvement and decided Christianity was the truth. Soon he became a zealous disciple of Christ, bringing many family members and friends to faith.

In 1854 Lu was falsely accused of treason. In prison he suffered countless horrible tortures. Finally on 14 December 1857 Jerome Lu Tingmei was led to the execution ground along with fellow believers Lawrence Wang Bing and Agatha Lin Zhao. The three martyrs were stripped naked and beheaded. Onlookers said that three bands of light, two red and one white, appeared around them and some non-Christians at a distance saw three globes of light in the sky.

Lawrence Wang Bing and Agatha Lin Zhao

Lawrence Wang Bing

Lawrence Wang Bing was born in 1802 to Catholic parents at Guiyang in Guizhou Province. During an earlier anti-Christian persecution, Wang's parents were arrested along with many other Catholics. They were sent into exile in Xinjiang, where they died. After his parents were arrested, young Lawrence was sent to live with his elder sister, but some time later she too was arrested, so Lawrence was sent to his aunt. Despite seeing his own family members unfairly treated, Wang remained a firm believer in God.

At the age of 20 Wang married, and he and his wife had two sons and three daughters. God blessed the work of Wang's hands and over time he became reasonably well off and owned a few acres of land. The other Christians who knew Wang considered him a godly man who treated others generously. He was subsequently appointed the Catholic leader of his community, even though he had never attended seminary. Wang was a gifted evangelist. Wherever he travelled he left behind new believers and strengthened the faith of believers.

Satan opposed Wang's ministry, and soon false

accusations were made against him. The authorities searched for him, so he fled to Maokou where he joined with his good friend Jerome Lu Tingmei. The local officials came to the evangelists and demanded a bribe, but they refused to pay. Wang and Lu were arrested. A beautiful young woman, Agatha Lin Zhao, was also seized. When she appeared before the magistrate the wicked man mocked her vow of chastity and insinuated that no young woman of such beauty could possibly be a virgin. This disgraceful slander infuriated Lawrence Wang Bing and Jerome Lu Tingmei. They spoke up in defence of Agatha, and in so doing angered the magistrate. Stung to fury, he condemned all three to death and they were executed the following day. After death a doctor was summoned to examine Agatha. He discovered she was indeed a virgin, and the magistrate admitted his mistake. The three Guizhou martyrs had left their old bodies behind, and were safe in the arms of their Heavenly Father.

Joseph Zhang Wenlan

Joseph Zhang Wenlan

Two years later troubled again flared in Guizhou, this time at Yaojiaguan, where four Catholics were brutally martyred for Christ. Joseph Zhang Wenlan was expelled from seminary while studying to become a Catholic priest. A sympathetic priest named Gu felt sorry for Zhang and secured a job for him as a children's teacher. Gu reapplied to the seminary on Zhang's behalf, asking them to forgive Zhang for his prior indiscretions. They reluctantly allowed him to return, but only on probation. In 1861 Zhang was working at the Yaojiaguan seminary when it became the target of a fierce persecution. One of the staff members, John Baptist Luo Tingyin, was captured and dragged away to the city. On the road the soldiers met up with Joseph Zhang Wenlan and Paul Chen Changping, who were returning from the town after a day spent buying provisions for the seminary. The soldiers bound the three Christian men and took them to an abandoned temple, where they entertained themselves by torturing their helpless victims for many days. The men held on to their faith in God.

On 29 July the three men and Martha Wang-Luo Mande were paraded through the streets on their way to the execution ground. People noted that the faces of the four displayed peace and joy. They prayed right up to the moment the executioner's sword separated their heads from their bodies.

John Baptist Luo Tingyin

John Baptist Luo Tingyin was born into a wealthy family in 1825. They lived at Qingyian, near the city of Guiyang in Guizhou Province. After a well-rounded education Luo opened a small medical clinic, where he treated patients and dispensed medicine, much to the appreciation of the local community. One day Luo heard the gospel of Jesus Christ. He was transfixed; the words seemed to burn in his heart and soul. He decided to become a Christian and at his baptism he took the name John Baptist. Within weeks he had led his parents and entire family to faith in Christ.

Some time later Luo gave up his medical practice and moved to a farm near Yaojiaguan, where he helped build the new seminary. In 1861 some corrupt local officials arrested Luo along with several other believers. His life was snuffed out at the age of 36.

Martha Wang-Luo Mande

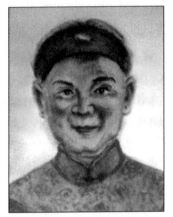

Martha Wang-Luo Mande

After Martha Wang-Luo Mande married it was found that she was unable to bear children, so she and her husband adopted two of their nephews instead. In the Chinese culture of the day Martha had to live with the deep shame and stigma of her barrenness for many years. Life became even more difficult when her husband suddenly passed away. Her two adopted sons became wild rebels and soon squandered all the family's savings. They left home and abandoned their mother. Martha moved to outside the southern gate of Zunyi, where she managed a small inn and made straw shoes in her spare time.

In 1852 Martha celebrated her 50th birthday, and in that same year she heard the gospel of Jesus Christ for the first time. She was fascinated by the new teaching and hungered to learn all she could about it. She believed and was baptized on Christmas Day 1852. The next year Martha set out on a three-day journey to the provincial capital Guiyang, where she had been offered a job in a convent for nuns. She helped with cooking and laundry, and loved the peaceful atmosphere that prevailed there. When the severe persecution broke out, Martha served the imprisoned Christians by bringing them food from the seminary kitchen and washing their clothes for them. The captors mocked and ridiculed Martha for her servitude, but she refused to be intimidated, believing that by serving her brethren she was indeed serving Christ.

On the day that the three Christian men were due to be executed, Martha was washing their clothes at the riverbank. As they were being led to the execution ground she followed along in spite of the soldiers' threats to cut off her head. Showing no fear, Martha Wang-Luo Mande declared, "If they can die, so can I." She was beheaded with the others.

Paul Chen Changping

The last of the four Yaojiaguan martyrs was Paul Chen Changping. He came from a family which these days would be labelled dysfunctional. While Chen was still young his father left home after a family feud. His father later met a Catholic priest, Lee Wanmei, who urged him to return home and reconcile with his family. When he arrived, however, he found his wife had remarried, and he was only able to gain custody of his son, Changping. Soon discovering he was unable to raise the boy alone, Changping's father handed him over to the church. By the time he was a teenager, Paul had become a fervent follower of Christ, and was baptized on Christmas Day

1854. Wanting to become a priest, Chen attended seminary but his peaceful progress came to an abrupt end when his father suddenly turned up at the seminary in 1857, demanding his son return home. Paul was determined not to go, and a loud argument ensued. The seminary leaders decided not to intervene, preferring to let the young man decide for himself. He decided to continue his studies. Paul Chen Changping was one of those held in an old temple and tortured mercilessly before being horribly murdered.

Jean-Pierre Néel

Jean-Pierre Néel

A fresh persecution broke out in Guizhou in February 1862. Five leading Catholics were killed, including the influential French missionary Jean-Pierre Néel. Born at Lyon in 1832, Néel's brief life of 30 years was intensely dramatic.

While studying at seminary, Néel expressed a desire to serve Christ in the neediest places on earth. He was assigned to Guizhou Province in China, where there had already been numerous martyrdoms of missionaries and their Chinese converts in years past. Néel knew that by going to China he was effectively signing his own death warrant, but he was ready and willing to follow Christ regardless of the cost.

Néel was arrested along with four Chinese Catholics when a mob of 100 men, some on horseback, descended on the place they were staying. The local magistrate was with the mob. He tied the Frenchman's pigtail to the tail of his horse, forcing Néel to walk or run according to the whim of the horseman. The other soldiers roared with laughter at the spectacle. Néel was cruelly tortured and threatened with death if he refused to betray Jesus. He replied, "If you want to kill me, do it now; to betray my God is impossible!"

The group of five Christians was beheaded on 18 February 1862, starting with Jean-Pierre Néel. It was said that immediately after Néel died, a beam of light appeared in the sky. The officials and all the non-Christians saw it and were surprised. The persecutors hung the heads of the five martyrs on the town gate as a warning to the people against faith in the Christian religion, but some believers came during the night and secretly removed them for burial.

The four Chinese martyrs included the 57-year-old John Zhang Tianshen, who had been a follower of Christ for just one month before being called to lay down his life; Martin Wu Xueshang, who was driven to the foot of the cross after a painful divorce; John Chen Xianheng, who had assisted Néel and preached the gospel over a wide area; and Lucy Yi Zhenmei, a 47-year-old virgin who was also put to death because she refused to deny her Lord.

The headless corpses of the five martyrs of Kaiyang were left where they had fallen. The next day some local believers went to gather the remains, only to find ten wolves feasting on the carcasses.

CHAPTER 8

THE TIANJIN
MASSACRE

Notre Dame des Victoires (now known as Wanghailou Catholic
Church), the site of the 1870 Tianjin massacre

Tianjin, today the third most populated city in China after Shanghai and Beijing, sprang to worldwide prominence in 1870 when eleven Catholic missionaries and approximately 100 Chinese believers were ferociously massacred. At a time when photography was not yet commonplace, shocked Europeans were left to imagine the carnage as they read the newspaper reports of the day.

In 1858, after a series of military clashes with Britain, France and the United States, the Chinese were forced to sign the Treaty of Tianjin, giving free trading access to those Western nations. Not content with that treaty, the British bombed the city in 1860 and coerced the Chinese into declaring Tianjin a "treaty port". Over the next few decades the British, French and Americans were joined by the Germans, Italians, Belgians, Austro-Hungarians and Japanese. Each nation claimed a piece of Tianjin for itself, building "concessions", each of which was a mini-city with its own prison, school and hospital.

The majority of Chinese people in Tianjin deeply resented the presence of so many foreigners in their city. This resentment boiled over into violence in the summer of 1870. The French were especially despised due to their perceived arrogance. In 1869 they constructed the provocatively named Notre Dame des Victoires on the site of a former temple and imperial garden. The cathedral was destined to be the focal point of the 1870 massacre. Over the course of history the cathedral was destroyed twice by the Chinese, only to be rebuilt each time by the defiant French.

The Catholic mission at Tianjin had grown into an extensive work. In one year more than 50,000 hungry people were provided meals, and 48,000 given medical treatment. The Holy Childhood orphanage housed 179 abandoned children. It was staffed by five French, two Belgian, one Irish and two Italian nuns. These ten sisters were receiving more abandoned children on their doorstep than they could cope with. Due to an epidemic, a total of 34 children in the orphanage had died in the months preceding the massacre. The anti-foreign sentiment in the city created a highly charged atmosphere and rumours abounded that the nuns were killing the children and using their hearts to produce drugs.

By mid-June 1870 the rumours were so widely believed that even some of the Tianjin Christians stayed away from the churches in protest. The missionaries remained indoors for fear of violence on the streets. Soon after noon on 21 June the fire-gongs were sounded across the city and a mob gathered. There was no fire to douse, however. The mob advanced to the French Consulate and burned it to the ground, murdering all the staff. They turned their sights on the Catholic orphanage about one mile away. Inside the nuns and children were aware of the savage calamity brewing outside. Maria Andreoni prepared a favourite lunch for the children, but none of them was disposed to eat.

By the time the frenzied mob reached the orphanage the men had been taken over by a spirit of hateful revenge. The ten nuns were stripped naked and barbarously stabbed and hacked to death before their corpses were thrown into a fire. Between 30 and 40 Chinese Christians associated with the orphanage were also slain. The mutilated and burnt remains were then gathered up and hurled into the nearby river. One gruesome report noted that

> A lance, twelve feet long and very thin, was passed through their bodies, coming out at the neck, then they were exposed in the street on each side of the great door – these were the trophies of the victory. Others were cut in pieces, and then distributed to the mob. These monsters even devoured the hearts of the sisters, and ate their flesh. They dragged out their eyes, cut off their breasts, and tore out their entrails.

By the end of the day 21 foreigners lay dead, including ten European nuns connected to the orphanage. Approximately 100 Chinese believers also lay dead. One man named Hou had his legs squashed in a wooden vice. He survived, but his legs were a horrific mess, with hundreds of worms crawling out of them. He finally perished about a year after the massacre.

The leader of the Catholic church in Tianjin was the Lazarist priest Claude Chévrier. Having arrived in China at the relatively advanced age of 45, Chévrier found the challenge of learning a foreign language difficult. In 1868 he was appointed to lead the mission, and was given responsibility for the construction of the Notre Dame des Victoires, a cathedral "named with strange disregard for Chinese feelings", according to a Christian historian. Less than a week before the massacre, Chévrier wrote,

> At this moment all the devils in hell seem to be let loose at Tianjin. The Christians will soon be exterminated, and I hope we shall be at the head of them. What consoles me is the thought that our Lord often chooses for the foundation of His works the greatest crosses and trials. So, in spite of all, I go on hoping.

Claude Chévrier

Vincent Ou was a native of the southern province of Guangdong. He impressed many with his gentleness and charitable spirit, and often did jobs that placed him in great personal danger, including helping foreign missionaries enter the empire. Finding himself in Tianjin at the time of the massacre, Ou was spitefully choked to death and then cut to pieces.

The ten nuns slaughtered in Tianjin came from several countries. Marie-Thérèse Marquet was a native of Belgium. Before leaving her homeland for China she told a priest, "It is very probable that I shall die in China." As the frenzied mob approached the orphanage baying for blood, Marquet rose from her knees and went out to speak to the leader. In a loud voice she asked, "What do you want with us? We only try to do all the good we can to your poor and sick. If you wish for our lives, take them. We are ready to die, but spare the children!" A sword flashed and the Belgian was slashed across the face. Marquet was killed on the spot, and then her hands and feet were cut off. She was 45 years old.

Maria Andreoni was once described as "one of those souls whose candour and innocence ravish the heart of God and gain every possible favour from heaven". Born in a small village near Florence, Italy, in 1836, Maria was raised in a Christian family whose main occupation was the making of straw hats. She was much loved by the other villagers, who called Maria "the angel of the village". When she was thirteen Maria suffered two serious illnesses, the second of which was so grave that her mother feared she would die. Maria propped herself up in bed and consoled her weeping mother, saying that God had shown her it was not time for her to die, and that before her death she would earn a crown.

Maria was a strikingly attractive young woman, and she received many marriage proposals from prospective suitors. Maria laughed them off, telling her family that each young man was "too ugly" for her. The vivacious Maria was in stark contrast to her austere sister Charlotte, who often found fault with her sibling. Charlotte was a serious-minded Christian who rarely laughed or showed any emotion. She criticized Maria for not being serious enough about her faith, to which she replied, "Never mind; with all your devotions, I shall be in paradise before you, and have a better place there."

Maria Andreoni made great progress with the Chinese language and was able to teach the children sooner than any of her co-workers. On one occasion in 1867 Maria told her colleagues that she had a vivid dream in which she was martyred for the cause of Christ. One by one the other nuns asked her if they were in the dream too, to which she replied, "Yes". When the elderly Sister Dutrouilh asked if she was in the dream, Maria replied, "No, we were ten of us, but you were not there." The other Sisters did not put too much weight in Maria's dream, but on 21 June 1870 Maria Andreoni and the other nine nuns were massacred at Tianjin, just as she had seen in the dream. Sister Dutrouilh had been surprisingly transferred to another station a short time before the massacre.

Maria was the second nun slain by the incensed mob. She was hacked with a hatchet, then impaled on a pole. When news of Maria's martyrdom reached Italy her parents said, "We are not surprised. Our dear Maria loved God so much that she was always speaking of the happiness it would be to her to be able to die a martyr."

Marie-Josèphe Adam was born near Verviers in Belgium. At the age of 22 she dedicated her life to being a nun. After years of study and Christian work, Marie-Josèphe was sent to Tianjin in northeast China in 1864, where she was much loved for her calmness, wisdom and generosity. She often spoke about the love of God and encouraged the other nuns and Chinese women to cultivate a simple lifestyle centred on glorifying Christ. When the mob arrived at the orphanage the 34-year-old was stabbed by a lance near her heart. As the life drained from her body, the Belgian's hands were folded on her chest as though she was praying for her attackers.

Born near Chevillé, France, in 1823, Marie-Anne Pavillion was appointed to join the team in Tianjin, arriving in late 1862. She proved to be a self-denying disciple of Christ, always humble and willing to help anyone in need. Marie-Anne's greatest joy was found in helping poor Chinese children. If a trip to the countryside was scheduled she would drag herself from her sickbed to go on it. When the nuns discovered a dying child Marie-Anne was known to shout out, "What a blessing! Here is another one for us!" She viewed children as little angels, and told her colleagues that if she were ever called to die for Christ, she would be happy to do so while helping children for him. She was granted her desire.

Amélie-Caroline Legras was born at Paris in 1834. In her late teens she had already cultivated an intimate relationship with the Lord Jesus Christ, and desired to serve him more fully. After working as a missionary for nine years at Alexandria, Egypt, she was asked to go to China and help in orphanage work. She was a quiet and calm woman who engaged in much fervent prayer with God. Many tears were shed as people whose lives had been impacted by this generous Frenchwoman heard about her martyrdom in the Tianjin massacre. She was literally cut in half by the mob.

Marie-Séraphie Clavelin was another who hailed from France. As a young woman she often struggled to understand the purpose of her life, and it was only by giving her body as a living sacrifice to God that she began to understand the joys of worship and service. Throughout her life Marie-Séraphie never forgot what a wonderful and undeserved privilege it was to serve God. This realization made her always willing to do whatever it took to see God's kingdom expand. Her desire was to go to the most far-flung location on earth if the need there was greatest. She was stationed for a time at Smyrna (now Izmir in Turkey), where she took care of abandoned children. Although she enjoyed her time at Smyrna, Marie-Séraphie's heart seemed to yearn for an even more distant land. She arrived in China in 1863. After seven years in China without a break, the 47-year-old nun perished in the Tianjin massacre. One account says, "She had a more horrible martyrdom than the others; for while still alive she had her eyes and her heart torn out. The agony caused her to utter agonizing cries, which these brutes in human form laughed at."

Born at Tours, France, in 1831, Marie-Pauline Viollet arrived at Tianjin in 1862. She enthusiastically engaged in the work, encouraging the other nuns at every opportunity and doing all she could to lessen the burdens of those around her. Her heart was especially touched by the little abandoned children that roamed the streets hungry and desperate. When the angry mob attacked the orphanage, Marie-Pauline mercifully fainted before being struck. This did not stop the assassins, who crushed her skull before burning her remains.

Marie-Aimée Tillet took her vows and commenced life as a Catholic nun when she was 25 years old. She worked as a nurse in her native France, but had such a burning desire to serve God as a foreign missionary that she begged her superiors for an opportunity to do so. After six years they finally consented and Marie-Aimée embarked on the long journey to China in 1866.

Like many missionaries before and since, Marie-Aimée went to China with a romantic notion of what it was like. When the harsh reality of her new environment set in, it left her devastated and depressed. She begged for permission to go home, but was gently told she had to stay and adjust, and after the initial shock wore off, her faith in Christ helped her gradually become an effective worker in God's harvest. Marie-Aimée's tender heart was often crushed when one of the orphans died. In contrast to her earlier desire to return to

France, she later told a colleague, "I feel the devil is furious at my being here, and that he is determined, if possible, to drag me away by force."

Marie-Aimée Tillet took refuge in the crypt when the mob broke into the building. They found her and diabolically roasted her to death on a blazing fire, holding her arms and legs down as the flames devoured her. She was just 34 years old.

Born in Paris in 1832, Marie-Angélique Lenu grew up in a wealthy family. Despite her frequent illnesses, she applied to become a foreign missionary and was sent to China in 1864. Her initial experiences were somewhat similar to those of Marie-Aimée Tillet, going through an initial time of "intense disgust with the country and its customs". Just when she was starting to feel more comfortable, Marie-Angélique was martyred for the cause of Christ. Just three weeks before her death she wrote to a colleague: "I am reminded that I am only a passenger on this earth, and my desire is to return quickly to our heavenly home." Marie-Angélique tried to hide from the mob under the veranda of the orphanage, but was discovered and cut to death with a sword.

Alice O'Sullivan was a much-loved jovial nun from Tipperary in Ireland. Born in 1836, her mother tragically died while Alice was just a baby. Her father was a devout Catholic, but could not raise Alice alone and so entrusted her upbringing to a servant woman. She grew up with several brothers, and consequently became something of a tomboy. When she was old enough her father sent her to a convent for her education. The nuns loved Alice and did all they could to share God's word with her. Alice firmly believed in Jesus Christ and dedicated her life to him. At the age of 20, she said goodbye to her beloved Ireland and travelled to France. After serving there for seven years she felt like God was moving her further afield. A priest asked if she would consider going to China. For weeks she struggled with the sacrifice required for such a commitment. Finally, in prayer, she believed the Lord gave her peace and she accepted the challenge.

In China, Alice O'Sullivan served the sick tirelessly, as she battled frequent homesickness for the emerald hills of Ireland. In 1867 she was given permission to return to Europe. Just before the ship departed she spent a time in fervent prayer, and to the surprise of all she emerged from the chapel saying, "I am not going home. Oh, I will not go." The other Sisters asked her what had happened to change her mind. She replied, "If I were to tell, you would not believe me." A close friend, Sister Azaïs, was to travel on the ship with Alice. At the moment of departure she said to Alice, "Goodbye till we meet again." Alice O'Sullivan answered, "We shall never meet again in this world. You shall return, but we shall be all gone." This and many other things that she said led many to believe Alice had been shown a vision of her martyrdom in the church that day, and she had realized that God wanted her to remain in China.

Now that her mind was made up, Alice set to work with a new vigour. She abandoned all desire to see her homeland again and was only interested in obeying God's will for her life. The smiling Irishwoman's ministry was concluded during the Tianjin massacre when she was knocked to the ground and butchered.

As news of the massacre reached Europe an old friend of O'Sullivan, Sister MacCarthy, surprised many by testifying, "When we were together in the convent Sister O'Sullivan, who was then only 16 years of age, said to me one day, 'Later on, you will see, I shall go to China and there die a martyr.' So I was not surprised when I heard that she had really had that happiness."

CHAPTER 9

MURDEROUS
MONKS IN TIBET

For generations of missionaries the forbidden land of Tibet remained an elusive prize. Thoughts of Tibet even today conjure up the most romantic of images, with the smiling Dalai Lama loved by Hollywood celebrities, and Tibetan Buddhism portrayed as a religion of peace and harmony. The gospel has struggled to gain a foothold on "the roof of the world" as Tibet is often called. Hudson Taylor once remarked that it was easier to go into a lion's den and steal her cubs than it was to win converts to Christ in Tibet.

A succession of missionaries in the late 19th and early 20th centuries laid down their lives for the gospel. Their killers were often jealous Buddhist lamas and monks.

Two Frenchmen, Nicolas Krick and Augustin Bourry, were killed while attempting to reach Tibet. They were slaughtered and cut into pieces in 1854 in the northeast Indian state of Arunachal Pradesh, while attempting to cross the border and establish a mission inside Tibet. It was later discovered that their deaths had been orchestrated by the Tibetan authorities, eager to prevent the missionaries from entering their territory.

Another Frenchman, Gabriel Durand, was killed at Mainkung in Tibet in 1865. A furious and spiteful attack by the Buddhist lamas led to several Catholic church buildings being destroyed in the region. At the beginning of 1865 Durand boldly moved back to a village near Bonga, hoping to recommence his former work. Another wave of attacks in

September of that year resulted in the Frenchman seeking to withdraw to a safer area. While he attempted to cross the Nujiang River on 28 September, the 30-year-old Durand was chased by an angry mob and struck by two shotgun bullets. He fell into the water dead. It later emerged that the Buddhist lamas at Mainkung had hired the murderers.

The town of Batang, today in western Sichuan Province but formerly inside Tibet, was a strategic base for Christian work into the vast surrounding areas. For decades a struggle between the missionaries and the local Buddhist lamas resulted in several deaths.

Jean-Baptiste Brieux was appointed to this remote and dangerous frontier town. The region was rife with bandits and violence, although for the previous 20 years the missionaries had generally been allowed to travel unmolested. Whenever Brieux wanted to go on a long journey to visit some of the believers under his care, he found the safest way was to attach himself to a large convoy of travellers. These trips often took weeks to accomplish, across some of the most brutal and breathtaking landscapes in the world.

On 8 September 1881 Brieux was attacked by Tibetan robbers while sleeping in a tent just outside Batang. While preparing for a night's rest a hail of rocks fell on the missionary, and several men rushed into his tent and stabbed him to death. Two of the priest's Chinese colleagues were kidnapped, but one managed to get free and report the events to the authorities at Batang. The magistrate immediately sent soldiers to investigate, and they found that four of the Tibetans who had been involved in the murder were taking refuge inside the Batang Buddhist monastery. The magistrate sent a note to the head lama, instructing him to hand the men over for questioning. The messenger was greeted with a hail of rocks. A small Chinese garrison was then sent to the monastery to arrest the murderers, and this time the

Buddhist monks responded by shooting and wounding three of the soldiers. The men were finally arrested and executed. The leader of the mission said of Brieux, "This apostle has sprinkled the ground of Batang with his blood. May this invaluable sacrifice advance the hour of God's merciful visitation, when Tibet opens its arms to us and the gospel!"

Further north in Qinghai Province, the first Protestant martyr in Tibet was killed in 1898. Two independent Dutch missionaries, Petrus and Susie Carson Rijnhart, entered Tibet

Petrus Rijnhart

from their base in Qinghai, hoping to get permission to begin medical work in Lhasa.

In 1898 the intrepid couple, with their little son Charlie, set out on an epic months-long journey towards Lhasa. It turned out to be a disastrous trip, with two of the three Rijnharts tasting death. After a harrowing journey across the deserts and mountains of northern Tibet, the Rijnharts were stunned by the death of their infant son. After burying him, Petrus and Susie decided to turn back along a southerly route. A gang of robbers trailed them, looking for an opportunity to strike. When the Rijnharts noticed the men, Petrus decided to walk back and talk to them, hoping such a direct approach would show them he was not afraid, and not worth robbing. He never returned, and was presumably murdered by the gang. For days Susie patiently waited for her husband, before finally realizing he was dead. She clung to her faith, but later wrote,

> I must admit it was a faith amidst a darkness so thick and black that I could not enjoy the sunshine. Evening found me still alone with God, just as I had been the night before. My unde-fined fear had shaped itself into almost a certainty, leaving me with scarcely any hope of ever seeing my husband again, and with just as little, probably, of my getting away from the same people who had seemingly murdered him.

Dr Susie Rijnhart put the incredible grief of her experience aside and courageously continued on without shelter and with little food. For two months she advanced, one step at a time, so that when she finally reached the China Inland Mission base at Kangding in Sichuan Province she was mistaken for a Tibetan beggar due to her dirty sheepskin clothes and her face being almost black from exposure to the sun.

Susie returned to her native Canada, where a close friend

Susie Rijnhart in traditional Tibetan dress

observed that she had "changed from a bright, dark-haired girl into a quiet, white-haired woman". After arriving home she was asked if it would be a "cross" to return to Tibet. "No," she replied, "it would be a cross not to return." She remarried and returned to medical mission work among the Tibetans in 1903, and had the great joy of seeing the establishment of the first evangelical Tibetan church in history.

In 1905 the frontier town of Batang experienced more trouble. French missionary Henri Mussot and his Chinese colleague Gong Wenhin were added to the long list of China's Christian martyrs. When Mussot's home was attacked by bandits he fled into the hills and barely escaped with his life. When the Frenchman later returned he found the Tibetans had burned his house down after plundering all the valuables they could find. A later attack at Batang, made with the complicity of the local authorities, resulted in Mussot being tied with a cord around the neck and led into the mountains. On the way the persecutors cruelly bashed him with their weapons, so that his torso was covered with deep bruises. Mussot was held inside the Buddhist monastery for three days where he endured a series of barbaric tortures. The Frenchman begged his captors to spare the life of his faithful Chinese servant, Gong Wenhin. The Buddhists were merciless, however, and Gong was bound and thrown into the river. Mussot was taken from the monastery, tortured with spikes, and finally shot. The torturers cut off his head and displayed it like a trophy above the entrance of the monastery.

At about the same time, Jean-André Soulié was also seized by the jealous Buddhist lamas. Soulié had sacrificially served the local people for years, treating their illnesses for free and providing free schooling for children of poor families. The Frenchman was held in high regard by the people, and the envious lamas could not bear it. The head lama at Batang devised a murderous plan with the chief of police. On 3 April 1905, while Soulié rode his horse towards Batang to visit a fellow missionary, he was surrounded by 60 hired Tibetan thugs from three different villages. The men seized Soulié, and blows and sword cuts rained down on him. His bruised and bleeding body was tied to a tree stump. The next morning the torturers were amazed to find Soulié still alive. They dragged him to Batang where they plundered the mission, destroying it with "a satanic rage". Soulié was barely conscious, but the wicked men proceeded to torture him to death. They pressed a crucifix into his feet and other parts of his body, while tearing up prayer books and demolishing the mission station. Soulié somehow survived for eleven excruciating days. Finally at around ten o'clock on the morning of 14 April, the head lama ordered one of his underlings to shoot the stubborn missionary. He was shot through the head and heart. A fanatic cut off his arm with a sword, and his body was buried under a pile of stones.

After several setbacks the resilient Catholic missionaries at Batang restarted the work and by 1924 the mission numbered two bishops, fifteen missionaries and 4,800 baptized converts.

Four days after Soulié's murder, eleven Tibetan Catholics were brutally slain at the village of Yanjing in Tibet. The church at Yanjing had been birthed in persecution. In 1865, after their community at Bonga had been pil-laged and burned to the ground, two mis-sionaries led a group of Tibetan believers to Yanjing and established a small mission. These French Catholic priests were men of outstanding quality. All who came into con-tact with them – including Protestant mis-sionaries – were impressed by their evident devotion and godly character. After Englishman Thomas Cooper visited the mission he reported:

A Tibetan Catholic

> The history of the mission may, from the date of its establish-ment, be traced in the blood of numbers of brave and noble-minded missionaries who have fallen by poison or the knife in the cause of their religion. Self-banished to this country without a hope of return, the French missionaries have worked on, and in spite of massacres by the savages ... their devotion has been rewarded by hundreds of genuine converts.

Several families responded to the gospel soon after the mis-sionaries started preaching in Yanjing, and other persecuted believers later joined the church. At the dawn of the 20th cen-tury the Christian community at Yanjing numbered more than 200 people.

This burgeoning church did not go unnoticed by the Buddhist leaders of Tibet. To have so many people forsaking their religion and embracing Christianity proved intolerable.

The Dalai Lama dispatched emissaries to Yanjing in order to force the Catholics to denounce their faith. The believers listened to the Dalai Lama's edict, and politely yet firmly replied that they could not change, for they had found the one true religion. In response, eleven Christians were bound to the pillars inside the chapel. The next morning, 18 April 1905, they were dragged out into a field known as the "Field of Blood" to this day. The persecutors read a message from the Dalai Lama, threatening death to all who refused to return to Buddhism. When the eleven again refused the offer they were shot dead and their bodies thrown into the river. Instead of intimidating the believers, this cruel act solidified their faith and helped them to renounce Buddhism. Yanjing has remained Christian ever since.

The orgy of Tibetan violence was not yet finished. A few

Yanjing Catholic Church, near the Field of Blood where eleven
Tibetan Christians were martyred in 1905

months later, near the town of Deqin in northern Yunnan Province, Pierre Bourdonnec reported that he was seeing a shift in the mood of the Tibetan people. They were becoming fed up with the corrupt Buddhist lamas, who exploited them for their own gain, and were more open to the good news of Jesus Christ. At the start of summer Bourdonnec was warned to flee the town by a friend. He made his way southward to Yanmen, where Jules Dubernard was stationed. On 19 July a local warned the two Frenchmen that the following day had been set for their massacre. That evening the duo and a number of local Christians fled into the hills. When they stopped for a rest the more elderly Dubernard, who was not able to walk quickly, begged Bourdonnec to go on alone. For the next few days Bourdonnec and several Christians walked onward through the remote mountains, sleeping in the open and not daring to light fires in case the smoke betrayed their presence. On 23 July Bourdonnec was exhausted and unable to go any further. The next day a mob found him and his two Christian friends: a woman named Joanna, and a servant Matthias. The trio were pushed along the banks of a river by the mob. When they came to a clearing the Tibetans shot them. The two local believers died instantly, but the bullets seemed to evade Bourdonnec for some minutes. Frustrated by their lack of skill with the gun, a Lisu tribesman shot a poisoned arrow which pierced Bourdonnec's leg. This was followed by many more arrows, planted in his body. As blood gushed out and he neared the gate of death, a man from the monastery ran up to the missionary and slashed Bourdennec's face with a sword, slicing his head in half above the jaw. This cruel act excited the lamas who were looking on, and they let out a cry of triumph. They cut off the heads of the two other victims and took their gory booty across the river.

The heads of the three martyrs, along with Bourdonnec's heart and liver, were carried like trophies to the large

Buddhist monastery at Deqin and presented to the head lama. The depraved man, with a broad grin from ear to ear, commended the murderers for their successful mission.

A few days later Jules Dubernard and his helper Raymond were seized by the wicked mob. When the crazed men approached their hiding place, Dubernard ordered his friends to depart in order to save their lives. He then knelt at the foot of a tree and prayed while awaiting death. The mob seized the venerable French priest and wounded him with many violent blows. Naked and covered in blood, Dubernard was forced down from the mountain; all the way they insulted him with vile words and blasphemed God. When they came to a clearing the mob threw large stones at him. The blood-covered missionary collapsed in a semi-conscious state. Undeterred, the callous men placed the nearly lifeless body on the back of one of their number and carried him down the hill. That night he was tied to a post in the middle of a field. The Tibetans mocked Dubernard by asking where his God was and taunted him by saying all his years of praying had been to no effect, for if his Jesus was so powerful he would come and deliver him from his perilous situation. When the Tibetans offered Dubernard a chance to denounce his faith, the old apostle raised his head indignantly, and told them they might as well slice him to pieces there and then, for he would never deny God. The Tibetans, finally exhausted from their exertions, fell asleep in a circle around their prey.

At daybreak three non-Buddhist men from the Lisu tribe were paid to kill Dubernard. Being "good Buddhists", the Tibetans were not permitted to take the life of another creature. For their evil deed the murderers were given a bull. The head lama at Deqin was overjoyed when he was presented with the head and organs of his hated enemy. For more than 40 years Jules Dubernard had loved the Tibetan people more than the lama had. He had served thousands of needy people without demanding anything in return, whereas the local monastery was known as a den of iniquity and the abode of lazy and corrupt Buddhist lamas. Dubernard's head was triumphantly hung on the monastery gate as a warning to the people not to follow Christianity.

Following the massacres of 1905 a few years of relative calm ensued for the missionaries on the borders of Tibet. The next martyrdom occurred on 26 May 1908, when the 25-year-old Frenchman Gustave Behr left the mission station at Batang for a walk around the town. He was seen strolling across the bridge behind the Buddhist monastery. By evening Behr had not returned and his co-workers were worried. They launched a search but no trace of the young missionary was found. It was not until nine days later that his corpse was fished out of the river a considerable distance downstream. The local magistrate conducted an autopsy and found suspicious contusions on Behr's body which indicated he had been struck dead before being thrown into the river in a bid to make it look like a drowning accident. Nobody was charged

Gustave Behr

A piece of France on the Tibetan Plateau: The Catholic cathedral at Cizhong,
defiantly built by Théodore Monbeig after the Tibetan
lamas destroyed the previous church in 1905

with the priest's murder, but he became yet another in a long list of missionary martyrs in Batang.

Undeterred by the frequent setbacks and deaths, the French Catholic missionaries continued to work throughout the Tibetan border areas, treating the sick, feeding the poor, and preaching the gospel to the lost. At the remote town of Litang the missionaries received a telegram from the magistrate on 12 June 1914, informing them that a European had been killed on a mountain slope just outside the town. All of the Litang missionaries were accounted for, so they thought it must be an explorer or a Protestant missionary. A short time later a letter arrived which had been written by Théodore Monbeig on 31 May, informing his colleagues that he intended to leave his home at Yanjing and come to Litang. The Catholics then realized the dead foreigner might be their missionary friend. Their fears were confirmed a short time later when they examined the corpse. They found that Monbeig had suffered "five blows from a rifle, six blows from a sabre, and two stone blows."

Théodore Monbeig was best remembered for constructing a French-style cathedral inside Tibet. After the massacres of 1905, he decided it was necessary to build churches like the ones found in his native France, made out of stone and with a bell-tower and beautiful bell. Reasoning that the enemies of the gospel would find it much more difficult to destroy a stone building, he set about the task of obtaining the necessary materials to realize his dream. The Tibetan Christians welcomed the audacious plan when they heard about it, for the Buddhists had often mocked their poor church buildings compared to the centuries-old citadels of wealth and power that were the Buddhist temples and monasteries. After many years of labour the new church was completed. The French-style cathedral still stands today at Cizhong, southeast of Deqin.

It serves as a reminder of the decades of selfless service performed by the Catholic missionaries in this remote location.

After 60 years of attacks the church in the Tibetan borderlands had suffered only a temporary setback. More workers soon came to replace those who had been martyred, and their faithful example led many people to inquire into the faith. Today there are approximately 9,500 Tibetan Christians in the border areas of Yunnan, Sichuan and southern Tibet where these courageous pioneers gave their lives.

CHAPTER 10 THE GUTIAN
MASSACRE

During the heat of summer, the missionaries in Gutian (then called Kucheng) in Fujian Province were in the habit of retreating to the nearby hill village of Huasang, which experienced a more pleasant climate due to its 2,000-feet elevation. The Stewart family and seven single women had enjoyed a conference in the last week of July 1895, which provided spiritual refreshment for the tired missionaries. Some of those present later said the conference was like "days of heaven on earth". In the final communion service on 31 July the missionaries rededicated themselves to the Lord's service with these words: "Here we offer and present unto Thee, O Lord, ourselves, our souls and bodies, to be a reasonable, holy, and lively sacrifice unto Thee."

A secret Chinese society called the Vegetarians had been stirring up trouble throughout the countryside. Little was known about this sect, apart from the obvious fact that they abstained from eating meat. They were not a religious sect as much as a motley collection of anti-government rebels. None of the sect's prior behaviour had suggested they were interested in killing Christians, so nobody could have predicted what happened on 1 August 1895. Suddenly, at a quarter to seven in the morning, more than 100 men from the sect descended upon Huasang village, and within a few minutes nine missionaries lay dead, two small children were fatally wounded, and the buildings were in flames.

The Stewart family

Robert Stewart

Robert and Louisa Stewart were Irish missionaries stationed in Gutian. Louisa had been instrumental in women's work, establishing a boarding school for girls in Fuzhou that resulted in numerous conversions to Christ. She also helped to establish a Christian hospital in the provincial capital.

The Stewarts had four children with them at the retreat centre, two daughters, Kathleen and Mildred, and two sons, one-year-old Herbert – who was murdered on his birthday – and a newborn baby named Evan. When the bandits attacked, eleven-year-old Kathleen Stewart and the other children were excitedly picking flowers for little Herbert's birthday picnic later that day. When the mob suddenly descended from the woods, the children rushed towards the trail to see what they thought was a procession. Annie Gordon, who had been reading the Bible under a tree, saw the men's spears and knew immediately of the danger. She shouted for the children to run. Kathleen somehow managed to escape the murderers' grasp, and rushed into her parents' bungalow.

Some of the attackers entered the bedroom and struck Louisa Stewart to the floor. They first killed her husband, telling him they had not come to take his money, but to take his life. Poor little Herbert was terribly wounded, and they killed his nurse, Helen Yallop, who had bravely tried to hide the baby under her clothes.

In spite of a terrible gash on her knee, which divided the joint, Mildred got up and went to the nursery with Kathleen, and together the brave little girls succeeded in pulling the wounded baby from under the dead nurse's body. They also rescued their baby brother Evan from the burning house after the Vegetarians set the mission houses alight with kerosene. The murderers believed they had killed all the foreigners, but the few they had missed hid in the woods until the murderers had gone. The shocked survivors didn't know what to do. The next day it was decided they should leave for the safety of Fuzhou, 80 miles (130 kilometres) away. During the arduous journey the little birthday boy, Herbert, joined his parents in heaven. "How glad father and mother will be to see him!" declared the brave Mildred when told of his death. The survivors finally arrived at the hospital in Fuzhou, where doctors attended to their wounds. In a strange irony, the same hospital that Louise Stewart had helped build now opened its doors to receive her children. A day or two after arriving in Fuzhou, the little baby Evan died. Even though his physical wounds had not been so great, it was as if his little spirit could sense the trauma of the situation.

The single women

Lucy Stewart

Lucy Stewart, who was not related to the Stewart family, was still in bed and had yet to dress for the day when the attack commenced. The mob entered her room, and after stealing everything of value they dragged her outside and slashed her to death. On her coffin were placed the words: "Miss Lucy Stewart, whose unselfishness and sympathy made her memory most fragrant – 'Receiving the end of your faith, even the salvation of your souls'".

Hessie Newcombe had also not yet risen from bed when the Vegetarians staged their early morning attack. The women ran out of the door at the back of the house, only to find themselves surrounded by dozens of armed murderers. As the four frightened women huddled closely together, one of them called out, "Sisters, never mind, we are all going Home together!" Hessie's body was found at the foot of a nearby embankment.

Anna Gordon was instantly hacked to pieces by the Vegetarians' swords and other crude weapons. She had struggled with loneliness since arriving in China, yet was fulfilled to be obeying the Master's call. At the funeral service in Fuzhou her coffin was marked with the following touching text: "Miss Annie Gordon, whose faithfulness and fortitude in loneliness impressed all who knew her – 'Where I am, there shall also My servant be'".

The band of wicked men continued their killing spree by butchering Eleanor (Nellie) Saunders, who was still asleep in the house. She was knocked to the floor. Elizabeth (Topsy) Saunders was horrifically slaughtered at the back of the house. The two Saunders sisters came from a strong Christian family in Melbourne, Australia. Their widowed mother took the news of her beloved daughters' deaths as an honour from God. She greeted two friends who called to comfort her with the words, "You've come to congratulate me, haven't you?" She determined to go to Gutian as a missionary in place of her two slain daughters, and did so.

Of the eleven missionaries and children killed at Gutian, perhaps none was remembered as fondly as the young English rose Elsie Marshall. Her life of just 24 years had touched so many that a biography was written soon after her martyrdom. Elsie was born in 1869 at Birchfield near the English town of Birmingham. As she grew up she developed a vivacious outlook on life. She loved to praise God and was constantly communicating with her Heavenly Father in prayer.

Elsie sailed for China on the steamship *Arcadia* on 14 October 1892, still a few weeks shy of her 23rd birthday. As the summer of 1895 commenced, Elsie was so involved in the work that she asked Robert Stewart if she could delay coming to the retreat centre until August. Stewart, with her well-being in mind, declined her request and told her to come with the other missionaries in July. The massacre took place on 1 August. The last letter Elsie Marshall wrote home before she was martyred could not be more appropriate. Mentioning the upcoming spiritual retreat, she wrote,

Elsie Marshall

I know He has some very precious lessons to teach us. One thing, I think, is to look on and see how God works. Another thing, not to be too much engrossed in the work itself to forget the Master, but to remember if He likes to call us away to other work He is at liberty to do so. We are His bond-slaves, just to go here and there as He pleases, and He has made me so glad to leave it all with Him now, and there's not a shade of worry.

Elsie was barely awake when screams rang out around the retreat centre that fateful morning. She was one of the four women hacked to pieces after being dragged from the house. Elsie was seen clinging to her Bible to the very end, though the hand with which she grasped it was nearly severed. Finally she fell under the savage blows raining down on her, and went to be with Jesus.

Flora Codrington was the only one of the adult missionaries to survive the massacre. She was terribly disfigured and mutilated in the attack but heroically refused to give up her call to China. After a brief time recovering in England she returned to Gutian, where she spent many more years serving Christ.

Although there had been numerous slaughters of Catholics over the centuries in China, the Gutian massacre was the first martyrdom of multiple missionaries in the 88 years since Protestants had arrived in China. Both the Christian and secular worlds were outraged at the Gutian massacre, and cries for vengeance were heard. The affected mission societies, however, would not entertain any such thoughts. They refused to receive any government compensation for the loss of lives.

CHAPTER 11

STORM CLOUDS ON
THE HORIZON

The size of both the Protestant and Catholic missionary forces reached its highest point in the years just preceding 1900. The church of Jesus Christ was being established in many new locations throughout China, and many encouraging signs were evident. At the same time, a growing discontent against Christianity and foreigners in general was reaching boiling point. The three years leading up to the Boxer Rebellion saw a number of Christians killed in various parts of China. These martyrdoms were like storm clouds on the horizon. The full brunt of the hurricane was to break in the summer of 1900.

Frédéric Mazel

Frédéric Mazel was born at Rodelle, France, in 1871. As a young man he put his faith in Christ's saving power, and by the time he reached his teenage years, Mazel wanted nothing more than to serve his King as a missionary. He was appointed to join the work at Xilin in south China's Guangxi Province. In March of the following year, 1897, Mazel was laid low with a burning fever. After receiving medical treatment he started on the journey back to Xilin, riding in a sedan chair. Mazel and his fellow travellers stopped at the town of Tianlin on 22 March. The Chinese men who had been hired to take supplies to the mission went on ahead, but a short distance from Tianlin they were robbed by bandits who stole their horses and mules. Mazel decided it was prudent to remain in Tianlin until the local magistrate had caught the thieves. Crowds of locals came to stare at the "big nose" foreigner. One man told Mazel, "It is you French who have attacked us, stealing our land. Now that we have met a man from that country, it will bring us much satisfaction to spill your blood in revenge." At four o'clock in the morning of 1 April 1897, a mob numbering between 30 and 40 men swooped on the house where Mazel was sleeping. He was shot dead in his bed, with one bullet lodged in his forehead, one in his chest, and one in his heart. One of the Christian servants travelling with Mazel was also killed in the attack. Frédéric Mazel's missionary career in China had come to an abrupt end after just eight months.

Nies, Henle, and Bertholet

Francis-Xavier Nies   Richard Henle

Just before midnight on 1 November 1897 a mob of men belonging to the Big Sword Society attacked the German Catholic Mission in the village of Zhangjiazhuang in Shandong Province. Three priests were asleep inside. One named Stenz managed to escape, but the 38-year-old Francis-Xavier Nies and 34-year-old Richard Henle were sliced to pieces.

Far away in Guangxi, on 21 April 1898, the French missionary Mathieu Bertholet and six new believers were

travelling towards the town of Dongjiang when a group of fifteen men ambushed them. Without any weapons, the bandits
blocked the way and shouted, "Anyone who tries to pass will
be killed!" At the same time the bandits blew on conch shells
to alert more of their numbers to come. Bertholet, realizing
the danger of the situation, tried to take refuge in a nearby
village but, as he approached, the gates were locked to bar his
entry. A group of bloodthirsty men encircled the priest.
Without a word they stabbed the 32-year-old Frenchman with
their swords and he soon passed from this world to the next.
Nearby, two young Chinese Christians, Dang Jiyu and Ben
Achang, were also hacked to death. The other believers were
taken captive and forced to pay a fine to secure their release.

Later in the year at Boluo in Guangdong Province the 33-
year-old Henri Chanès and thirteen Chinese Christians were
slaughtered. During the eight years he ministered at Boluo,
Chanès counted more than 1,500 new believers. In October
1898 several of the new converts were mistreated because of
their faith and Chanès complained to a local magistrate on
behalf of his flock. The authorities had no interest in seeing
justice done for the Christians, and helped orchestrate the
massacre on 14 October. Chanès and the thirteen Chinese
believers were slain inside the church.

William Fleming and Pan Xiushan

Protestant missionaries first entered south China's Guizhou
Province in 1877, almost 300 years after the Catholics had
arrived. In 1896 the China Inland Mission started to reach out
to the many non-Han Chinese minority tribes living in the
province.

In October 1898 William Fleming arrived in Panghai to
oversee the work for a few months while the resident missionaries had a period of rest on the coast. Fleming was a

William Fleming in
Chinese dress

native of Broughty Ferry, near the Scottish town of Dundee. At
the age of 17 he became a sailor and travelled the seas for six
years before his life changed dramatically while in Australia.
He wrote home, telling his family that he had given his life to
Jesus Christ, had left the navy, and was studying to becoming
a missionary. Fleming departed for the Orient in 1885.

With local Christian Pan Xiushan acting as his inter-
preter, Fleming travelled widely among villages of the Hmu
tribe for three weeks, preaching the gospel. While they were
away from Panghai, the Hmu burned down 300 houses in the
Chinese part of the village, in protest over which day of the
week the market should be held on. The atmosphere was
tense, so Fleming decided to make his way to Guiyang and
wait for the trouble to blow over. He never made it. On 4
November Fleming and Pan left for Guiyang. After travelling
about fifteen miles (24 kilometres) they stopped for lunch at
Chong'anjiang village. When they crossed the river on a hand-
pulled raft they were accompanied by three men, one of whom
carried a long sword. These men had been appointed by the
headman of Chong'anjiang to kill Fleming and Pan. As they
stepped onto the bank on the other side of the river, the

people of the village crowded to watch the spectacle. Just as they reached a bend leading up the hill, the man with the sword came up behind Pan and struck him to the ground, killing him instantly. Fleming struggled with his attacker for some time before finally being done to death.

William Fleming was the first ever martyr belonging to the China Inland Mission. God had protected their many workers in the 33 years since Hudson Taylor founded the mission. Pan Xiushan was the first of his tribe to follow Christ. His death was an inspiration to many Hmu people, who knew Pan had died unjustly. Little more than six months after the martyrdoms, a missionary among the Hmu wrote,

> There are quite a few persons who profess to be interested in the Gospel and want their names put down as enquirers. Several parties have come to see us. One was deputed by 40 or 50 men to come, and another by a whole village of 30 or 40 families. Already our brothers' lives and labours are bearing fruit.

Sidney Brooks

Sidney Brooks

The English missionary Sidney Brooks is widely recognized as the first martyr killed by the Boxers. He died in Shandong Province in the last week of 1899, even though the Boxer Rebellion is generally recognized to have commenced in the summer of 1900.

Brooks had studied at St Augustine's College in Canterbury, England. He became an Anglican missionary and arrived in China in 1897, accompanied by his sister. Brooks travelled to Pingyin in southwest Shandong Province, while his sister established her home at Tai'an, approximately 150 miles (243 kilometres) away. Brooks threw himself into language study and preaching, and saw little of his sister. She married a missionary, H. J. Brown, and the two newlyweds had only just returned from their wedding in England at Christmas 1899. Brooks excitedly made the journey to Tai'an, where he greatly looked forward to sharing a Christmas break with family members. They had a wonderful time together, and Sidney longed for the day he would be able to return to England to see his many loved ones and enjoy the familiar surroundings of home.

On 28 December, after lovingly bidding farewell to his sister and brother-in-law, Brooks mounted his donkey for the long ride home to Pingyin. At ten o'clock the next morning, as he rode past a village, there was a terrible commotion. About 30 Chinese men brandishing large knives rushed towards him, yelling in a frenzied state.

Brooks was startled. He had no idea what he had done to deserve such a hostile reception. Little did he know, but the men were Boxers, a secret society that were to butcher tens of thousands of Christians across China the next summer. Brooks had found himself in the wrong place at the wrong time, and when the anti-foreign Boxers saw a white man calmly riding his donkey through their village it was more than they could take. They decided to make the Englishman the firstfruits of their blood orgy.

Brooks realized his only hope of survival was to flee, so he forced his mount into a faster speed, but the pursuing Boxers soon overcame the donkey. Brooks leaped from the beast and ran into a temple, hoping he would be safe inside a house of religion. This hope proved to be a false one, for the temple headman had witnessed the chase and wanted nothing to do with protecting the missionary. He grabbed Brooks and tried to push him out of the temple. Brooks struck the man to the ground with his fists. Instantly the temple monks rushed at Brooks from all sides. With his back to the wall he threw punches with both hands, knocking his assailants over.

The bloodthirsty Boxers waited impatiently outside the temple for the condemned man to be brought out. Finally by sheer weight of numbers Sidney Brooks was overwhelmed by the monks, who dragged him to the door and tossed him at the feet of the diabolical Boxers. They set upon him, bashing the defenceless missionary with their knife handles and pricking him with their blades. They kicked him, punched him, and tore his face with their nails.

Brooks tried hard to reason with the men, offering them money for his release. They laughed and spat in his face. The only thing they wanted was his blood. Throwing Brooks to the ground and binding his hands behind his back, the Boxers cut a hole through his nose, ran a rope through and led him around the village, shouting and dancing about him. The villagers joined in the celebration.

In this horrible fashion Brooks was dragged along the path to another village a short distance away. Caring nothing about the man whose life they had in their grasp, the Boxers stopped for lunch so they could discuss how to kill Brooks in the most gruesome manner. The Englishman was stripped to his blood-soaked underwear and made to wait, despite the temperature being below freezing. He shrieked aloud in his pain, but his sufferings only served to delight the fiends.

Somehow, out of utter desperation and terror, Brooks managed to free his hands and raced away. The callous Boxers laughed at this development, focusing their attention on their meal. Three horsemen were sent in pursuit and soon overtook him. Brooks jumped into a deep gully, taking his last stand. The Boxers sprang on him like vultures, cutting off his head and taking it back triumphantly to show their wicked companions.

It later emerged that Brooks had told his sister and brother-in-law of a premonition he had of his own martyrdom. When Brooks visited them for Christmas he seemed depressed. When they asked the cause, he replied that he had received a disturbing dream in which he saw himself walking through the halls of his former school in England. He was back in England and walking through the halls of his former school. He stopped to read the tablet bearing the names of all who had gone out from that school as missionaries, together with the name and field and the date of departure, when he saw another tablet, bearing the inscription: "To those who were martyred for the Faith". He saw his own name recorded on it.

PART TWO

The Boxer
Rebellion of 1900

CHAPTER 12 | PRELUDE TO THE
SUMMER OF
SLAUGHTER

A poster produced by the Boxers portraying foreigners
as a dragon attacking China

Starting in the late 1890s an increase in blasphemous literature and posters appeared in China, produced by enemies of
the gospel who desired that all missionaries be killed or
expelled once and for all. A number of secret societies operated throughout the countryside, sometimes in compliance
with local officials. In the years preceding 1900 a sect was
established under the Chinese name *Yi He Quan* (literally,
"Righteous Harmony Fists"). A missionary, noting their pen-
chant for practising boxing drills, dubbed them "Boxers".

In Hunan Province, anti-missionary placards were

produced declaring things such as "Attack and beat the foreigners" and "All dealings with foreigners are detestable. These men have no fathers or mothers. Their offspring are beasts." The situation was exacerbated by a severe drought that gripped north China. Many believed the drought was heaven's judgement on China for allowing so much foreign influence into the country.

On 21 June 1900 the empress dowager Cixi issued an edict that stated in part, "The foreigners have been aggressive towards us, infringed upon our territorial integrity, trampled our people under their feet. They oppress our people and blaspheme our gods. The common people suffer greatly at their hands and each one of them is vengeful. Thus it is that the brave followers of the Boxers have been burning churches and killing Christians."

With the support of the empress, the Boxers knew the imperial troops would aid in the slaughter. Christians perished in countless cruel ways. Thousands were burned alive, buried alive or dismembered. Most were decapitated by the long, curved swords carried by the Boxers. Sometimes a martyr's body was not allowed to be buried for three days, as the Boxers had heard that Christians could rise from the dead.

Most Chinese Christians were offered their freedom if they would denounce Christ. This act of betrayal usually required a person to bow down to an idol or sign a paper declaring that he or she was no longer a follower of Jesus. While many believers compromised under pressure, many more did not, and died as genuine martyrs of the faith. For decades, critics of the missionary endeavour had claimed Chinese Christians were shallow in their faith, motivated by having their physical needs met. The term "rice Christian" was coined to describe such church members. After the Boxer Rebellion had ended, however, many of the critics were forced to acknowledge they had been wrong.

The Boxer slaughter did not end up being a nationwide rebellion, but was mostly confined to the northern provinces. In other regions sympathetic governors and magistrates chose to ignore the imperial edict, or delayed it sufficiently to allow the missionaries to escape and the Chinese Christians to go into hiding. While thousands of believers were killed in Shanxi Province, not a single missionary perished in neighbouring Shaanxi. The governor, Duan Fang, had befriended several Protestant missionaries. He not only refused to publish the imperial edict to kill missionaries and Chinese Christians, but offered protection and assistance to safeguard them. The same occurred in Gansu Province.

The slaughter would have been much more widespread if not for the brave actions of two telegraph officers at Nanjing in Jiangsu Province. When they received the empress dowager's telegram to "Kill all the Christians!" they were supposed to send it on to all the southern provinces. Instead, the two officers boldly changed the command from "Kill all the Christians!" to "Protect all the Christians!" and thousands of lives were preserved.

A. H. Smith's writings from the time provide a sobering insight into the deeply intense, demonically motivated experiences that believers were compelled to endure during the Boxer Rebellion. He wrote,

> Some groups of Christians were pillaged over and over again, while elsewhere there was nothing but rapine and sudden death, the whole storm having passed over in an afternoon, leaving scarcely a living representative of the hated faith. "Destroy Christians root and branch," was often the war-cry, which the Boxers sought to carry into literal effect by killing not only human beings, but every cat, dog, and chicken belonging to the home of Christians, cutting down every tree, uprooting flowers, and laying waste the courts and gardens of the ruined

A group of missionaries in Shanxi Province in 1898.
Twenty-one of these were martyred for Christ in 1900.

houses. In a room occupied by a refugee Christian family, a for-
lorn little kitten was pointed out to a lady visitor, with the
remark: "A whole village was out all night hunting for that cat.
They said it must be found and destroyed or it would bring
calamity to the town. It was picked up and sent to relatives at a
distance and so escaped."

The majority of the population seems to have become convinced that it was the "will of heaven" for Christians to be
slaughtered. Smith continued,

The cruelties of the persecutors found expression in the most
hideous forms. All the barbarities practiced upon foreigners
were shared likewise by their followers. Men, women, and children were chopped into pieces and their bodies thrown into
running streams to be dispersed beyond power of doing injury.

> Great numbers were burned alive, and children were flung back into the flames after they had once broken forth. Yet in one case known to the writer a lad who had twice been bound and thrown into the Grand Canal, and had each time succeeded in getting free, was allowed to escape, because it must be "the Will of Heaven."

The Boxers' desire to obliterate Christianity in China badly backfired. In the years immediately following 1900 widespread sympathy was evident towards Christians, and a new openness to the gospel was displayed. In Jiangxi Province a single Protestant missionary reported 20,000 converts in 1901 and 1902.

The Catholic Church in China also grew rapidly following the Boxer violence. In little more than a decade after the tumultuous summer of 1900 the Catholic Church had almost doubled in size.

In the following pages we profile some of the martyrdoms that took place during the Boxer Rebellion, grouped together by province.

CHAPTER 13   BEIJING

Postcard of a young
Boxer

The Boxers surprised many by the highly coordinated attacks they were able to launch against Christians in the summer of 1900. Many had underestimated the Boxers' size and organization, downplaying them as a motley collection of gangsters.

Beijing was the main target of the Boxers' wrath. Emboldened by the knowledge that the Chinese military would not oppose them, the Boxers desired to rid the capital city of all foreigners and their Chinese sympathizers. Christians were especially hated because the Boxers believed the new religion was causing great offence to the spirits of their ancestors, and only a blood sacrifice could placate their wrath. The Boxers claimed to have supernatural powers to help them discover who the followers of Christ were, boasting they could see a cross on the forehead of any true believer.

Hill Murray's Blind School in the western part of the city

had 30 sightless boys and eight girls in attendance. On the night of 13 June the Boxers decided to kill all of them. The school buildings and dormitory were set alight. All of the children tried to run into the courtyard, but the heartless Boxers forced them back inside the buildings and burned them to death. The worst atrocities in Beijing took place on the following night and into 15 June. William Pethick, who led the first rescue party into the city after the slaughter, said, "Never have I seen anything like it, men, women and children bound together with burning coals under and around them; killed, dead and dying on every hand; weak ones carrying aged and sick on their backs – and worse."

Dr Ernest Morrison, a reporter for *The Times* newspaper of London, was an eyewitness of the evil as approximately 6,000 Chinese Christians were butchered in the streets and alleys of Beijing. Morrison's report provides us with a clear picture of one of the darkest days in the history of Christianity in China.

THE MASSACRE OF NATIVE CHRISTIANS

As darkness came on the most awful cries were heard in the city, most demonical and unforgettable, the cries of the Boxers – Sha kuei-tsz (kill the devils) – mingled with the shrieks of the victims and the groans of the dying. For Boxers were sweeping through the city, massacring the native Christians and burning them alive in their homes. The first building to be burned was the chapel of the Methodist Mission in the Hata-men Street. Then flames sprang up in many quarters of the city. Amid the most deafening uproar, the Tang-tang or East Cathedral shot flames into the sky. The old Greek Church in the north-east of the city, the London Missionary Society buildings, the handsome pile of the American Board Mission ... It was an appalling sight.

On 15 June rescue parties were sent out by the American and Russian Legations in the morning, and by the British and

German Legations in the afternoon, to save if possible native Christians from the burning ruins of the Nan-t'ang. Awful sights were witnessed. Women and children hacked to pieces, men trussed like fowls, with noses and ears cut off and eyes gouged out. Chinese Christians accompanied the reliefs and ran about in the labyrinth of network of streets that formed the quarter, calling upon the Christians to come out from their hiding-places. All through the night the massacre had continued, and Boxers were even now shot red-handed at their bloody work…

But to our calls everywhere no reply was given. Refugees, however, from the east city had managed to escape miraculously and find their way, many of them wounded, to the foreign Legations, seeking that protection and humanity that was denied them by their own people. As the patrol was passing a Taoist Temple on the way, a noted Boxer meeting-place, cries were heard within. The temple was forcibly entered. Native Christians were found there, their hands tied behind their backs, awaiting execution and torture, some had already been put to death, and their bodies were still warm and bleeding. All were shockingly mutilated. Their fiendish murderers were at their incantations burning incense before their gods, offering Christians in sacrifice to their angered deities.

The Catholics in Beijing had large cathedrals located in each of the quarters of the city. The 60-year-old Lazarist missionary Jules Garrigues was one of many Christians burned to death inside the East Cathedral. The missionaries had instructed the Chinese brothers to ring the church bell continuously if the Boxers arrived at the gate, in order to alert the Christians. When a mob started to set the building on fire, the bellman rang the alarm with all his might. The fire caught the tower and crept to the floor beneath his feet, but still he kept ringing. The floor finally gave way and he and the bell fell into the inferno.

The West and South cathedrals were also burned to the ground, resulting in the death of many Christians. The Catholics at the North Cathedral decided to stay inside the church and defend themselves against the Boxers. Bishop Favier led about 3,400 believers – men, women and children – and with the aid of a handful of French marines held the Boxers at bay for two months until the Allies liberated the city.

In June 1900 thousands of foreign and Chinese Christians rushed to the foreign legations around the city. A legation in those days was somewhat equivalent to an embassy today, in that the land it occupied was considered the sovereign territory of that foreign country, and its occupants were therefore permitted to operate according to the laws of their respective lands, including having their own troops for security. The British Legation covered an area of six acres. Inside the walls

The ruins of the Presbyterian Church in Beijing

were found streets with houses, a library, post office, shops, stables, graveyard and a church. It was there that more than 2,000 people – mostly Christians – fled for refuge. The Boxers and Chinese soldiers laid siege to the British Legation for eight weeks in the summer of 1900, yet somehow by the provision of God the Chinese were never able to enter inside the walls and massacre its inhabitants. The stress on the refugees huddled inside was immense. In addition to the mid-summer heat approaching 40° C (104° F), the people cramped into the quarters had cannonballs and thousands of bullets fired above their heads every day. They suffered from a lack of food and water, from flies and filth; and perhaps worst of all, the fear and uncertainty of not knowing what would happen next.

After eight stressful weeks a multinational army liberated Beijing and the siege of the legations ended on 14 August. The missionaries had not understood why the Chinese kept shooting their bullets so high above the compound walls. They were later told by Boxers and Chinese troops that they had been bothered by the presence of white-clothed men standing on top of the walls and towers, and so had spent much of their ammunition on them. The more they shot at these "men", however, the more there seemed to be. No men were ever atop the walls during the whole eight-week siege. It was later estimated that some 3,900 mortar shells had been lobbed at the British Legation during the eight-week ordeal, yet not a single person had died from any of them!

The Chen family

Chen Dayong and his family laid down their lives at Yanqing near Beijing. Employed by the Methodist mission, Chen and his wife had four sons and six daughters, all of whom grew up as committed Christians. When the Boxer violence broke out in 1900 Chen was preaching in a small town outside the Great

Chen Dayong

Wall. The local Christians urged him to flee into the mountains where they would help conceal him from the murderers.
"No," Chen replied. "I will not leave until all the members of
my flock are first hid away."

On 5 June a man saw the Chen family and immediately
rushed back to the town and told the Boxers, who quickly rode
out and overtook them and stripped them of all their possessions. Chen's daughter, who was nicknamed Apple, ran
screaming into her mother's arms, from where she watched
the murderers cut off her father's head. The Chens' fourth
son, Chen Weifan, cried out in terror, "Oh, mother, what shall
we do? What shall we do?" She replied, "We will all go to our
Heavenly Father together", her faith never wavering to the
last. She and her thirteen-year-old daughter were hacked to
pieces, locked in one another's arms.

Some months later the Chens' third son travelled to Yanqing and recovered the remains of his family members and gave them a proper burial. It might seem natural for this son to have feelings of revenge for the ruthless murder of his parents and siblings, but he had already forgiven those who had committed the dastardly acts. The local authorities asked him if they should track down the murderers and inflict on them the same punishment, but he told them it was not necessary. They asked if he wanted to apply for compensation for the property his family lost, and again he replied, "No". The only request he made was, "I should like to go and preach the gospel to the people who murdered my parents."

Wang Zhishen

Wang Zhishen was a senior student at Beijing's Methodist University when the new century arrived. One of the best students in his class, he was polite and courteous. Wang had become a committed Christian a few months earlier when the Holy Spirit saved him at a revival meeting. After some of his friends heard that Wang had become a Christian they ridiculed him, but he was unperturbed. God had touched his life so deeply that he could not be swayed by their opposition.

Wang was captured by the Boxers and offered the choice of denying Christ or death. To make it easier for him to decide, it was proposed that some of his friends be allowed to worship the idols in his place, which would secure his release. "No," said Wang, "I will neither burn incense to idols myself nor allow anyone to do it for me; not to mention the fact that it would be denying my Lord, I should never dare to look my teachers in the face again."

Wang's persecutors stood there stunned, not knowing what to do next. The young Christian began to exhort them to repent of their sins and accept Christ before a fate worse than death overtook them. The Boxers commanded him to be quiet, but he refused. To silence him, they cut off his lips, then his tongue, and then cut him up limb from limb until he expired. Wang Zhishen had followed Christ only a short time, yet his courageous witness impacted many lives.

Zhang Yong and family

Zhang Yong, his wife and
baby daughter

When the Boxers started searching door by door for Christians, Zhang Yong went into the countryside to find a hiding place for his family to move to. He returned to the capital on 13 June to find the massacre had already begun. Zhang's wife, along with her child and sightless mother-in-law, were forced out into the street and wandered about the city disorientated and full of fear. As morning broke, a Boxer grabbed her by the sleeve and ordered her to follow him. She was taken to one of the city gates for execution. The place where she stood was slippery with blood and filled with the stench of a pile of mutilated bodies. She clutched her precious baby to her breast and bravely prayed, "O Lord, give me courage to witness bravely for you until the end."

The Boxer chief placed a stick of incense in her hand, and told her if she would burn the incense before the idols her life would be spared. "Never!" Mrs Zhang boldly proclaimed. The bloodthirsty crowd started to shout "Kill! Kill! Kill!" Mrs Zhang turned to them and in a confident voice said, "My body, cut in pieces, will remain scattered on the ground, but my soul will escape you, and go to be with Jesus."

God miraculously opened a door of escape for Mrs Zhang and her baby. As the Boxer chief went to fetch the sword that would end her life, a soldier called out, "You hateful thing, you deserve to die; but it is a shame that the baby should be killed; and if you die who will care for it? Quick! Run for your life!" The wife of Zhang Yong survived the ordeal, but her husband, child, father, mother, younger sister, and the blind old mother-in-law were all numbered among the dead.

Shu Shan and family

Gao Xin was an evangelist in charge of the mission station at Fuho. His household consisted of his mother, his wife Shu Shan, an eight-year-old son, a three-year-old daughter who was deaf and unable to talk, and a baby boy aged fifteen months. On 7 June Gao Xin decided to flee into the mountains north of their home. It was impossible to take the three children with them, so Shu Shan and the children were sent to stay with relatives. When Gao's aged mother was asked what her plans were she replied, "I shall stay here. Can we not bear a little suffering for Jesus? If it is his will, we shall meet again; if not, let us trust him, even unto death."

A picture taken before the troubles of 1900: Gao Xin with his wife Shu Shan, two of their children, and Gao's mother and grandmother

For weeks Gao Xin walked long distances in a bid to stay ahead of the Boxers. One night he had a horrible dream. He knew something terrible was happening down on the plains, but he had no alternative but to press on. He later learned that his entire family had been slaughtered by the ruthless Boxers, among a total of 42 Christian martyrs in Fuho.

The Boxers surrounded the house where Shu Shan and her children were hiding. The ruffians knelt in a circle and cried out, "Kill! Burn!" Shu Shan's relatives were no longer willing to shelter her and the children, and told them to leave. In despair, Shu Shan stumbled across the fields, carrying the heavy fifteen-month-old baby and sometimes the three-year-old girl, while her eight-year-old son walked by her side. Shu Shan tried to spare the life of her oldest son by sending him to stay with some other relatives, but he calmly said, "No, mother, if we are to die, let us all be together. I am not afraid."

Without food or money, the desperate Shu Shan decided

to return to her home. The Boxers watched from the village as the brave mother and her three children trudged, one painful step at a time, towards their home. Inside the gate they found the mangled corpse of Gao Xin's mother. A mob of Boxers, along with dozens of villagers, stared at the pitiful family. Shu Shan turned to them and requested, "If you kill me, kill all my children. Don't keep them alive to suffer after I am gone." The Boxers, however, announced that the spirits would allow the three-year-old girl to live, and told the crowd that anyone who wanted her could come and take her away. A young man named Ho came and took her. Another man knelt and requested that the life of the baby also be spared, but the Boxers refused.

Shu Shan was suddenly dragged out of the house into the yard. She stood, with her baby nestled in her arms, as her dear son was slowly stabbed to death. A spear was thrust through his back, then as he ran screaming round and round the tree one merciless Boxer after another cut at him with their swords and spears. The frenzied and traumatized Shu Shan had a thought as she clasped her doomed baby close to her heart. No matter what, she would not allow the cruel men to torment her beloved baby. She dashed the child against a tree, killing him instantly. The Boxers took their revenge by slowly torturing Shu Shan to death.

A shallow grave was dug in the backyard, and the corpses were flung into it. Poignantly, some burnt pages from a hymn book blew into the grave before it was covered up.

Yun Yi

Yun Yi took refuge in a relative's house when the Boxer attack commenced, but they turned her out into the blood-stained streets to fend for herself. That night she wept bitterly, as the sound of Christians being butchered echoed throughout the

Yun Yi with her family. Yun Yi is
seated on the right.

city. When the Boxers found Yun Yi they tried to force her to worship idols. She steadfastly refused to bow down or burn incense to any image, and told her captors, "I am a Christian. I believe in Jesus." Some of the onlookers were amazed to find no fear at all on her face, and assumed it was because she was not really a Christian and therefore didn't understand the danger she was in. "That is not true," Yun Yi calmly replied. "I have been a Christian for years. I belong to a Christian family." At this the bloodthirsty men shouted with rage and declared she was not fit to live.

A teenage boy, crazed by the innocent blood he had already shed, hacked Yun Yi's head from her neck. Her mother, who survived the Boxer madness, later said, "When I first heard of all she suffered, I felt as if my heart would break, but afterwards, when I thought about it calmly, and heard how brave a confession she had made and how fearless she was in the face of death, I felt glad that my girl had proved herself a true witness for Christ the Lord."

Two hundred and twenty-two Orthodox martyrs

The Russian Orthodox Church was first established in Beijing in 1655, but had grown to only several hundred members by

1900. The leader of the Orthodox mission in Beijing at the time, Archimandrite Innocent, recalled the events that unfolded on the night of 10 June:

> In the middle of the night gangs of Boxers with flaming torches spread over Beijing, attacking Christian houses, seizing Christians and forcing them to deny Christ. Some, terrified by torture and death, indeed renounced the Faith in exchange for life and burned incense before idols. Others, undaunted, confessed Christ. Their fate was horrible. They were ripped open, beheaded, burned alive.

The Orthodox catechist Paul Wang was slain as he knelt and offered a prayer to God. Ia Wang, a mission schoolteacher, was slashed with Boxer swords and buried alive, the Boxers believing she was dead. A passerby heard her groaning and took her to his house, but when the Boxers heard about it they returned and tortured her to death.

The most well known of the 222 Orthodox martyrs killed by the Boxers in Beijing was Mitrophan Zizhong. When the Boxers set the mission buildings ablaze on 10 June a large number of believers – about 70 – rushed to Zizhong's home, hoping to be sheltered from the crazed mobs. At about 10 p.m. the Boxers surrounded the house, and every Christian inside was butchered. When the Boxers burst through the gate they found Mitrophan sitting in the front yard. They stabbed his chest countless times, and he fell dead under a date tree. His wife Tatiana and two of their sons, Isaiah and John, were put to death. Boxers used their razor-sharp swords to slash the eight-year-old John's shoulders and chopped off his nose, ears and toes. When people asked him if it hurt, the brave young boy answered, "It does not hurt to suffer for Christ." Some of the survivors later said that John's shoulders and legs had wounds which were deeper than an inch, yet he didn't seem to feel any pain. Thus the entire family of Mitrophan Zizhong was killed except his son Serge, who later became an archpriest of the Orthodox Church and carried on the faith that his family had honoured for so long.

Thousands of other Christians were counted worthy to lay down their lives for Jesus in Beijing. Many gave courageous and clear testimonies before they were slain. Fifty-three Christians in the district of Shunyi were killed. One of them, a woman named Li, was last seen walking through the streets of the city with her hands tied behind her, and rough Boxers on every side. Over and over she sang the one hymn she knew, "Jesus loves me, this I know." Moments later she met Jesus face to face.

Just before Dou Weicheng was killed he told his persecutors, "Men, you may kill my body, but you cannot harm my soul. It will return to God. I shall see you at the Day of Judgement. I urge you to repent of your sins."

A doctor named Wang told the Boxers, "You may kill me, but I will not worship your gods in any way. There are four generations of Christians in my family. Do you think I would let my child see his father deny his Saviour? Kill me if you must, but I will not betray my Lord." The Boxers almost reluctantly ran Dr Wang through with a sword, lamenting, "What a pity to kill such a man."

CHAPTER 14

THE TONGZHOU MASSACRE

A memorial scroll listing the names of 130 martyrs killed in Tongzhou in 1900

Tongzhou was a small country town at the time of the Boxer Rebellion, but it has since grown into a city with about 700,000 people, located a short distance east of Beijing. Protestant missionaries commenced work in Tongzhou in the 1860s, and by the turn of the century a growing number of people were believing in the truth of Christ Jesus.

Some of the most sickening, yet God-glorifying accounts of martyrdoms came from this town. At the Tongzhou north gate two teenage boys were making their escape into the country when the Boxers seized and questioned them. These nameless young confessors said boldly, "We are of the Jesus Church." When about to be tied up they told their persecutors, "You need not bind us. We will not try to get away. Every step we take to your altar is one step nearer heaven."

Other heroic martyrs in Tongzhou included a female schoolteacher named Liu who was captured along with her widowed mother. When given the chance to denounce Christ and live, Liu fearlessly proclaimed, "I can never deny my precious Saviour. You can kill me, but you cannot compel me to deny Jesus and worship false gods." Her body was hacked to pieces in a barbaric manner, and thrown into a well. An old Christian man was buried in the ground up to his waist, then kerosene was poured over the upper part of his body and he was set alight. A little girl was not afraid to die for Jesus. She lifted a fearless face to the Boxers as they were about to hack her to pieces, and boldly declared, "Yes, I believe in Jesus." A crippled woman named Chen was alone in her house. The cowardly Boxers debated whether they should drag her out or just burn her alive in her home. They asked Chen why she believed in the "foreign religion", but before she had a chance to respond, the bloodthirsty men set upon her and sliced her with their knives. Her lifeless body flopped to the floor, her spirit having already left this world to be with Jesus.

Deacon Li Yunsheng

Li Yunsheng was a deacon in the Tongzhou church and also worked in the local magistrate's office. Most magistrates at the time grew rich from bribes and other underhanded dealings. Li, however, was known as somebody who could be trusted and was respected for his honest dealings.

When the Boxers launched their campaign against the Christians in Tongzhou, many felt Li would be safe because of his position. During the first days of June, when the mission-aries and many local believers fled to Beijing to avoid the Boxer advance, Li told his friends, "I shall not run away. This is my home, and here I shall stay, for life or death." A short time later the churches, mission compounds, the college and Christian houses in the city were ablaze, and dozens of fol-lowers of Christ were butchered, yet still Li remained. The magistrate, in a bid to protect Li's life should the Boxers come for him, instructed Li to burn his Christian books so that evi-dence could not be found against him. Li refused to burn his Bible, however – it was too precious to him. He read it and prayed daily, asking God to intervene.

On one occasion Li said out loud, "One day the church and the college will be rebuilt, and the Boxers will come to jus-tice." He was overheard and the Boxers were notified. A band of 40 men forced their way into the magistrate's compound and demanded Li be handed over. When the magistrate refused, the men broke into the inner rooms and dragged the deacon out. A search soon found his Bible, which was used as evidence that Li Yunsheng was a Christian worthy of death. They tore the Bible into pieces, and as they led him away, Li confidently stated, "I believe in my Lord Jesus. Though I am going to my death, it is with a willing heart. I do not regret being a Christian."

The Boxers chose a manure pile as the altar on which to offer up their victim, and 40 swords hacked and cut the dea-con's body until all that remained were some entrails and bone fragments.

Sister Tang

Even before her martyrdom, the life of Sister Tang was full of pain and difficulty. Her mother was a notoriously wicked woman and her husband an abusive drunkard. Her daughter-in-law was partly mentally retarded, and her son worked in an idolatrous temple and was one of the first men in Tongzhou to join the Boxers. The only bright spot in Sister Tang's life was Christianity. She gained peace and joy from reading her Bible and singing hymns to the Lover of her soul. Blind in one eye and nearsighted in the other, she was often seen holding her beloved Bible as close as possible in order to make out the words. Tang's abusive husband once stormed into a Bible study in a drunken rage, severely beating his wife as he dragged her home. Her small collection of Christian books had to be replaced several times after he burned them. Sister Tang refused to hate her husband, and often prayed for his salvation during church meetings.

After the Boxer massacres began in Tongzhou, Sister Tang's wicked son came to her with a pot of opium, encouraging her to commit suicide by swallowing it rather than be cut to pieces by swords. She steadfastly rejected his idea, telling him it was a sin for Christians to take their own life, and that she would rather endure the Boxers' wrath. The next day they came to her house and seized her. As Sister Tang was dragged through the streets she called out in a loud voice, "This is my time of suffering, but it will be brief; then I shall have an eternity of joy. But for you who are killing me, there will be everlasting sorrow." The Boxers hacked Tang's body into small pieces, but she had already gone to a place with no more pain or sorrow.

Teacher Wang

The Wang family was one of the wealthiest and most respected in Tongzhou. Teacher Wang was especially looked up to, having been a Confucian scholar for 25 years. Because of his great learning, he had acted as a translator and teacher to the missionaries, and had been befriended by them. For many years he had heard the gospel preached in the Tongzhou chapel. Hundreds of fervent prayers had gone heaven-bound pleading for Wang's salvation, but when the awful summer of 1900 came around Teacher Wang was still unable to confess Christ as his Lord and Saviour. As his pure-hearted Christian friends were slaughtered one by one, Wang's heart sank into deep grief. He could not understand why the best people in the land should suffer such an ignominious fate.

One day Teacher Wang and a friend walked past a Boxer temple in the northern suburbs of Tongzhou. The friend said, "Let's go in and see the fun." Wang recoiled with a look of horror on his face. The Boxers, who suspected that he was a Christian, noticed his reaction. They dragged Wang to their shrine and commanded him to bow down. He replied, "For many years I have worshipped only the one true God; I will not worship your idols." Immediately the furious Boxers severed his head from his body. After years of not being able publicly to declare his faith in God, Teacher Wang had finally done so in the most dramatic way. He went to heaven with his confession still on his lips, to meet the King of Kings who said, "Whoever acknowledges me before men, I will also acknowledge him before my Father in heaven."

Brother Zhang

Zhang was a Christian businessman who lived in a village near Tongzhou, yet he spent much of his time doing business in Beijing. When the Boxer insurgents started to go house to house throughout the capital slaughtering Christians, Zhang immediately departed and rushed home to protect his family. He gathered them together and encouraged them to be faithful to God regardless of what fate awaited them.

Neighbours began to warn the Zhang family, saying the Boxers knew they were Christians and would soon come to hack them to pieces and burn their house down. Zhang decided he and his family should flee into the mountains, but as they were leaving the village the Boxers arrived and seized them. They stripped Zhang naked and bound him with ropes to a cart and led him to the magistrate's office.

When the magistrate questioned him, Zhang gave a clear testimony of his faith in Christ. "This is my faith," he declared. "I am not afraid and am quite ready for death. Whatever happens I shall not give up my religion." The statement was recorded by the magistrate's secretary and given to Brother Zhang, who signed it, even though he knew that by doing so he was effectively signing his own death sentence. After this Zhang knelt down and began to pray. The magistrate seemed perplexed about what to do. He didn't want to kill such a brave and honest man. Finally, like Pilate of old, the magistrate was not willing to stand up for the truth. He turned around and left the court, and a few seconds later Zhang's body was hacked to pieces by the Boxers. Zhang's martyrdom made a great impression on the magistrate and other officials who witnessed it.

In all, 130 Christians were martyred for Christ in Tongzhou.

CHAPTER 15

HEBEI PROVINCE

Hebei was one of the worst affected parts of China during the Boxer Rebellion. Many missionaries were slaughtered, while the number of Chinese martyrs numbered in the thousands. The trouble in Hebei started when the provincial governor issued a proclamation declaring: "All foreign teachers of religion are deceivers and propagators of devilish and injurious doctrines. All who have joined their churches must recant at once, or they and their families will be killed, their houses burned, and property confiscated. Missionaries must get back to their own countries."

All across Hebei the same story of death and destruction was repeated. It was months before some Christians discovered the fate of their loved ones. One young woman named Zhang was studying in another province at the time of the Boxer attacks. Only in March the following year did she learn that her father, mother and younger brother had been killed.

Protestant martyrs

Throughout Hebei Province whole Protestant communities which had taken years to establish were wiped out in a day. In and around the remote town of Kalgan (now Zhangjiakou) in northwest Hebei, 31 members of the Congregational Church were slain. Most of them were thrown into a well and covered with large rocks and dirt.

At the town of Zunhua a total of 163 Methodist believers

were massacred, including 17 students of the Christian Girls' School. The Satanic plan to obliterate Christianity from Zunhua failed miserably. Within a few years following the Boxer Rebellion the church attendance in the city surpassed the pre-1900 levels. Today at least 20,000 people in Zunhua follow Jesus Christ.

A similar tale unfolded at Jizhou in southern Hebei, where the Christians were hunted down like animals and put to the slaughter. In many places extremely barbarous methods were used to kill the prey. Most of the 147 martyrs at Jizhou passed into eternity without any earthly record of their sufferings and deaths. A brief mention should be made of a woman named Zhang, who had been a Christian for fifteen years. When the Boxers offered her a chance to live by denouncing Christianity, Zhang replied, "I have served him for fifteen years and I am not going to turn my back upon him now. I fear none of you, nor do I fear death, as I shall go home to him who died for me." A few moments later she was in the place her heart had long yearned for.

Zhou was a colporteur employed by the mission. The Boxers arrived at his house, tied him up along with his aged mother, and dragged the duo to a temple where five other Christians were already awaiting execution. The Boxer leader promised to free them if they would burn incense and worship the idols, to which Zhou replied, "For seven years I have served Christ, and he has never failed me, and he will not forsake me now. I cannot and will not worship any save Jesus." Zhou then began to sing a hymn in a display of fearless defiance. The Boxers responded by hacking his 80-year-old mother to pieces right in front of him. Zhou was killed as he prayed for his murderers.

At Qingyuan a 16-year-old boy named Liu Liandeng was bound with his hands behind his back. Liu showed no fear at all. He lifted his face toward heaven and bravely sang:

My home is in heaven, my home is not here,
Then why should I murmur when trials appear?
Be hushed, my sad spirit; the worst that can come
But shortens my journey and hastens me home!

Upon hearing these words the Boxers broke into mocking laughter. They shouted at Liu, "We will soon see if that is true or not. We will make your home here for ever, down in the grave!" Almost the same instant they finished speaking, sharp swords hacked at Liu's neck, severing his head from his body and sending the spirit of this courageous teenager to the side of Jesus.

A young man, Jin Shaojian, was a seminary student at Gucheng. Although he followed Christ, Jin frequently seemed depressed and burdened by trouble. Jin and his father fled southward. Their money was soon exhausted, so Jin decided to sell some of his clothes at a local shop. While he was doing so, Jin was overcome with compassion for the crowds of people on the street outside, and it occurred to him that he should preach the gospel to them. The listeners marvelled at the courage of the young preacher.

Jin and his father travelled onwards. When they received news that the Boxers were on their trail they hid in a brick kiln. The once depressed Jin was now so full of joy that he couldn't restrain himself from worshipping God. The Boxers heard his singing and dragged him out of the kiln. He was taken to a local chapel and tied to the doorposts. Even then he worshipped Jesus to his heart's content, showing no fear. At last one of the Boxers said, "You are a stranger and we do not wish to kill you. If you promise to follow no longer the foreign doctrines we will let you go!" Jin Shaojian replied, "You talk about foreign doctrines and ask me not to follow them. That would be easy! What you really mean is that I am to give up Christ, my Lord. You have no right to try to control my heart or to ask such a thing of me. I shall never give up my belief in Jesus!" This confession infuriated the Boxers. They cut off one of his ears and asked, "Are you a preacher now?" "Yes, now and until death," he replied. A few moments later he was viciously cut into pieces by the wicked men.

Charles Robinson and Harry Norman

Harry Norman

Among the dead in the town of Yongqing were Protestant missionaries Charles Robinson and Harry Norman. Robinson was a native of Leeds, England. He went to China while engaged to Miss Rule, and studied Chinese in preparation for his bride's arrival. When the day to welcome his fiancée arrived, Robinson exuberantly travelled to the coast, only to be devastated by the news that she had died during the long ocean voyage. Robinson decided to remain single and continued to pursue his call to China.

Harry Norman grew up at Portland, near Weymouth in the south of England. While working as an apprentice carpenter his heart was attracted to overseas missionary work. In the summer of 1891 Norman arrived in China where he taught children, displaying boundless care and compassion for their welfare. On one occasion Norman took a boy who was considered a "no-hoper" by the other teachers and personally trained him as a carpenter, paying the boy's expenses in the process.

Before daybreak on 1 June 1900 the Boxers attacked two Christian villages outside the city. Robinson and Norman fled to the local magistrate's office, unaware that the Boxers had gained his tacit approval for their slaughter of Christians. The

Boxers came to the office and demanded the missionaries be handed over. Charles Robinson and Harry Norman were immediately hacked to pieces by the bloodthirsty men.

Methodist martyrs of the Kaiping Circuit

One of the key Methodist areas in China was known as the Kaiping Circuit, which took in a number of towns and villages in Hebei Province. In total, 45 faithful Christians were murdered there. A report noted that the methods of cruelty used against the Kaiping victims included

> Burning alive, beating to death, dismemberment, disembowelling, drowning, snipping to pieces under a straw-cutter, throwing from a precipice, saturating with oil and then burning, burying alive – such were some of the cruel tortures through which our brethren and sisters entered into the glory of heaven.

Zhang Shouchen, a preacher from the town of Xiaoji, was burned alive in his home, along with his wife and seven other family members. At Tangshan the body of a young Christian teenage boy, Zhang Yuwen, was chopped into pieces, nailed to a wall, and offered for sale at 500 *taels* per piece. His father was asked three times if he would denounce Christ. "No, no, no, not even if you kill me!" was his response.

Catholic carnage in Hebei

Hebei had the highest number of Catholics in China, and subsequently the proviince suffered the highest number of Boxer martyrdoms. At the conclusion of the Boxer Rebellion the bishop of Southeastern Hebei counted more than 5,000 Catholic martyrs in his vicariate alone between June and

August 1900. There were numerous massacres of Catholic families throughout Hebei. Just a few brief testimonies among the thousands who perished in Hebei are listed here, but thousands more departed this world to heaven without any earthly record of their testimony.

On 16 July the Boxers killed more than 100 Christians at Xuanhua, and torched hundreds of houses. Three large carts containing Catholic nuns were attacked and all the occupants butchered. The maniac Boxers even burned the carts and cut the mules into pieces and burned them too. When a Catholic believer visited the scene he found only ashes and the hoofs of the mules.

John Ma Taishun joined the Catholic Church as a teenager and later became a widely respected doctor. He also worked as a catechist, helping fellow believers better understand their faith. When Ma was alerted that the Boxers were coming to his village, he fled into the fields nearby, concealing himself while the Boxers plundered and murdered. Not finding the Christian doctor at home, the Boxers searched for him and soon found his hiding place. Ma's friends and neighbours tried to get him to denounce his faith, but he responded, "I firmly believe in God. If you want to kill me for that, do it and

John Ma Taishun

don't hesitate. I am willing to suffer and die for God's sake." As he recited the Lord's Prayer the Boxers beheaded him and burned his body.

Rosa Fan Hui was a 45-year-old schoolteacher. The Boxers cut off her arm with a knife, then slashed her face, peeling off her cheek. Rosa kept calm and prayed fervently. She told her persecutors, "Wait till I finish my prayers. Then you can kill me." When she was done with her prayers, she said, "I have finished now. Go ahead!" All their swords and knives fell on her at once and she dropped to the ground, half dead. They then threw her into the river and watched her drown.

Mary Guo Li was the 65-year-old wife of a well-known Christian leader. The couple were blessed with numerous children and grandchildren, all of whom grew up in the Christian faith. When the Boxer persecution began she encouraged her family and other believers to stand firm and not deny the Lord. On 7 July, Mary, her two daughters-in-law and four grandchildren were led to the execution ground to be beheaded. As she neared the place of death some of Mary's relatives watched with tears in their eyes. She turned to them and said, "Don't cry. We are going to heaven to enjoy eternal life." With the flash of a sharp blade, Mary and her six family

Mary Guo Li

members departed from this life into the presence of Jesus Christ.

Lang Yang was married before she had become a Christian, and soon after her conversion she gave birth to her

Lang Yang and Paul Lang Fu

only child, a son named Paul Lang Fu. When the Boxers attacked the village they caught Lang Yang, tied her to a tree, and began interrogating her. Seven-year-old Paul returned from play and began to cry when he saw his mother there. She told him, "Don't cry, child, come here." The Boxers then set fire to the house, pierced her body with a sword and cut off the boy's arm. Both were then thrown into the fire.

Peter Liu Zeyu refused to flee before the Boxers came to his village, saying, "To be killed by the Boxers is martyrdom and a great grace from God. Why do we reject it?" One of his friends challenged Peter's stance by asking, "It would be all right if they just killed you, but they may torture you for a long time. Can you bear that?" Liu replied, "Before God, the greater the suffering, the greater the merit. I trust myself to God's mercy. I desire to suffer more for him." On 17 July a Boxer raised his sword and in one blow severed 57-year-old Liu's head from his body. A Buddhist monk, amazed at Liu's courage and faith, grabbed a knife from one of the Boxers, cut open the martyr's chest, scooped out his heart and raised it in the air to show it to the people who were watching.

Two French missionaries, Modeste Andlauer and Remigio Isore, were martyred together at Wuyi on 19 June. Both men had laboured in Hebei for 18 years when the Boxer persecution commenced.

Before coming to China, Isore met with his provincial superior and asked to be posted to Zambia. Africa at the time was a hostile place where missionaries rarely lasted more than a few years before succumbing to violence or disease. When asked why he wanted to be sent to such a difficult place, Isore replied, "Because I long for martyrdom." The provincial superior, who had just returned from visiting China, replied, "You don't know what you are asking for. You want chances for martyrdom? There are more in China. Fine, you will go to China."

Modeste Andlauer   Remigio Isore

When the rebels took over the city of Wuyi they posted guards at all four gates to ensure no one escaped. The believers were meeting for devotions when the Boxers captured the city. Hearing the commotion outside, many tried to escape by climbing over the walls, but Andlauer and Isore came inside the church, shut the door, and began to pray at the altar, earnestly preparing themselves for martyrdom. At six o'clock in the evening the Boxers smashed the church doors open and hacked the two Frenchmen to death with swords and spears.

Four orphan girls

The four young girls who refused to
betray Christ

Among the thousands of Christians massacred in Hebei is a touching story of four Chinese girls from the Catholic orphanage at Wangla village. The oldest of the four was 18-year-old Lucy Wang Cheng. The others were Mary Fan Kun (16), Mary Ji Yu (15) and Mary Zheng Xu (11).

On 24 June the Boxers invaded Wangla village, burned down the church, and massacred all Catholics who were too slow to escape. The Boxers decided to spare the four girls, planning to use them as sex-slaves. The Boxer leader, a brute of a man named Ying Zheng, made a proposal of marriage to the eldest of the orphans, Lucy Wang Cheng. For four days he tried to persuade her to accept the offer, using both threats and manipulation. Lucy considered it a betrayal of her faith and her God, and she refused. She encouraged the other three girls by exclaiming, "We are daughters of God. We will not betray him." Seeing they would get nowhere in their lustful endeavours, the Boxers decided to kill their captives. The younger girls started to cry, but Lucy told them, "Don't cry. We are going to heaven soon. God has given us life; he will take it back. We should not be reluctant givers, but offer ourselves cheerfully." The girls were offered one last chance to deny Christ. They unanimously replied, "No! We are daughters of God. We will not betray him." At that the four brave girls were slain.

Mary Du Tian and children

Mary Du Tian, a 42-year-old mother of five, was murdered along with three of her children. They hid in a pit covered with reeds, but the Boxers were tipped off to their location. As they prepared to shoot them all, Mary's 19-year-old daughter, Magdalen Du Fengju, suddenly leaped up and ran to a friend's house, only to find that the door was locked. She slumped down in the doorway and awaited her fate. The pursuing Boxers let out a fiendish howl when they caught up with her. They shot her and then ran back to the pit. There, Mary Du Tian and her two sons Matthew and Timothy refused to denounce Christ and were slaughtered.

The villagers had started to dig a ditch to bury the dead bodies when a friend of Magdalen discovered she was still alive. The bullets had severely wounded her, but she was still breathing. The friend pleaded with Magdalen to deny her faith in order to save her life, but she whispered, "Impossible.

I want to go to heaven and be happy with my mother and brothers." The Boxers threw all four into the ditch. Magdalen peacefully took her place among the others, pushing the bodies of her mother and brothers to one side. She covered her face with her sleeves and was buried alive.

Eighteen members of the Zhao family

Zhao Mingxi and Zhao Mingzhen

Zhao Mingxi and Zhao Mingzhen were brothers who had put their trust in Christ earlier in life. At the time of the Boxer persecution Mingxi was 56 years old, and his brother Mingzhen was 61. When the Boxers reached their village, the brothers were arrested along with 16 family members and relatives. As they were led to the place of execution, the Zhao brothers knew they were about to die, but were concerned about the spiritual condition of some of their relatives. They loudly proclaimed the gospel to them, telling their loved ones to call out for God's mercy and to ask his forgiveness for their sins. They then prayed, "God, please help us; so that we may sincerely offer our humble lives to you. Please open the gates of heaven to us and receive our souls, so that we may enjoy eternal life with you." Their prayers were answered when the entire group of 18 people was callously butchered to death by the Boxers.

Elizabeth Qin Bian and her children

Elizabeth and Simon Qin Bian

Elizabeth Qin Bian was a widow who suffered martyrdom with four of her six children. When the Boxers came Elizabeth and her children hid in a friend's house, spending seven days in constant prayer. When their hiding place was discovered they fled to another village, where a rich man offered to protect them from the Boxers if Elizabeth's youngest son, Simon, would agree to marry his daughter. The fourteen-year-old Simon said, "Mother, do not deem my bodily life worth more than my soul. I have decided not to leave you. If we die, we die together!"

Insulted by this rejection, the rich man informed the Boxers of the Qin family's whereabouts. The Boxers soon caught up with them. Simon asked the Boxers to let the others go, knowing the rich man was really only after him for spurning his daughter. He knelt down and prayed to the Lord.

Without a word the Boxers killed him, before pursuing the remaining children and their mother. The Boxers killed another son, Paul, by nailing him to a tree. They then took the women back to the village, and tried to entice the daughters to deny Christ and marry some men from a neighbouring area. The girls replied, "We are God's daughters and will keep our virginity for life. We believe in him and there is no changing our mind. To kill or not is your business, but it is impossible for us to deny our faith."

As Elizabeth Qin Bian was led to the execution ground with her children, she turned to a group of watching women and said, "Please go home; what will happen to us will frighten you. As for us, God will reward us with eternal life, so we are not afraid of death – to die is to return home." As they walked on, her daughter Mary started to cry. Her mother held her hand, telling her not to be afraid. This devout widow and two of her children were led to a pear garden, where they were killed in a barrage of gunfire.

It has been estimated that by the end of the carnage between 15,000 and 20,000 Catholics had been killed throughout Hebei Province. Today Hebei is the strongest Catholic region in China, with more than two million believers meeting in both government-sanctioned and underground Catholic congregations. The blood of the martyrs has again proved to be the seed of the church.

CHAPTER 16

THE ZHUJIAHE MASSACRE OF 3,000 CATHOLICS

The remains of Zhujiahe Catholic Church after the Boxers
set it alight, burning hundreds of Catholics to death

Of all the ghastly and spine-chilling episodes of evil committed against God's people in China, one of the worst occurred when approximately 3,000 Catholics were massacred by the Boxers in the village of East Zhujiahe in Jing Xian, Hebei Province. The Boxers were assisted in the day-long slaughter by 10,000 soldiers of the imperial army.

Approximately 300 of the 400 inhabitants of East Zhujiahe were Catholics. The village served as a mission centre and contained an orphanage, schools for girls and boys, and a large church. Because the village had a wall encompassing it, many Catholics from surrounding areas took refuge there when the troubles started in May 1900. The number of people in the village swelled to approximately ten times the normal size. Under the leadership of the missionaries, the refugees worked hard to fortify the village walls. More than 1,000 able-bodied men planned to defend the women and children by force if necessary.

On 15 July the Boxers made several attempts to enter Zhujiahe, all of which were unsuccessful, although a large number of Christians were killed in the skirmishes. At the same time General Li Pingheng was leading his army to Beijing to defend the capital against the invasion of foreign troops. The route for the army's journey took them directly through Jing Xian, so the Boxers, allied with the local magistrate, asked Li for help to exterminate the 3,000 Catholics holed up inside the walled village. Li sent 10,000 of his men to wreak revenge on the Christians. Realizing they would soon be slaughtered, the missionaries in Zhujiahe abandoned their plans to defend the village and focused their energies on preparing the believers for martyrdom.

The army laid siege to the village for three days. Finally, on a day that lives on in infamy – 20 July 1900 – the Boxers and soldiers broke through the wall. More than 3,000 of the refugees were put to the sword, burned alive, or drowned inside the well.

A number of Christians, including missionaries Leon Mangin and Paul Denn, were shot dead inside the crowded church by the soldiers. The heartless men then decided to lock the remaining believers inside the building and burn them to death, even though most of those present were women and children. The Boxers and soldiers encircled the doors and windows to ensure none of the believers could escape the flames. The church roof was made of reeds, so it burned rapidly. Many tried to escape through the windows, only to be hacked to death outside. It was a pitiful scene. One report said, "Women and children fled to the orphanage, where some jumped into the well. They either died by drowning or suffocation, but others were immobilized by the dead and could be heard crying for help for days. Nothing more tragic had ever been seen."

During the commotion 51 Catholics did manage to escape the fire. The Boxers rounded them up but decided not to kill them that day, as they were exhausted from hours of continual slaughter. The Boxer chief went to the detainees and offered them their freedom if they would denounce Christ. Only two of the 51 did so and were released. The remaining 49 voluntarily entered their names on heaven's scroll of martyrs.

For months thousands of bodies were left strewn about Zhujiahe. Dogs, wolves and birds of prey feasted on the carcasses, while robbers came and took jewellery and clothing from the bodies. Remarkably, 87 years after the Zhujiahe massacre, remains were still being discovered. In 1987 the skeletons and belongings of 58 martyred nuns were retrieved from an old well in the village. It is believed the nuns took their own lives rather than be abused by the Boxers. The horror

The gruesome remains of human bones after the Boxers set fire to Zhujiahe Catholic Church with hundreds of believers locked inside

that the people of Zhujiahe experienced in those dark days can scarcely be imagined.

Paul Denn   Leon Mangin

Two French missionaries were among the slain at Zhujiahe. When Leon Mangin was first appointed to missionary service in China he told a fellow priest, "I was granted what I asked for. Now I only wait for the gift of martyrdom." When the Boxers entered the church where Mangin and a large number of Chinese Christians were hiding, a 50-year-old woman named Mary Zhu Wu stood in front of the Frenchman to protect him. She was shot dead, and moments later Mangin saw the Lord face to face. The Boxers set fire to the church, and the refugees sheltering inside were burned to death.

The 53-year-old Paul Denn had served in China more than half his life. Before his final breath, Denn said in a loud voice, "Dear people, do not be disturbed! Have a little patience before we all go to heaven." Denn was shot but only wounded, and crawled around the altar until the church was burned down. Both missionaries thus died with their flock, giving witness to the faith.

CHAPTER 17 LITTLE ANNA WANG
AND HER FAMILY

Anna Wang

The Wang Family

On 21 July 1900 the Boxers captured a number of Catholics at the gate of Majiazhuang village in Wei Xian, Hebei Province. The 68-year-old Joseph Wang Yumei – one of the Catholic leaders of the area – was martyred first, while the others were locked in a room and told to choose between their faith and death. The captives were held inside the East Room, and told if they went to the West Room it would indicate they did not want to believe in God and they would be released unharmed. Some chose to deny Christ by changing rooms, but most of the believers remained in the East Room, sealing their commitment with their own blood.

The next morning the Christians were led out for public execution. Many locals were appalled to see that the Boxers intended to kill little nine-year-old Andrew Wang Tianqing.

They remonstrated with the rebels, demanding they release him. Andrew's mother, Lucia, held on to her son and boldly announced, "I am a Christian. My son is also a Christian. If you want to kill me, kill us both. Please kill my son first. Then, kill me next." The cold-hearted Boxers agreed to her proposal. Little Andrew willingly knelt down, bent his body, and extended his neck to the executioner while smiling and looking directly at his mother. The axe fell and this brave little boy went to heaven. Lucia Wang and her five-year-old daughter were brutally decapitated. A further five women and a ten-month-old baby were also slaughtered. The Boxers even cut off a leg of the infant, threw it into the air and cut it in half, throwing the remains beside its mother.

One of the Wang family members killed was little fourteen-year-old Anna Wang. Anna was one of the Christians locked up in the East Room by the Boxers. After a while her stepmother decided to deny Christ and she stood up to go to the West Room. She grabbed Anna's arm in an attempt to pull her out of the East Room. Anna cried out, "I want to believe in God. I do not want to leave the Church! Jesus, help me!" She remained in the East Room.

When darkness fell the Boxers lit some candles that they had stolen from the church. Anna told her terrified companions, "These candles are from the church. Look how beautiful the flames are! However, the glory of heaven is a billion, billion times more glorious than these beautiful flames!" She encouraged the other believers and led them in prayer. An eyewitness provided this stirring account of Anna Wang's death the following day:

> Kneeling straightly, she folded her hands and prayed loudly with her eyes looking up at the sky. She was radiant and dignified. Suddenly, she appeared to have been transcended to heaven, as if she were no longer in this world. Instead of acting

as someone about to be executed, she appeared as if she were in the middle of a celebration. The head of the bandits was so surprised when he looked at her. He raised his axe, yet stopped in the middle, hesitating and murmuring to himself unintelligently. Finally, he went in front of her and appealed to her: "Leave your church now!"

Deep in her prayers, Anna Wang did not hear him. The bandit touched her forehead and asked her again whether she wished to deny her faith. Anna Wang woke up, took a step backward and screamed: "Do not touch me." After that, she calmed down and said: "I am a Christian. I will never deny God. It is better for me to die."

The executioner continued to have a deeply troubled conscience, and tried to tempt Anna by offering her the chance to marry into a rich family and so save her life. She calmly replied, "I will never leave my religion. Besides, I am already betrothed." She was part of the Bride of Christ, and nothing could sway her from her dedication to the Bridegroom.

Anna's refusal to compromise greatly incensed the executioner, who cruelly cut a piece of flesh from her shoulder and asked again, "Are you going to deny your faith?" The young girl replied, "No!" The Boxer then cut off her left arm. Anna Wang continued to kneel, smiled calmly, and said, "The door of heaven is open." She then whispered, "Jesus, Jesus, Jesus." In a flash, her head rolled down to the ground.

Two eyewitnesses said, "After Anna Wang was beheaded, she was still kneeling very straightly and did not fall down until a bandit kicked her body. Even after her holy body fell, she still lay on the ground very straightly." An elderly woman named Wang Lau said, "When Anna Wang was martyred, I saw her ascending to heaven, wearing a blue and green silk dress with a flower crown on her head. She looked very, very beautiful."

More than a century after the martyrdoms of the Wang

family, Hebei remains the strongest Catholic area in China. Generations of believers have been emboldened by the heroic example left for them by these martyrs. One hundred years after the defenceless Wang family, and numerous others, were butchered in Wei Xian, the Communist government ordered the requisition of 30 acres of land to build a grand Boxer museum complete with an artificial lake and landscaped garden. To this day most Chinese view the Boxer Rebellion as a great moment in the nation's history. Whatever the political motivations of the Boxer uprising, it is sad and pathetic that an event that slaughtered little boys and girls should be remembered with any fondness at all.

CHAPTER 18

THE YANSHAN SLAUGHTER

Ruins of the London Missionary Society's chapel at Yanshan

Most of the Christians in Yanshan, located in eastern Hebei Province, fled when the Boxer onslaught commenced. They found shelter wherever they were able, many laying in ditches during the day and among millet fields at night, where they poured out their hearts in agony before the Lord. Because the attacks took place during the summer the lives of many Christians were spared, for the millet was so tall it enabled them to hide without being seen on a plain that is otherwise completely treeless.

By the end of the summer the Boxers had slaughtered nearly 250 Protestant Christians in Yanshan, not counting the many who later died from starvation and deprivation. Many of the dead were young boys and girls from the missionary-led schools. Among the slain was a 16-year-old boy named Hao Shude, who was a student of the boarding school operated by the missionaries. With his hands tightly bound behind his back, the young man boldly exclaimed, "I am not afraid to die! Though you may kill this body of mine, you can do no harm to my soul." He was thrust through with a spear. Friends came and buried his body, but the Boxers disinterred it and burned it to ashes, fearing the teenager would rise again.

Pastor Shao and his family

Pastor Shao

The leader of the Protestant church at Yanshan was Pastor Shao, who had been faithfully serving for almost 30 years at the time of the Boxer Rebellion. Shao was a lamp-maker by trade when he first heard the gospel. Although he was not able to read well, Shao was convinced of the truths of Christianity and forced himself to read the New Testament, which became his constant companion. After Shao and his brother started following Christ the whole household changed. Their widowed mother induced Shao's wife to join with her in bitterly opposing Shao. Her cruelty knew no bounds. She frequently destroyed their beloved Christian books, and the angry woman would often order her grown-up son to lie down upon the ground and beat him furiously with a bamboo rod. According to Chinese law if Shao had retaliated against his mother at any time he could have been sentenced to death.

Through all these trials Shao continued to grow spiritually. The hardships produced in him a strong zeal for the gospel, so that he committed himself to God regardless of the cost. When the Boxers started their slaughter most of the Yanshan Christians fled into the hills, hoping to preserve their lives. Pastor Shao refused to flee, saying, "As long as God's house is here I shall remain." On 16 June the Boxers arrived in large numbers and burned the chapel and other buildings to the ground. The Shao family was captured and dragged into the mission compound. In a bid to disturb the preacher's calm demeanour, the barbaric Boxers murdered his wife and young daughter before his eyes. Shao continued to remain calm until he was viciously cut into thin slices and burned. The few bones that remained were later buried at the foot of the city wall. The sacrifice of Pastor Shao and his family was not in vain. Today Yanshan County contains at least 20,000 Christians among its 400,000 population.

Li Liushi and five relatives

One of the "Bible women" at Yanshan was Li Liushi, who was used by the Lord to bring the gospel to her home. She was a much-loved woman, celebrated for her hospitality and graciousness. Because of the God-given wisdom displayed in her life, even non-believers sought Li's advice and counsel. Such was her reputation that when the Boxers first came to Li's village they allowed her to go free, although five of her relatives were captured and executed.

A Boxer named Huang Dang – who didn't share the same sentiments as the other Boxers – came to Li Liushi's home with a mob of men and seized the Bible woman. To Li's horror, she recognized the man as being one she had taken and nursed as a child during his mother's illness. The boy's parents were impoverished, and she had taken the child into her home for long periods of time, loving him as if he were her own son. "Let someone else seize me," she exclaimed, "and not you, Huang Dang, for whom I have cared as my own flesh and blood! I am willing to go, but let someone else bind me! I am not sorry for myself, but I am grieved to the heart that you should do this thing." Huang pretended not to understand her. "I have no idea what you are talking about," he said. "I hope to be the first to smite you."

Li Liushi bowed her head and prayed, "Lord, I pray you, forgive him, for he knows not what he is doing." She continued praying for a few minutes until the men who had come for her grew impatient and dragged her off along the path. On the way Huang suddenly became filled with a demonic rage against the old woman. He attacked her with his sword, slashing her to death. Li Liushi was murdered by the same hands that she had lovingly helped when he was a little boy.

Fan Haoze

One of the better-known martyrs at Yanshan was a man named Fan Haoze. Fan and his family fled to the village of some relatives far from Yanshan, only to find that the relatives refused to accept them. They threatened to murder Fan and his family if they didn't depart immediately. The Boxers rushed to the village to find they had already left and gone into hiding. The Boxers seized one of his cousins, a non-believer, and threatened to behead him in Fan's place. When Fan heard this he came out of hiding at once, saying, "It is I only who am a believer in Jesus. I do not wish to involve anyone else in trouble on my account. You can do with me what you will." He was bound and dragged to a place outside the village. A deep pit was dug, and Fan Haoze was lowered into it until his head was below the level of the ground. The Boxers urged him to give up the faith of the foreigners and save his life, while they filled the pit with earth up to his knees. He kept on speaking kindly to his persecutors about the love of Jesus. "How can I give him up? How can I deny such a Master?" he asked.

The murderers were so angry they pierced Fan's body with the points of their spears until blood flowed. Then filling the grave until only his face remained uncovered, they offered him a last chance of life. "No, I can never give up Jesus," he said. The Boxers then hurriedly covered Fan's head with dirt, stamping it down over the still living body, until Fan Haoze breathed his last and went home to the Lord Jesus whom he loved so much.

Liu Zhaosan

Liu Zhaosan was the gatekeeper of the mission at Yanshan. He was a rough-looking man who had never learned to read or write. Liu had spent many years as a soldier before becoming a devout Christian later in life. When Liu applied for baptism in 1895 he found it difficult to answer all the questions. He said, "I cannot answer clearly, because I am an uneducated man. I only know this – there is a river; on one side of it is hell, and on this side is heaven. I know that I have crossed this river and am now on my way to heaven."

Liu and his wife hid from the Boxers in a riverbed outside the town. During the hot daytime Liu and his wife separated, but during the night they met together underneath a bridge and encouraged one another to be faithful and to persevere to the end. One night the two were overheard by a traveller passing by on the bridge. The Boxers captured Liu and prepared to slay him. "Just wait a minute," Liu said, "I will sing one of our hymns to you."

The Boxers, with a mocking spirit, allowed his request. In a clear and loud voice Liu sang the well-known hymn, "He leadeth me, oh blessed thought". By the time he reached the verse, "Glories upon glories hath our God prepared", the Boxers had become transfixed by the spirit of the song, and exclaimed, "Good! Good!" One of the Boxers suggested they would be better off letting Liu go free. The others, however, scoffed at the idea. They quickly bound him with strong cords and secured him in front of the mouth of a cannon, which they fired, sending the martyr into the place of joy he had sung about.

CHAPTER 19

THE BAODING MASSACRE

Christian women who were living in the Presbyterian mission at Baoding. The Boxers killed all of these women.

The American Congregational Church founded the mission at Baoding (formerly spelt Paoting) in Hebei Province in 1873. The first convert came to Christ five years later. By the late 1890s more than a dozen foreign missionaries resided in the city. The main church numbered approximately 120 believers, while the entire district under the administration of the Baoding church had a total church membership of about 600 baptized believers. In early 1900 the Christians knew a perilous change was coming. Posters were placed around the city announcing the Boxers' plan to exterminate all Christians. A few weeks before the carnage began, missionary Frank Simcox wrote a letter to his home church, saying,

The Church has become a Martyr Church, and we rejoice to know, she has proved that she is able to suffer for the Lord. Hundreds of homes have been destroyed, and all have held fast. When the history of the Martyr Church of China is written, it will be a beautiful record of suffering for His Name! Dark and troublous times are ahead of us, but we trust in the Heavenly Father's love, that all is for the best.

The missionaries and more than a dozen Chinese believers belonging to the Presbyterian mission were killed on 30 June in the northern suburbs of the city. A group of more than 20 Boxers and a mob of local troublemakers gained entry to the mission compound by setting fire to a pile of cornstalks placed against the wooden gate. Approximately 20 Christians were slaughtered, many of whom were burned to death.

The site where the China Inland Mission and American Board missionaries were slaughtered on 1 July 1900

On the following day, missionaries and Chinese believers associated with the China Inland Mission and the American Congregational Church were massacred outside the south wall of the city. In total, eleven foreign missionaries and four children were killed in Baoding, in addition to around 50 Chinese Christians.

Meng Zhangzhun and children

Meng Zhangzhun – the first pastor at Baoding

THE BAODING MASSACRE 199

Pastor Meng Zhangzhun was known for his God-given ability to win souls for Christ, and for his humility and dependence upon Christ's sustaining power. When the Boxers were preparing to attack Baoding, Meng was visiting another district. Despite the obvious danger, Meng immediately returned home. "The church members will need me," he said as he hastened away. A prominent Christian asked Meng, "Why do you not hide away for a time?" He replied, "I am the shepherd of the flock. Can I leave them? The missionaries have stayed by us; I shall stay and live or die with them." A group of Boxers suddenly rushed into the chapel and stabbed Meng in the head before dragging him to a temple. After mercilessly torturing him throughout the night, Meng's head was severed from his body and he went into the presence of his Lord and Master. On 1 July three of Pastor Meng's children were slaughtered at the mission compound, along with his sister Meng Du and her three children.

The Simcox family

Frank and May Simcox were born a short distance from each other in the US state of Pennsylvania in 1867 and 1868 respectively. They were united in matrimony and in a common goal to serve Christ in China. Frank Simcox was asked to make a speech at his college graduation in 1893. He took a Bible in his hands, raised it above his head, and boldly declared: "God only knows whether we shall live to learn the Chinese language so as to be able to proclaim the Gospel in the Chinese tongue. If we shall not live long enough to learn the language and shall only live to place our feet on Chinese soil and hold up this dear old Book in the sight of a perishing race, I shall feel that our going to China has not been in vain."

Every heart was inspired by Simcox's words, and the reality of his pledge became more apparent later when he spilled

Frank and May Simcox and their sons Paul and Francis, all martyred for Christ

his blood on China's soil. After commencing work at Baoding the Simcox family welcomed the addition of two boys. Paul was born first, followed by Francis three years later. The two boys saw that one of their friends had a baby sister, so they decided they wanted one too! Every night they prayed to God, asking him to send a little sister to them. Their prayers were duly answered when baby Margaret was born. Paul and Francis were proud of their role in the whole affair, and didn't hesitate to tell people that their sister had come about solely as a result of their prayers!

After lunch on Saturday 30 June, a group of Chinese Christians was gathered in the Simcox home. They prayed together, asking the Lord to protect them and, if that was not in his plan, to prepare them for a death that would honour Jesus. At about four o'clock in the afternoon a group of 20 Boxers and a mob of ruffians descended on the house. After the Christians managed to barricade themselves inside for three hours, the heartless men set fire to the building. May Simcox, with baby Margaret in her arms, pleaded for the life of her little daughter. The Boxers paid no attention and mother and baby passed into their heavenly home together when the flames consumed them. One eyewitness account says,

> Paul and Francis rushed from the building into the open air to escape suffocation from the dense clouds of smoke. They were immediately set upon by the crowd, cut down and their bodies thrown into the cistern. The other inmates of the house perished in the flames. About 20 Chinese Christians and servants living in the Compound also perished.

The entire Simcox family was martyred for Jesus Christ. Francis was seven years old, Paul five, and Margaret just eleven months.

Cortlandt and Elsie Hodge

Cortlandt van Rensselaer Hodge was born in New Jersey in 1872. His father was a pastor, and many of his uncles and

Cortlandt Hodge   Elsie Hodge

other relatives were among the eminent theologians and sci-
entists of their day, for it was an era where the divide between
science and theology was much narrower than it is perceived
to be today. Cortlandt's uncle, Dr Charles Hodge, was a world-
renowned theologian.

As a boy, Cortlandt was frequently immersed in the
atmosphere of missions. His father's church often hosted visiting missionaries who shared heroic stories of faith and
courage with the wide-eyed youngster. He later attended
Princeton University, graduating in 1893. He then proceeded
to the University of Pennsylvania, where he completed medical studies, becoming a fully fledged doctor in 1897.

Elsie Sinclair was a native of Cedar Rapids, Iowa. The
other missionaries nicknamed her "Bonnie" because of her
cheerful disposition. Cortlandt and Elsie were married in
West Philadelphia in 1899, and just three weeks later the newlyweds sailed for China.

During the Boxer attack the Hodges decided to take
refuge with the Simcox family. Cortlandt and Elsie Hodge

were burned to death together aged just 28 and 26 respectively. Their deaths were considered a terrible waste by some back in America. God, however, accepted their sacrifice as a precious offering.

Tracy Pitkin

Tracy Pitkin

Horace Pitkin – better known by his middle name Tracy – was born in Philadelphia in 1869. He came from a respected family, eight generations removed from the pioneer William Pitkin (who arrived in New England in 1659), and related to Elihu Yale, the founder of the prestigious Yale University. Some of Pitkin's classmates at Yale went on to become highly successful in the eyes of the world (including Henry Luce, the founder of *Time* magazine), but Pitkin's heart was set on different goals.

On 7 May 1897, Tracy Pitkin and his wife Letty arrived in

China after stops at Paris, Rome, Greece, Palestine, Egypt and India en route. The Pitkins' reputation had preceded them. They were renowned for their literary and musical abilities. Tracy was a gifted pianist, and Letty an accomplished singer. Pitkin devoted himself to what many people considered a lowly position as a missionary, despite coming from one of the wealthiest families in America at the time. In an era when missionaries were caricatured as impoverished and lacking all but the most basic necessities, it must have seemed strange when the Pitkins had a Steinway grand piano delivered to their new home in China.

While the Pitkins were still learning Chinese, God blessed them with a little boy, Horace. Letty struggled with life in China. She suffered from neuritis, an inflammation of a nerve resulting in much pain, loss of reflexes, and muscular atrophy. Tracy sent her and little Horace back to America for medical treatment in May 1900. The trip spared their lives. On 2 June Tracy Pitkin wrote, "It may be the beginning of the end. God rules and somehow His Kingdom must be brought about in China. It's a grand cause to die in. Jesus shall reign, but we do hope a long life may be for us in this work."

In many ways the experience of the China Inland Mission and Congregational Church workers was worse than their Presbyterian brethren, because they had to endure the night of 30 June knowing that their colleagues across the city had been slaughtered, and that the same fate awaited them the next day.

At dawn the next morning, with heavy rain falling, the Boxers attacked the mission. The missionaries leaped out of a window and took refuge in a small room in the school yard. They were soon dragged out and mutilated one by one. Later the bodies of nine martyrs, including Tracy Pitkin, were lifted from a pit where they had been thrown. Ironically, Pitkin had been preparing to preach his first sermon in Chinese on the day of his martyrdom. God graciously allowed his servant to give a message more powerful than words, the laying down of his life.

Mary Morrill and Annie Gould

Mary Morrill   Annie Gould

Born near the city of Portland, Maine, in 1863, Mary Morrill received a good education and was known for her academic ability and strong character. She led the girls' school at Baoding and did a sterling job, even though her heart yearned to be a travelling evangelist. The arrival of Annie Gould in 1893 freed Morrill up to pursue this call. Gould was also from Maine, having grown up just 50 miles from Mary. The two of them became such close friends in China that people who knew them always spoke of them as one. The duo travelled widely around the province, encouraging believers and sharing the gospel wherever the opportunity arose.

In her final letter home on 30 May 1900, Morrill wrote,

> Long before this letter can reach you the cables will have carried all kinds of news and conjectures. Miss Gould and I cannot leave if we would and would not if we could. Do not feel too troubled about us. The danger is all around and near, but God is nearer. Despite all apprehensions, we are happy, and even try to be jolly.

Gould's final heartfelt letter to her family said,

> I know perfectly well the possibility of danger, but generally speaking, it does not weigh on me, or when it does, I just cry out and pray for grit. I can't tell you exactly what I fear; not death, nor even violence at the hands of the mob, for the physical suffering would be over soon, and God can give strength for that. Perhaps you can understand why with all this disturbance and my sleepiness I can't put my thoughts on paper. If I live, I will send you another letter soon. Pray for Mary and me. If not on earth, we will meet in Heaven.

The Boxers burst into the mission and dragged Mary Morrill and Annie Gould to a temple. Annie fainted from shock and fear, and remained in a more or less comatose condition for some time and was unable to walk. She was bound hand and foot and slung on a pole, as pigs are carried in China. The two close friends were beheaded and their corpses flung into a shallow grave near the moat.

The Bagnall family

Benjamin Bagnall joined the British navy at the age of just 17 and served for ten years, rising to the rank of warrant officer. While on a tour of duty through Asia he first gained a burden for missionary work among the Chinese. As soon as he was discharged from the navy in 1873 he joined an independent mission in China.

Benjamin and Emily Bagnall with their little daughter Gladys were brought to a Boxer temple in the southeast corner of Baoding. They were accompanied by William Cooper, a national leader of the China Inland Mission who was visiting Baoding at the time. At around six o'clock in the evening the captives were led out of the city to the place of execution.

The Bagnall family

The angelic Gladys Bagnall

Little Gladys was speared to death first, notwithstanding her mother's entreaties for her life. Then the adults were cut down one by one, and the remains dumped in a shallow grave. The Bagnall's two sons, William and Howard, survived the Boxer Rebellion because they were away at boarding school in Shandong Province.

Chinese martyrs at Baoding

Many were the tales of horror from Baoding. It is hard to imagine the grief one young Christian named Wang Jiude must have felt when he was told, "Your grandfather, mother, two sisters, two brothers and their wives, and four nieces have all been killed."

A man named Zhang returned to his home, knowing the Boxers would soon come to kill him. Unafraid, he wrote the words "I am a member of the Jesus church" on a piece of paper and posted it on his door. A few days later, as he was sitting down to eat, a cry went up, "The Boxers are coming!" Zhang said, "They must wait until I have asked for the blessing." He sat with his head bowed in prayer as the Boxers rushed in and hacked him to death.

The many Chinese Christians killed at Baoding in 1900 included Dou Lianming. When his captors ordered him to bow down and burn incense before the idols Dou refused to do either, which led to one of the ruffians shouting, "He is a devil!" The composed Dou replied, "I am not a devil, but a Christian", and he started to explain to the crowed what it meant to believe in Christ. Unimpressed by his sermon, the crowd shouted, "Kill him! Kill him!" He was bound and dragged away to a street that had been set aside for slaughtering Christians and other people the Boxers deemed unfit to live. On the way, Dou continued to exhort the crowd, urging them to repent of their sins and follow Jesus Christ. Just

Dou Lianming

before they executed him, Dou Lianming shouted his last words in this world: "Though you can destroy the bodies of the Christians you can never destroy our souls! Hereafter we shall live eternally in the Saviour's presence."

A "Bible woman" named Gao and her adopted daughter Jessica were praying on the morning of 29 June when the Boxers pounded on their door with shouts of "Kill! Kill!" Gao calmly went to the Boxer leader and presented herself without fear. "Please permit my daughter and myself to put on our long garments and hair ornaments, then we will go with you," she said. When the Boxers approached the duo to bind them, Gao objected, saying, "We are women, why bind us? We are believers in the Lord; if we promise not to run, we surely will not do it." At the gateway of their house, Gao stopped and addressed their terrified servants, who were not yet Christians: "Sisters, I have been the cause of great fear coming to you today. Farewell. If I am permitted to see you again, I shall rejoice; if not, I hope that we may meet in heaven. I should be so glad if you all believed in Jesus."

They finally arrived at a temple, where Gao and Jessica were forced to stand in the courtyard under the blazing sun. Gao looked in her daughter's face and asked, "Are you afraid?" "Mother," Jessica replied, "Jesus is with you and me; is there anything to fear?" When they were praying, Gao's face began to glow, and she said to her daughter, "Jessica, I see Jesus has come; do you see him?"

Before being decapitated by the Boxers, Gao knelt in their midst and prayed, "Father, forgive these men. They don't understand what they are doing." A moment later she sealed her commitment to Christ with the sacrifice of her life. Miraculously, Jessica's life was spared at the time because of her great beauty. The ordeal took its toll on the 19-year-old's frail body, and she peacefully slipped into eternity a few months later.

CHAPTER 20 THE TERRIBLE
ESCAPE

Not all missionaries in the interior provinces of China waited
for the Boxers to do their work in the summer of 1900. Two
separate groups staged remarkable attempts to escape to the
safety of Wuhan in Hubei Province, which at the time was
under foreign control. A third group succeeded in reaching
Tianjin. Most of the missionaries survived the brutal journey
in the back of carts, seeing the miraculous hand of God almost
daily. Their extraordinary experiences were later recorded in
bestselling books. It is difficult to imagine the stress the fleeing missionaries endured during those long months. Several
adults died from injuries received in the attempt, as did several small children who were not able to endure the physical,
mental and emotional strain.

Hattie Rice and Mary Huston

Hattie Rice   Mary Huston

Hattie Rice hailed from Haydenville, Massachusetts. She started for China in 1892, and was appointed to work in an opium refuge at Lucheng in Shanxi Province. There she met Mary Huston, with whom she was closely linked in both ministry and in death. The two became inseparable friends.

On 12 July, while attempting to escape the Boxers, Rice became dehydrated from the oppressive heat and from walking all day. She collapsed from exhaustion near the town of Zezhou. Cruel, hate-filled men beat the missionaries and robbed them of all their possessions, even the clothing they were wearing. Seeing young Hattie Rice lying motionless on the ground, the crowd of onlookers began to stone her and a callous man ran his cart over her naked body in an attempt to break her spine. Mary Huston tried to shield her friend's naked body until clothes were brought. Hattie died shortly after.

Mary Huston came from Pennsylvania in the United States. She sailed for China in December 1895 as a member of the China Inland Mission. When Hattie was cruelly murdered, Mary and the other missionaries were in a state of shock and despair, yet somehow they kept moving. Because of the chaos Mary got separated from the other fleeing missionaries. Part of her brain was exposed from a bashing received at the time of Hattie's death. When the other missionaries arrived at Zezhou they pleaded with the magistrate to send a cart back to find Mary. Days later the cart returned with the body of Hattie Rice, and a severely wounded and ill Mary Huston. The missionaries tried to help their co-worker by protecting her from the sun, but they knew it was no use. After a time of prayer, Mary Huston passed away without saying a word.

It was later said of Rice and Huston, "They had taken nothing from China and given everything."

Jessie and Isabel Saunders

Isabel (left) and Jessie Saunders – innocent victims of the Boxer Rebellion

Alex Saunders and his wife were the first Protestant mission-aries at Pingyao in Shanxi Province. For years they laboured away in almost total isolation. When the Boxers started their killing spree, two parties of Shanxi missionaries tried to flee to the city of Wuhan in Hubei Province, 1,000 miles (1,620 kilometres) south. The children who went along were espe-cially courageous. At every town mobs of furious people came out and abused the foreigners.

Jessie Saunders was born in China in 1893. The Chinese people loved her dearly, as she was the personification of innocence. Very early on in her life she loved Jesus, and some-times said, "When I see him I will look for the marks of the nails in his hands and feet." Often as she passed people in the street she would ask her parents, "Do you think they have heard about Jesus?" When the escaping party were badly beaten in one town, seven-year-old Jessie reminded her par-ents, "If the people loved Jesus they would not do this." After a number of days on the road Jessie was struck with a fever and the missionaries stopped in an abandoned barn. While her loving mother fanned her, the little girl looked up, smiled, and announced, "Jesus was born in a place like this." A few days later on 27 July, Jessie's baby sister, Isabel, died from beatings and exposure to the hot sun. Her grief-stricken mother wrote, "She had been so patient and passed away so peacefully, we could only rejoice for her that she was safe for evermore."

After her little sister's death, Jessie grew weaker and often told her mother that she wanted to go to a comfortable place. Her wish was granted a week after Isabel's death. The two precious children were buried together on the side of the road.

Mary and Edith Lutley

Mary and Edith Lutley were two girls among a group of missionaries who fled their base at Linfen in Shanxi Province on 15 July. The group were like lambs to the slaughter – completely at the mercy of the Chinese villagers who lived along the route on the long journey southward.

Forty-five days of dreadful anxiety and barbarous treatment later, the carts reached the safety of Wuhan. The two little Lutley girls were not among those who made it alive. On 3 August Mary died from an illness resulting from the hardships of the journey. Bounding along hour after hour on rough potholed roads was a terrible experience for the sick child, and in the end her body simply expired. She was buried outside the wall of a town they were passing through. Two weeks later on 17 August her sister, Edith Lutley, also died while being pushed along in a wheelbarrow.

After a time of grieving at their home in Great Somerford, England, Albert and Mrs Lutley returned to China without their two precious daughters and recommenced the work that God had called them to. They reported that crowds of people responded to the gospel in a far greater way than they had prior to the Boxer Rebellion.

Margaret and Brainerd Cooper

Margaret Cooper and her little
son Brainerd died from injuries
received while fleeing from
the Boxers

Among the saddest stories to emerge from the Boxer year was the death of Margaret Cooper and her baby son, Brainerd. During the terrible escape the Coopers went through a harrowing experience. One account says,

> Mobs followed them from one village boundary to the next, hurling sticks and stones, shouting, "Death to the foreign devils!" Robbers stripped them of everything but a few rags. Emaciated from hunger and thirst, shoeless, barebacked in the scorching heat, desperately trying to hold up filthy, torn Chinese trousers, they staggered from village to village half alive.

In one place the people viciously attacked the missionaries. E. J. Cooper was severely beaten and left for dead, covered in blood and bruises. Somehow he recovered and crawled back to his family's side. His wife Margaret was unmoved by all the trouble, and told her husband that she wanted to return to Lucheng once conditions had improved. Her crushed body did not match her willing spirit, however. On 6 August she was close to losing consciousness. E. J. Cooper turned to his dear wife and said, "Jesus is coming for you." Margaret replied, "No, I am too strong to die, I just want to rest a little while." She closed her eyes and entered into her eternal rest. Just three days after the survivors reached Wuhan, little Brainerd was laid to rest beside the body of his mother. The 18-month-old toddler had survived the whole journey only to succumb at the very end, partly due to the deprivation of the experience, but also because his little heart was grieving at the absence of his mother. Somehow, by the grace of God, E. J. Cooper found the strength to write to his mother:

> The Lord has honoured us by giving us fellowship in His sufferings. Three times stoned, robbed of everything, even clothes, we know what hunger, thirst, nakedness, weariness are as never before, but also the sustaining grace and strength of God and His peace in a new and deeper sense than before. Billow after billow has gone over me. Home gone, not one memento of dear Maggie even, penniless, wife and child gone to glory. And now that you know the worst, Mother, I want to tell you that the cross of Christ, that exceeding glory of the Father's love, has brought continual comfort to my heart, so that not one murmur has broken the peace of God within.

Vera Green

A small band of five Westerners managed to escape miraculously from a remote part of Hebei all the way to freedom in foreign-controlled Tianjin. China Inland Mission workers Charles and Eliza Green, their two children Vera (aged five) and John (two), and an unmarried female missionary, Jessie

Vera Green

Gregg, decided to take up an offer from a local temple-keeper to hide in his temple on a nearby mountain. Soon after arriving there, locals alerted the Boxers and the party of five was forced to flee on foot into remote caves. The Boxers searched everywhere for them. Local Christians then arranged for the group to shelter in an isolated farmhouse. After four weeks the Boxers found out where the missionaries were hiding and surrounded the building. They shot Charles Green in the head, yet miraculously he survived. Realizing there was no point in trying to defend themselves, the besieged Christians committed their lives into the hands of God and surrendered to the Boxers. For some unknown reason they were spared. More afflictions awaited the besieged missionaries, however. They were beaten and abused from town to town as they were sent as prisoners to appear before a succession of magistrates.

Little Vera Green had been suffering from dysenteric diarrhoea for weeks. Her parents helped her as much as they could, but she slipped further towards death's door. Eliza Green remembered those sad days while she witnessed the demise of her little daughter:

After nearly a fortnight's illness, she fell asleep. In the solemn hush of that hour God drew very near, and bound up our broken hearts, as with faltering lips we said, "He is worthy." We did not sorrow as those who have no hope, for we know that those who sleep in Jesus, God will bring with Him, and it is only "till he come." His purposes through her had been fulfilled. She was undoubtedly used of God to preserve our lives. Her bright, loving ways touched the hearts of the people and led them to spare us. Yes, her work was done, and in a very real sense her life was laid down for Jesus' sake and for China.

Flora and Faith Glover

The Glover family going out to preach, March 1900

Flora Glover was born on New Year's Day 1872 in Dover, England. As a young woman she was known for her joyfulness and strong desire to obey God's Word. Flora married Archibald Glover, and before leaving for China the couple was blessed with two children – Hedley and Hope.

The Glovers were among a group of missionaries who tried to flee to safety through Boxer-infested towns and villages. Near the town of Shunde they were stoned and left for dead, but somehow the Lord delivered them. The missionaries tried to send messages through some Chinese Christians travelling with them, but they were murdered. At Handian, bitter mobs shouted abuse at the missionaries, even tearing the clothing from their bodies and robbing them of everything they had. Some sympathetic people further down the road threw rags to the Glovers with which they covered their nakedness. At the next town the whole population came out to murder the foreigners, but once again for some unexplained reason their plans failed. One night the bedraggled group slept in a graveyard and scavenged for food.

For the next nine weeks the party of desperate missionaries inched southward, enduring obscenities and abuses every day. How Flora Glover, in the seventh and eighth months of pregnancy, made it successfully to Wuhan only heaven knows. The survivors were immediately rushed to hospital, where just four days after the arrival, on 18 August, Flora gave birth to a baby daughter, Faith. Due to the physical and emotional stress of the escape the little girl was emaciated and struggled from her first breath. It was no surprise when she passed away on 29 August, the span of her life encompassing just eleven days. Despite the sorrow and hardship of the previous months, Archibald Glover wrote to his mother, "You all shared in our sufferings, and perhaps the suffering of suspense was even more trying to you all than that which we were called to go through. But now we can rejoice together in the common mercy of our God, and with one heart and one mouth glorify Him, having indeed tasted that the Lord is gracious."

The Glovers were transferred by boat to Shanghai so that Flora could receive the best available medical treatment. Her body had been destroyed by the ordeal, and the death of her newborn added woe upon woe. Her emotional state was already fragile, and losing her baby daughter seemed to crush her beyond repair. Despite her valiant fight, Flora Glover passed into glory on 25 October. The following day Archibald Glover again raised his pen to break the news to his wife's family back in England. With a trembling hand he wrote,

In the Lord's good pleasure, sweet darling Flora departed to be with Christ yesterday morning at 4 a.m. It was a very sudden call at the last – so quiet and gentle that it was a literal falling asleep. In those last precious moments, I held her hand and breathed into her ear such sweet consolation for her departing spirit as the Spirit gave me. The breathing got slower, until it culminated in three deep breaths, taken at intervals of several seconds – like deep sighs of relief – and her gentle, lovely spirit was with Christ

My heart is broken, dearest parents, and the hand of God is heavy upon me. But I praise Him, in all the anguish of the stroke. For His tender love has been covenanted to me in Christ as Father, and "He keepeth covenant and mercy with them that fear Him."

CHAPTER 21

MANCHURIA

The Boxers inciting people against the missionaries with a puppet show.
The pig puppet represents the foreigners.

The northeast region of China, now the three provinces of Heilongjiang, Liaoning and Jilin, was formerly known as Manchuria. Just prior to the Boxer attacks of 1900 thousands of people had made commitments to Christ. In 1899 the Presbyterian Church alone reported more than 5,000 baptisms in less than twelve months, and more than 7,000 names were on a list of applicants for baptism.

Approximately 1,400 to 1,500 Catholics were slaughtered by the Boxers in Manchuria, while the number of Protestant martyrs numbered 311. Many thousands more Christians suffered intensely throughout the summer, hiding in remote hills and forests, and struggling to stay alive by eating raw grain, wild berries, and even bark from trees.

Slaughter at Shenyang

At Shenyang, the capital of Liaoning Province, rumours that the Boxers would launch their attack on 24 June did not scare the Christians, although many calmly made plans to leave the city. That Sunday morning more than 400 believers gathered in the main church for one final worship service, while their horses and mules waited outside the church ready to leave immediately after the service ended. After the sermon the believers all remained on their knees while the pastor cried out to God for help. He told the precious flock that they were truly like sheep among wolves, and advised them of three things they should pray: for grace to remain faithful, for the restoration of peace to the church, and for the welfare of the nation.

The final hymn sung was "Soldiers of the Lord, arise!" Then the congregation quietly dispersed. Later that same day an imperial edict arrived at Shenyang calling for the extermination of foreigners. A bounty of 2,500 *taels* was promised for every "devil" (foreigner) killed, with 500 *taels* for every "devil's slave" (Chinese Christian). An imperial edict did not become law, however, until the viceroy of a province signed it and posted it on the gate of the capital city. The viceroy of Manchuria was sympathetic to the Christians and delayed signing the decree for as long as possible to help the missionaries and their converts escape. Thousands of believers fled north into the vast Mongolian plains, and nearly all the Protestant missionaries in Manchuria managed to escape with their lives.

Fewer Catholics attempted to flee, and in the first week of July several hundred Catholics in Shenyang were slaughtered. The Boxers then set their sights on the town and villages in the countryside, pillaging and slaughtering anyone they believed was connected to the Church. Among the dead in Shenyang was the French bishop, Laurent Guillon, who had never been afraid to confront those in authority and to make a bold stand for righteousness. After Guillon took charge of the Catholic work at Shenyang the effectiveness of the mission was greatly increased. Between 1894 and 1898 more than 10,000 conversions were recorded.

When the Boxers mobilized thousands of people, Guillon took refuge inside the cathedral along with missionary Noël-Marie Emonet, a Chinese priest Jean Li and two nuns. Crammed into the cathedral were also several hundred terrified Chinese believers. Together they managed to barricade themselves inside for more than a week. The Boxers, with the help of imperial soldiers, finally broke the Catholics' resistance by firing a canon from the city wall which caused the buildings to catch on fire. The main gate was battered in, and several hundred Christians were barbarously slaughtered.

Other heroic martyrdoms

It was perhaps not surprising, considering the large number of church members who were new converts, that approximately one-third of the Protestants in Manchuria chose to renounce their faith in order to escape death. Many more Christians, however, were faithful until the end.

Most were beheaded, but others were wrapped in cotton-wool soaked in oil and burned alive. One was given a "fiery crown", a thick ring of oily cotton wool being placed round his head and set ablaze. Others were hacked to pieces limb by limb, being offered a chance to recant after each slice.

Mrs Xiao was a wealthy woman who, even though she had only recently believed in the Lord, spent much time and energy spreading the gospel. Explaining her decision to follow Christ, Xiao said, "The Lord called me with his own voice, and I was constrained to follow him." The Boxers came to her home and demanded her money and property, but she stood her ground and was prepared to witness for the Lord. She was consequently killed. Until the last breath Xiao kept praying for her attackers, and proved to be a splendid monument of God's grace. According to an eyewitness, "The fiends cut off her ears and lips, and slowly hacked her quivering, agonized body to pieces. Yet she kept praying to the last."

Another Christian woman refused to renounce her faith. Before being decapitated she asked for permission to pray for a moment. Kneeling down, she prayed for some time; then stood up and sang the hymn, "At the gate of heaven". While she was worshipping with all her heart the executioner's sword fell on her neck, and heaven's gate opened wide to receive her. Another Christian told the Boxers, "You may not only behead me, but cut my body into fragments. Every portion, if you should ask it, would answer that it was a Christian."

The Chinese Christians later said that the single greatest

loss the Protestant Church in Manchuria had experienced was the martyrdom of Elder Xu. He served the congregation in west Shenyang and was about to be ordained head pastor. Xu was at Faku when the Boxers commenced their attack. They discovered his hiding place, and Xu and his son were brought back to Faku where they were publicly beheaded. The merchants of the town pleaded for Xu's life, out-

Elder Xu, a martyr and key leader of the church in Manchuria

lining all the positive things he had done for the community, but the Boxers would not listen and viciously decapitated their defenceless victims. As a mark of respect, the merchants provided coffins and hired labourers to stitch the heads back on to the bleeding bodies for burial.

Li Gudang was a preacher with the Presbyterian mission. After being dragged to the execution ground he was asked, "Will you continue to preach the Jesus religion?" "As long as I live," Li boldly replied. The wicked men cut his eyebrows off, and he was asked the same question again. Then his ears were sliced off with a knife, and finally his lips. After each mutilation Li was offered a chance to deny Jesus Christ, but he still answered that while he lived he could not help but preach the way of salvation to sinners. When he felt that he was close to fainting, he said, "I may be unable to speak, but I shall never cease to believe." The demonized Boxers leaped onto the evangelist and cut his heart out of his chest. It was exhibited at a theatre for several days.

The Boxer violence reached all the way to China's most northerly and coldest province, Heilongjiang. The 27-year-old French Catholic missionary Louis Leray was shot dead by the Boxers on 16 July. Four days later Jean François Georjon was captured. The Boxers cut off his arms and ears, then folded back the skin of his face and finally sliced his head off. The Room of the Martyrs at the seminary of the Paris Foreign Missionary Society contains the chain with which the torturers secured Georjon before his death. Three more Frenchmen, Jean Viaud, Edouard Agnius and Jules Bayart were killed at Guangning. The Boxers swooped on them and cut them to pieces. Their bodies were thrown into a nearby river.

The satanically inspired plot to exterminate Christianity in northeast China failed miserably. At one stage the leaders of Shenyang announced that their city had been completely "purged of the foreign poison", but in the aftermath of the Boxer slaughter a missionary reported, "On the whole the church members now seem more impressionable and more spiritually alive than ever before. One noticed it in their prayers and the readiness with which they took the spoiling of their goods. Attendance is about double what it was before the trouble."

At Guangning, where many of the worst atrocities occurred, the Martyrs' Memorial Church was opened in 1903 in honour of all the Christians who had laid down their lives three years earlier. A plaque was unveiled which said, "To the Glory of God and in memory of more than 300 Christians martyred during the Boxer rising". A revival later broke out in the very same church. The Canadian missionary Jonathan Goforth led powerful revival meetings in Manchuria between 1908 and 1910 in which thousands of people entered into a relationship with Jesus Christ.

CHAPTER 22 BLIND CHANG

Blind Chang

One of the greatest examples of God's saving grace is found in the extraordinary testimony of a man named Chang Shen, who came to be universally loved and known simply as "Blind Chang". In April 1886 the missionaries in Shenyang were feeling discouraged at their lack of progress when a 36-year-old "poor ragged blind man" found his way to the gate of the mission hospital. Chang was in the final stages of dysentery. His appearance was destitute, with just a few rags covering his nakedness. All hospital beds were taken at the time, but a Chinese evangelist had compassion on the desperate man and gave up his couch so that he might be provided for. Chang received medicine and loving care, and before too long his health had improved.

The hearts of the hospital staff melted when they heard Blind Chang's story. He had walked almost 120 miles (194 kilometres) to visit them, and along the way had been attacked and robbed of all his money and warm clothes. Chang had belonged to a notorious Buddhist sect known as the Vegetarians, which had caused much trouble in China and was not afraid to use violence as a means to achieve its goals. In 1895 the Vegetarians were behind the massacre of eleven missionaries at Gutian in Fujian Province.

As a young man Chang could see, but while he was swindling people out of their money as a fortuneteller he started to lose his sight. Chang was well known throughout the entire region as a drunkard, womanizer and gambler, and a man of such immoral practice that his name was used as a curse word. Chang's family had disintegrated after he threw his only child, a daughter, out of the house. She was forced into a life of begging and prostitution in order to survive. A short time later Chang also drove his wife away. Seventeen days later he was struck totally blind. His neighbours said it was the judgement of the gods for all his evildoing.

The missionaries allowed Chang to stay on their premises for free. While he was there he attended the chapel services and heard the gospel for the first time. Immediately, and without reservation, he gave his life to the Lord Jesus Christ. Dugald Christie said, "Never had we a patient who received the gospel with such joy, and the rapidity with which he grasped the leading truths of Christianity was remarkable." Another missionary, Mr Inglis, described Blind Chang as "A remarkable man, with a soft voice and mellow beyond any Chinese I have ever met. He speaks with great rapidity, his words seeming to flow from his lips like the ceaseless murmur of a brook."

A month after becoming a Christian, Chang decided to return home to his remote village in Jilin Province, and asked to be baptized before he left Shenyang. The missionaries, however, told him to wait because they wanted to test the sincerity of his faith over time. This upset Chang, but he decided to return home anyway. He explained, "None of my people have heard even the name of Jesus, or of his offer of the gift of eternal life; and do you think that I can keep that to myself any longer? I do wish for baptism, but I cannot delay my return." When Blind Chang started proclaiming the gospel in his home village of Taipinggou ("Valley of Peace"), the people laughed at him. They mocked his new faith, saying, "It is all very well for him to reform, for he cannot gamble without his eyes."

Despite this opposition Blind Chang remained steadfast in his commitment. As the weeks and months rolled by it became obvious to the villagers that a dramatic change had taken place in Chang's heart, and his character had been radically transformed. Villagers often sat in the shade of a large spreading elm tree near the village on hot summer days. Chang also sat under the tree, as it afforded him the best opportunity to share the gospel with people. The elm tree, along with the house next to it, was later purchased by the mission and became the site of the first church and school in the area.

In October 1886 missionary James Webster visited Chang's home to check if he had remained true to the faith. Instead of just one poor blind man to baptize, Webster was astonished to find approximately 200 new believers in Chang's village and in surrounding communities. Blind Chang had walked throughout the district, unhindered by the muddy swamps and rugged hills, and had shared the Good News with everyone who would listen. He loved to teach the people the one hymn that he had learned in the hospital:

Jesus loves me, he who died
Heaven's gate to open wide;
He will wash away my sin,
Let his little child come in.

Jesus loves me, he will stay,
Close beside me all the way;
If I love him when I die,
He will take me home on high.

After baptizing Chang and an initial eight new converts, Webster was overjoyed. He wrote,

> I have never witnessed a more interesting scene, nor joined in a more solemn and joyful sacramental service. The nine men were headed by their blind guide, who had to be led by the hand to receive the sacred rite. Professing to come to Christ and to believe in Him, and to venture their all in thus believing, they declared their intention to forsake the idolatry of their fathers, casting it forth root and branch; expressing their desire through grace to turn from evil and serve the living God – and all this with a warmth of purpose impossible to describe.

Blind Chang proved to be an evangelist without parallel. Everywhere he went he testified to the power of a changed life through Christ, and such was the notoriety of his past life of vice that nobody could question the validity of his testimony. With the use of a staff, Chang made his way around dozens of villages. His preaching was always with great power and authority. The spectacle of a blind man giving his testimony and exhorting people to repent and believe in Jesus never failed to gather a crowd. It was said of Blind Chang, "Missionaries followed after him, baptizing converts and organizing churches."

After a while the missionaries told Chang about a school

for the blind in Beijing. Amazed by the news that he could learn to read God's Word by Braille, Chang set off for the nation's capital, where he received a warm welcome from missionary W. H. Murray. Within three months Chang had mastered the art of reading and writing. Murray wanted him to stay longer, but Chang was again anxious to return home and share the blessings he had received. He recommenced his daily preaching, reading the Word of God to crowds of amazed people who were surprised to see a blind man read with his fingertips. Within a few years he had memorized the whole New Testament, the Psalms, and several other Old Testament books. By 1895 Chang had more than 500 converts under his care, many of whom had been the worst of society – among them highway robbers, opium addicts and prostitutes.

Blind Chang was away visiting the Christians at Deshengguo when the Boxer Rebellion commenced. The believers there knew Chang would be a prime target, so they hid him inside a cave, hoping the threat would soon pass. At the same time, some 125 miles (203 kilometres) across the province at Chaoyang, a group of Boxers rounded up a group of 50 Christians for execution. A local resident told the Boxers, "You are fools to kill all these. For every one you kill, ten will spring up while that man Chang Shen lives. Kill him and you will crush the foreign religion." The Boxers promised to spare the 50 Christians if someone would bring Chang to them.

When a man arrived and relayed the information to Chang, the blind evangelist reached out his hand and said, "I will gladly die for them. Take me to them for it is better that it be so." For days the duo travelled along the stony paths towards Chaoyang, praying that the Boxers would not lose patience and slaughter the captured believers before they arrived. When they reached the city on 19 July, Blind Chang was arrested and bound. Three days later he was taken to the temple of the god of war. Chang calmly yet firmly explained his faith in the following account of the conversation between the blind disciple and the Boxers:

> "I worship Jesus, the Saviour of the whole world. I refuse to deny Him. If you kill my body, today my soul will be with Him in Paradise."
>
> "Unless you renounce Jesus and burn incense to Buddha, you must die."
>
> "I am quite willing to die," answered Blind Chang. "I do not believe in Buddha."
>
> "Kneel down, then," commanded the Boxer judge.
>
> While the executioner's blunt sword was making three cuts at his neck, he kept on praying – "Lord Jesus, receive my spirit."
>
> Then a strange thing happened. When Blind Chang's head rolled on the ground, the Boxers threw away their weapons and fled in fear, no man pursuing!
>
> "We have killed a good man," they cried, as they vanished conscience-stricken, leaving the other Christians unhurt.

The Boxers refused to let the local Christians bury Chang Shen's body. They had heard a rumour that he would rise from the dead, so they forced the believers to buy oil and incinerate the remains.

Due to the sacrifice of 50-year-old Blind Chang the lives of many Christians were spared. It was only after his death that people started to understand the full scale of the suffering and hardship Chang had endured during his years of ministry. A teenage boy, who had served as the evangelist's guide on several journeys, recounted how Chang had often met with bitter persecution and endured great hardships. Children were encouraged to pelt him with rocks or bricks, and curses were hurled at him as the people drove him from their doors. Worst of all, huge mongrel, half-starved dogs were sometimes set upon the blind evangelist. What such attacks must have meant to someone unable to defend himself from their onslaughts is hard to imagine. Yet none of these things moved him, for Blind Chang had already died to self and this life held no attraction to him, apart from the times he presented Jesus to people who needed him.

When the Boxer Rebellion concluded the government of Manchuria realized they had allowed the murder of a unique and holy man of God to take place. A stone monument was erected in honour of Blind Chang.

CHAPTER 23

ZHEJIANG

The coastal Zhejiang Province is one of the strongest Christian areas in China today. The large city of Wenzhou contains hundreds of thousands of believers and has come to be known as the "Jerusalem of China". Zhejiang escaped most of the Boxer troubles in 1900, although nine Protestant missionaries and their children perished along with a number of Chinese believers.

The China Inland Mission commenced work at remote Quzhou in western Zhejiang in 1875, and at the start of the 20th century a small church had been established.

The Thompson Family and Josephine Desmond

David and Agnes Thompson

In 1900 Quzhou was home to three female missionaries plus the Thompson family – consisting of David and Agnes Thompson from Scotland and their two sons, Edwin (six) and Sidney (two). When news of the Boxer atrocities in other parts of China reached Quzhou the missionaries considered fleeing for the coast, but in the end they decided it was safer to remain where they were. On 20 July – the day before his death – David Thompson wrote:

> I know not what to say or think; everything up here is growing worse. We hear all kinds of evil reports, which make us fear, but by His grace we are able to rise above all, and take hold of our God and Saviour. As yet we do not see our way clear to move, for if we leave without a very strong escort we shall be robbed; so we will just "stand still and see the salvation of God." Pray for us. Now I will close; and God, our Father, take care of us, or *take* us. His Will be done.

The local magistrate, a man named Wu, assured the missionaries he would protect them. This was a sincere offer, but on 21 July a mob of enraged locals seized the magistrate, along with his family members and servants, and slaughtered them – 31 people in all.

A short time later the Thompsons' home was attacked and all their possessions were looted. The Thompsons escaped, but when they raced to the military official's residence for help they were turned away and told, "We cannot be troubled with your affairs now." With all their hopes dashed they faced the cruel mob, which rushed at the missionaries with knives and other weapons. David Thompson was stabbed to death and his body left in the street. One of his children was killed in the same manner. When Agnes Thompson pleaded for the life of her second son the mob responded by dashing him against a rock and stabbing him to death before her eyes. She was then cruelly murdered.

Josephine Desmond was born in West Newton, Massachusetts, in 1867. Her parents were staunch Catholics, having migrated from Ireland before she was born. Josephine entered into a personal relationship with Jesus Christ while attending school. After serving two years as a missionary among a Native American tribe in South Dakota, Desmond departed for China in 1898 and was with the Thompsons when they were savagely slaughtered on the streets of Quzhou. Josephine Desmond was 33 years old and had served in China for just 18 months when she was mercilessly murdered.

Josephine Desmond

Etta Manchester and Edith Sherwood

Etta Manchester   Edith Sherwood

Etta Manchester was raised in a God-fearing family at Edmeston, New York, but the process of knowing Christ was a gradual one for her. It wasn't until she was 19 that she definitely knew she had passed from death to life. Wanting to serve Christ in the neediest place, she sailed for China in 1895. In the spring of 1900 she received a letter telling of her father's failing health. Etta was making plans to return to America when the Boxers killed her.

Edith Sherwood was a 46-year-old Englishwoman who had loved the Lord with all her heart, mind and strength from a young age. Even as a schoolgirl she was active in sharing her faith with people. Sherwood later worked among the sick and poor in the north London suburb of Barnet. She was also involved with outreach to soldiers and for a time assisted at a mission in Paris. During these years of fruitful ministry she formed an acquaintance with David and Agnes Thompson. Their resolve and zeal rubbed off on Sherwood, and she ended up going to China with them in 1893. Although she commenced her missionary career at a relatively late age of almost 40, Edith Sherwood played a key role at Quzhou.

The homes of Etta Manchester and Edith Sherwood were located to the north of Quzhou. At about noon on 21 July a mob came rushing into their home and began plundering whatever they could lay their hands on. The women tried to escape but were severely wounded. Etta and Edith somehow managed to pull themselves up and hid in a neighbour's house for the next two days. The pressure was so great that the neighbours finally decided they could not give their own lives to protect the missionaries, and they handed them over. A mob rushed upon them from all sides, dragged them to a nearby chapel, and stabbed them to death.

The Changshan missionaries

George and Etta Ward

The Ward family was cruelly murdered in Zhejiang in the summer of 1900. Raised in a wealthy family, George Ward met Christ in 1890 during a meeting at the YMCA in London. From the start the fruit of his salvation expressed itself in good works, and before long he was burdened by the needs of the mission field. Ward applied to the China Inland Mission, offering to meet all of his own expenses if they accepted him. He accompanied David and Agnes Thompson to China in 1893, and was stationed at Changshan in Zhejiang Province.

On 20 July 1900 the local magistrate sent the Wards a note advising them to flee, for he could no longer guarantee their safety. George Ward thought he should remain at his post, but made arrangements for his wife Etta, their five-month-old son Herbert, and Emma Thirgood to leave the next morning. Ward still didn't believe there was any serious danger, and promised his wife that if the city was attacked he would leave immediately.

Within hours of his family's departure a crazed mob attacked Changshan. George Ward fled on foot with a Chinese evangelist and a servant named Li Yun. Travelling on small pathways in an effort to escape detection, the trio made their way unmolested until the following afternoon, when they stopped at a small village named Sanmojia. A crowd of unfriendly people surrounded Ward and his colleagues. Ward pushed past them and ran along a path, only to find it came to a dead end at a pond. The mob laughed at him as he returned, then set upon him with sticks and clubs, beating the missionary and Li to death. The Chinese evangelist was left for dead, but managed to crawl away during the night and reported what happened.

Etta Ward was an American from the state of Iowa. She met Christ at the age of twelve and departed for the Orient as a missionary in 1894. For the first three years she worked at Changshan in Zhejiang Province, where her inner charm and beauty attracted the interest of George Ward. After their marriage in 1897 the Wards saw a sudden surge in their work. In two years the number of Christians in Changshan doubled. In 1899 the arrival of a baby boy, Herbert Calvin, added to their joy.

Etta, her little son Herbert, and Emma Thirgood left Changshan by boat on the afternoon of 21 July 1900. By evening they had only managed to travel about ten miles (16 kilometres) from the city when they looked back and saw a red glow in the sky above Changshan. They assumed the Boxers were burning the city so they proceeded towards Quzhou, arriving there at daybreak. The city was in an uproar due to the massacre of the Thompson family and other missionaries the previous day. The boatmen were scared and refused to take the two women and child any further. They threw the missionaries' baggage onto the river bank and ordered them to get off the vessel.

After waiting on the riverbank for a long time a boat came up and offered to take the besieged trio to Hangzhou. They were relieved, but just as they started placing their luggage on the boat the same mob that had viciously killed the Thompsons arrived. The leader demanded money, at which Etta Ward took off her wedding ring and offered it to her persecutors. The leader snatched it from her and sneered, "We want your life, not your gold rings." They stabbed her in the arm and she fell to the ground. Somehow she managed to fend off the blows aimed at her baby boy, until the brutal men stabbed mother and child together, and with one blow cut their heads off. In an instant Etta and her precious child were reunited in heaven.

Having witnessed the diabolical attack, Emma Thirgood knew there was no chance of escape. She knelt in prayer and committed her soul to God. While still in this posture she was hacked to death.

CHAPTER 24

INNER MONGOLIA

Catholic carnage

A group of Boxers before they commenced their murder spree

Catholic work had been underway in Inner Mongolia for more than 200 years by the time of the Boxer Rebellion. Dutch and Belgian missionaries dominated work in the province. Their main strategy was to buy up large tracts of farmland and turn them into productive communities, in which Chinese and

Mongol converts could live and work. One of the motivations behind this plan was to avoid a repeat of the mass starvation that occurred during periods of long drought. The strategy led to many thousands of new believers, but also contributed to the high number of Boxer martyrdoms that occurred in Inner Mongolia. The Boxers knew the Catholics lived in these farming communes, and subsequently it was almost impossible for them to escape or hide.

Bishop Ferdinand Hamer, the son of a Dutch grocer, was born in 1840. He arrived in China at the age of 25, and went on to spend many decades of faithful and effective service. Hamer was about to celebrate his 60th birthday when the Boxers launched their attack. Local believers urged him to flee before it was too late, but he chose to remain at his post and not abandon his Chinese friends, even though he ordered the other missionaries under his care to leave. Hamer had given his life to the Chinese and Mongol Christians, and now he was prepared to die with them.

After Hamer was put in prison his fingers and toes were cut off, and he was taken from village to village and paraded by the Boxers until death brought his sufferings to a conclusion. On 24 July Hamer was stripped naked and covered with cotton cloth, soaked with oil. His hair was pulled out, and his nose and ears cut off. The bishop was then tied to a pole with his feet up and head down, and the cotton was set alight. There was a dreadful scream, and then silence. Two hungry beggars ate the martyr's heart.

Several hundred Chinese Catholics were also put to death in Taiyuan. Many of the young women and girls were sold to Muslim traders, to be used as concubines and sex-slaves.

On 13 August two Belgians, Amand Heirman (37) and Jan Mallet (29), took refuge in a village with about 1,000 Chinese Catholics. The believers successfully repulsed three separate Boxer attacks. Local officials then resorted to deceit in a bid to flush the missionaries out of the village. A number of carts and armed soldiers were sent with assurances that the missionaries would be safely taken to Beijing. They had hardly gone a mile when they looked behind and saw the church building on fire, while the officials, seated on the roof of a house, looked on laughing. Heirman and Mallet were chopped into fragments by the soldiers. Many native Christians were then put to death.

After the Boxer slaughter in Inner Mongolia had run its course, investigations into the impact on the Catholic communities there brought shocking results. One report in 1902 found that every one out of 347 villages where Christians lived had been attacked by the Boxers. More than 1,500 believers had been cruelly slain. The suffering of those who survived was so great that it is believed the number of martyrs doubled in Inner Mongolia over the next few years.

The Scandinavian Alliance Mission

The Scandinavian Alliance Mission was founded in Chicago in 1890, with the goal to help Scandinavian Christians living in North America become missionaries. Work in China commenced in 1895 when a red-bearded Swede, David Stenberg, arrived in Inner Mongolia to work among the Ordos tribe. Born at Jonköping, Sweden, in 1872, Stenberg went to America and studied at the Chicago Theological Seminary. It was said of him, "There is nothing bad about him, he is pure gold. He was a favourite with all." Wanting to integrate himself totally into Mongol culture, Stenberg wore only Mongol clothing, rode a camel, and travelled with nomads.

At the beginning of the 20th century the Scandinavian Alliance Mission had 35 people (21 adults and fourteen children) in Inner Mongolia. The majority of them worked at Hohhot. After seeing little fruit for their endeavours, they decided to copy the Catholic strategy. Using funds raised by churches in the United States they purchased a large tract of land and founded a farming colony. They then invited poor Mongols to come and live on the farm, provided them with tools and a plot of land, and shared the Christian message with them. By May 1900 Inner Mongolia was full of rumours of violence and impending death to the Christians. Stenberg wrote, "At present we have to bear with very evil reports. The fight is severe. We expect a breaking out, but we know God is on our side, and after this hour of darkness shall dawn the day of salvation for the Mongols."

In June seven of the missionaries and seven children tried to flee across the desert on camels. Before they had gone far they were intercepted by robbers who took everything, even their clothes. In the trauma two of the female missionaries gave birth. French Catholic missionaries later found the bewildered group wandering around the desert, subsisting on roots. They took the Scandinavians back to the Catholic mission station and took care of them.

Among the rescued missionaries were Carl Lundberg, his wife and their three children. In a letter home, dated just six days before his martyrdom, Lundberg wrote,

Carl Lundberg

> The robbers stripped us even of some of the clothes we were wearing, so that we were both hungry and cold. In our vicinity lived four Catholic priests, who invited us to come to them; and we went. We have now been here eight days, but even here it is very dangerous, as Boxers and soldiers intend coming to destroy

it. Those of us here are Mr. and Mrs. Emil Olson and three children, Mr. and Mrs. Albert Anderson with two children, one only a few days old, Miss Emelie Erickson, myself and wife and two children. Our way to the coast is cut off. If we are not able to escape, tell our friends we live and die for the Lord. I do not regret coming to China. The Lord has called me and his grace is sufficient. The way He chooses is best for me. His will be done. Excuse my writing, my hand is shivering.

Five days later Lundberg penned a final note, "The soldiers have arrived and will attack our place. The Catholics are prepared to defend themselves but it is in vain. We do not like to die with weapons in our hands. If it be the Lord's will let them take our lives."

The Catholic priests and two of the Scandinavian missionaries, Olson and Anderson, tried to escape. Before they could get far they were captured and beheaded. The others were killed with guns and swords. Another group of missionaries with three children set out for the coast. They ran into an ambush planned by the magistrate and all were killed.

At another location, Olaf Bingmark, his wife and two young sons first sensed there was trouble on the horizon when the Chinese children stopped attending their school. Rumours were rife that Bingmark was extracting the eyes of Chinese boys to use in his medicine. A Chinese peddler named Zhao, whom the Bingmarks had helped many times, betrayed the Bingmarks and helped the Boxers gain access to their home. They were dragged outside and attacked with swords and stones while an artist stood by sketching the violence. The picture showed the two little boys kneeling and asking for mercy.

Standing: Carl Suber, N. J. Friedstrom (who escaped), David Stenberg;
Sitting: Hilda and Clara Anderson, Hannah Lund

The Swedish Mongolian Mission

Another massacre took place in a different part of Inner
Mongolia during the month of September. Those martyred
were also Swedish missionaries working under the leadership
of another organization – the Swedish Mongolian Mission,
which had been established under the presidency of Prince
Bernadotte of Sweden that same year.

Born in Sweden in 1872, Carl Suber graduated from the
Chicago Theological Seminary in 1896 and left almost immediately for Inner Mongolia. A year later the work was
strengthened by the arrival of three unmarried women:

Hannah Lund, Hilda Anderson and Clara Anderson. One who knew them said, "There could not be found any braver souls; they were fully consecrated to the Lord's service." In the autumn of 1899, a married couple, the Hellebergs, and a single man, Emil Wahlstedt, arrived in China. They were all to die the following year.

In August 1900 all the missionaries attempted to flee north into Mongolia. Half a day into their journey they met a man who advised them to turn back. Stenberg and the women decided to ignore the advice, as a Mongol chief had promised to protect them. Two of the men, Friedstrom and Suber, remained where they were, but after sensing that Stenberg and the women had fallen into danger, Friedstrom searched for them while Suber remained with the caravan. When Friedstrom did not return, a Mongol was sent to investigate what had happened to the missionaries. He returned with the horrifying news that soldiers had killed them all, decapitating them and preserving the heads in salt, so that they could later take them to Beijing and get the money reward that had been offered for killing foreigners.

Stenberg and the three women were killed on 1 September, and Suber perished about ten days later. Friedstrom was the only member of the group to escape. Providentially, a sandstorm covered his tracks just after he left.

CHAPTER 25

SHANXI

Protestants in the martyr province

IN
LOVING MEMORY
OF THE
MISSIONARIES & CHILDREN
OF THE CHINA INLAND MISSION WHO LAID DOWN THEIR LIVES
FOR CHRIST'S SAKE DURING THE ANTI-FOREIGN OUTBREAK 1900.

CHIH-LI	SHAN-SI	SHAN-SI	SHAN-SI
WILLIAM COOPER	EMILY WHITCHURCH	GEORGE McCONNELL	ALFRED WOODROFFE
BENJAMIN BAGNALL	DUNCAN KAY	ISABELLA McCONNELL	ELIZA M HEAYSMAN
EMILY BAGNALL	CAROLINE KAY	Kenneth McConnell	EMMA G. HURN
Gladys Bagnall	Jennie Kay	ANTON P. LUNDGREN	ELIZABETH BURTON
Vera Green	STEWART McKEE	ELSA LUNDGREN	ANNIE ELDRED
	KATE McKEE	HATTIE RICE	S. ANNIE KING
CHEH-KIANG	Alice McKee	W. MILLAR WILSON	PETER A. OGREN
	Baby McKee	CHRISTINE WILSON	Mary Lutley
DAVID B. THOMPSON	JANE STEVENS	Alexander Wilson	Edith Lutley
AGNES THOMPSON	MARGARET COOPER	MILDRED CLARKE	Jessie Saunders
Edwin Thompson	Brainerd Cooper	F. EDITH NATHAN	Isabel Saunders
Sidney Thompson	CHARLES S. I'ANSON	MAY R. NATHAN	NATHANIEL CARLESON
EMMA A. THIRGOOD	FLORENCE E. I'ANSON	EDITH DOBSON	MINA HEDLUND
EDITH SHERWOOD	Dora I'Anson	EDITH SEARELL	SVEN A. PERSSON
GEORGE F. WARD	Arthur I'Anson	MARY E. HUSTON	EMMA PERSSON
ETTA WARD	Eva I'Anson	MARGARET E. SMITH	GUSTAF E. KARLBERG
Herbert Ward	WILLIAM G. PEAT	JOHN YOUNG	OSCAR A. LARSSON
M. ETTA MANCHESTER	HELEN PEAT	ALICE YOUNG	ANNA JOHANNSEN
JOSEPHINE DESMOND	Margaretta Peat	DAVID BARRATT	JENNIE LUNDELL
	Mary Peat	FLORA C. GLOVER	JUSTINA ENGVALL
	MARIA ASPDEN	Faith Glover	ERNST PETTERSON

ALSO OF
WILLIAM S. FLEMING killed in KUEI CHEO 1898.

HE will swallow up Death in Victory,
and the LORD GOD will wipe away Tears from off all Faces.
Isaiah XXV. 8.

ERECTED BY THEIR FELLOW-WORKERS in the CHINA INLAND MISSION 1901.

Memorial stone listing the 189 China Inland Mission martyrs of 1900

For many Christians around the world and inside China, Shanxi has been known as "the martyr province" ever since the ghastly Boxer summer. The scale of carnage inflicted on the Protestant missionary force in particular is brought into perspective when it is considered that between 1661 and 1893 there were 130 Protestant missionaries martyred in all parts of the world, while during the summer of 1900 a single organization, the China Inland Mission, lost a total of 189 people (136 adult missionaries and 53 children). When Hudson Taylor, founder of the China Inland Mission, first heard news of the slaughter he said, "I cannot read; I cannot think; I cannot even pray; but I can trust."

More than 150 Protestant missionaries were slain in Shanxi Province, encouraged by the wicked governor Yu Xian, who urged as many Chinese as possible to join the Boxers. After murdering the missionaries, the Boxers turned their attention on the Chinese Christians. Across Shanxi hundreds were hunted down like animals and subjected to barbaric treatment. A full account of their sufferings has never been published, but the few anecdotal testimonies that surfaced provide an insight into what these believers endured for the sake of Christ. They were beaten to death, perished in prison, hanged, drowned, buried alive, mutilated and vivisected. Some were placed under the blades of straw cutters and sliced to death.

The China Inland Mission was one of few missions at the time that afforded young unmarried women the opportunity to pursue their missionary dreams. Among the single women who gained a martyr's crown in Shanxi were Emily Whitchurch and Edith Searell.

Whitchurch was martyred at Xiaoyi after 16 years of selfless service in China during which time she displayed Christ's love by treating opium addicts and sharing the gospel with all who would listen. Whitchurch was a close friend and

Emily Whitchurch

Edith Searell

co-worker of Edith Searell, who hailed from Christchurch in New Zealand. When Searell boarded the ship to China in 1895 a friend mentioned that she did not know how long it would be before she saw Edith's face again. Edith replied, "Well, there is nothing I would count a greater honour than to wear a martyr's crown." In May 1900 she became seriously ill with pleurisy. In one of her final letters she wrote to a friend,

> You speak in your letter of the possibility of one place being safer than another. I think from the human standpoint all are equally unsafe; from the point of view of those whose lives are hid with Christ in God, all are equally safe! His children shall have a place of refuge, and that place is the secret place of the Most High. Shall we murmur if we have less of time than we expected? The less of time, the more of heaven.

The work of Emily Whitchurch and Edith Searell on earth was done, and their reward awaited them. When the mission premises were attacked by a raging mob all the Christians who were still on the compound gathered together for prayer. After committing themselves to God they started to sing, and in the midst of their songs of praise a mob burst in and beat them to death with pieces of broken furniture, finally throwing their bodies into the baptistery.

Courageous Chinese martyrs

In one part of Shanxi a Christian woman named Meng was spinning yarn on her loom when the Boxers arrived at her door. She rose and invited them in, saying quietly, "Gentlemen, I am ready, but just allow me to change my dress." She left the room, prayed for a moment, and put on her best clothes. Coming back, she turned to them and said, "Now you may do as you wish, for I will not deny Jesus. I am ready." In a moment her head was severed from her body.

Twenty-two Chinese Christians were slaughtered in the town of Fanshi on the first day of July. An angry mob of Boxers and townspeople set the chapel on fire and the beloved pastor, Zhou Yongyao, was bound and thrown alive into the flames. He burned to death. A few hours later a Christian named Gao Zhongdang was seized in the street and beaten almost to death. The cruel Boxers then took him and threw him into the chapel, which was still on fire. For a time Gao remained conscious and asked some bystanders to give him water. In response, one man threatened to urinate on the suffering Christian, bringing howls of laughter from the onlookers. Unlike many martyrs who were blessed with a quick death, Gao Zhongdang's suffering lingered on throughout the night into the next day, when he finally perished.

At Linfen 27 Christians were massacred, while 18 others had knife wounds in the shape of a cross dug into their foreheads. The hellish Boxers kept their victims in the scorching sun to make the scars permanent. Later these men were beaten with 500 strokes with the bamboo, after which they were imprisoned for several weeks. For the rest of their lives they bore on their bodies the marks of Jesus.

Catholics in Shanxi

The Cemetery of Boxer Martyrs, built at Taiyuan in 1901

There was no place in the entire province where the Boxer persecution did not reach. Even remote mission stations in the Luliang Mountains were affected, and hundreds brutally put to death. Many Catholic children in Shanxi showed great courage when facing death. In one location as the Boxers led them away to be executed the children declared, "You are bringing us great honour! This is our day of great joy!"

Shortly before his death, an ex-soldier Joachim Li Fu exhorted his fellow Christian prisoners: "Think well on the sorrows of Jesus. Stand firm against those who will try to rob you of your faith. Torture is only a trifling thing compared to the pains of hell. If they come to put you to death, lift your pigtails high off your necks so that they can cut your heads off the more easily. It will be over in a moment and paradise will be yours."

The missionaries and their co-workers had done a sterling job for many years helping the needy in society. The governor miscalculated how important and difficult this work had been. After the foreigners were slaughtered on 9 July the governor ordered the 200 orphans under the mission's care to be sent to a government building. One night 20 carts were dispatched to transport the frightened children, who were bound together in pairs and placed in the back of the carts. On the way to their new location the children started to cry so the soldiers threatened to beat them unless they kept quiet.

The governor soon found that taking care of 200 orphans is hard work. There was only enough food provided for each child to eat two small pieces of bread daily. They became so hungry that they began to eat grass from a nearby field. Each day the local magistrates came and interrogated the children, doing all he could to make them turn away from their faith in God. This invariably failed, and the little ones declared in unison, "No, no, we will never give up our religion!" Two Christian teachers, Anne Zhen and Frances Li, were brought in to help take care of the frightened orphans. As soon as the magistrates appeared each morning the children knelt down and began to pray aloud, putting the scheming men to shame.

When the wicked governor was foiled in his designs he decided to torture the women teachers and some of the strongest children in the presence of the others, hoping the traumatic experience would break their resistance. Twelve children were singled out and, with the two women, were suspended from a beam with their hands tied behind their backs. After a long time the sufferers were taken down from the beam. One of them faced the magistrates and boldly rebuked them for their cowardice: "You men," she said, "ought to be ashamed of yourselves to ill-treat these little girls in such a cruel way. What harm have they done? You are worse than dogs."

When the governor heard what had taken place he was infuriated and summoned Anne and Frances to his presence, threatening them with death if they would not denounce their faith. The two Christians defiantly replied, "We will never submit to you." Yu Xian roared, "I will have you cut in pieces!" "Do as you wish," the women said.

Anne Zhen and Frances Li were dragged out into the street and literally sliced to pieces, their limbs being cut off one by one as they called on the name of Jesus. When the brave women finally perished the soldiers gathered their warm blood in cups and forced the little children to denounce Christ or drink their teachers' blood. The children, faced with two vile options, decided it was worse to turn against the Lord and so drank the blood. The governor was defeated. Realizing he could do nothing to make the children turn against Jesus Christ, he ordered the massacre of all 200 orphans. The local magistrates, however, could not bring themselves to carry out the order and their lives were spared.

The repentant catechist

Another group of Christians were holed up inside the Taiyuan house of a catechist named Matthias Li Jinzhao. On 14 July the Boxers raided Li's house and arrested everyone present. When they began to bind the Christians one of them protested, "You have no need of chains or ropes; we will go freely wherever you wish." After being threatened with death, one of the group declared, "Here we are now. Put us to death here. We have nothing left in this world. Why send us back to the homes which you have already destroyed?" The group was cast into gloom when Matthias himself, who had been a tower of strength up to that point, began to waver and proposed a compromise with the Boxers to secure their freedom. He claimed it was possible to strike a deal outwardly with their enemies while remaining true believers in their hearts. As he prepared a list of the names of all present for the Boxers, every other believer strongly objected and fell to their knees in prayer. As

Matthias Li Jinzhao made his way towards the Boxer head-quarters with the list in hand he was suddenly seized with ter-ror. He saw Bishop Grassi, who had been martyred a few days earlier, walking towards him! The bishop came up to him, placed his hand on his shoulder and asked, "How is it, cate-chist, that you show such a bad example to the Christians? Return immediately and I promise that you will soon be with me in heaven." Overcome with fear and sorrow, Matthias hur-ried back to the house and, rushing in to his companions, threw himself on his knees and related with tears and sobs what had occurred. "Oh, pray for me, for I am a wretched sin-ner," he cried. Encouraged by the vision, Li took his stand for Christ and was one of 42 Catholic men and boys slain by Boxer swords the following day. The Christian women were allowed to go free after the governor's wife pleaded for the females to be spared.

One of the martyred men was Anthony Guan Lun. His wife Christina was forced to witness the deaths of her hus-band and two sons, Anthony and Francis, aged five and ten respectively. Francis cried out when his father was put to death, "Mama, mama, what are they doing to daddy?" "Close your eyes, darling, and keep quiet," she sobbed. The little fel-low obeyed and covered his eyes with his hands, but soon afterwards whispered, "Mama, I'm thirsty." His mother replied, "Wait a moment, darling, and our blessed Lord will bring you a drink." She had hardly completed her sentence when a Boxer decapitated the little boy.

The trembling Christina clasped her youngest infant, only nine weeks old, while the Boxers laughed at her tears. A Boxer callously asked, "Is that a boy or a girl?" Christina hes-itated before answering. All she had to say was "It's a girl", and the baby's life would be spared. But even under such duress she would not lie to her persecutors. With total abandonment to God's will, she truthfully said, "It's a boy." The Boxer ordered her to put the baby on the ground, where a blood-soaked sword pinned the infant to the earth.

In some cases God intervened and saved the lives of those who stood up for the truth. In the days following the massacre at Taiyuan on 9 July, an additional 70 Chinese Catholics were rounded up from the suburbs of the city and brought before the governor. He told the captives, "You rebellious subjects! I have killed the foreigners, now you must give up the foreign religion." The elder believers in the group replied, "We are trusting the Lord Jesus to save us from our sins, we cannot deny him." Yu Xian asked the group, "Why will you die? You are Chinese people, and I do not want to kill you." Finally the leaders of the 70 Christians, on behalf of the whole group, declared, "We are trusting in the Saviour to save us for ever, we cannot forsake him." The enraged governor picked out two teenage girls and cruelly beheaded them. Their blood was caught in a basin, mixed with water, and the remaining 68 Christians were made to take a sip, after which they were allowed to go home.

Approximately 8,000 Catholics were killed by the Boxers in Shanxi. After peace was restored, a Franciscan friar named John Ricci was ordered to go through the province and collect all possible details concerning Catholic martyrs. The result was that 2,418 Causes for Beatification, "out of hatred for the Faith", were sent to the Vatican for consideration.

CHAPTER 26

THE TAIYUAN MASSACRE

Governor Yu Xian, the Butcher
of Shanxi

The date of 9 July 1900 has gone down in Christian history as a day of infamy. Forty-six foreign missionaries, 33 Protestants and thirteen Catholics, were savagely massacred in Taiyuan City, the capital of Shanxi Province in north China. The instigator of the carnage was the governor, a wicked man named Yu Xian who held a grudge against Christians. On 27 June he issued a proclamation urging Chinese believers to renounce their faith or face death. On the morning of the massacre, hundreds of onlookers crowded into the palace courtyard to witness the macabre scene, many shouting their approval as heads were severed from their bodies.

A few years after the Taiyuan massacre a scholar, who was an eyewitness to the events that dreadful day, explained that he had been in the courtyard when the missionaries were slaughtered. What impressed him the most was their fearlessness and inner calm, even in the face of death. There was no panic and no last-minute cries for mercy. Just before the carnage began a little golden-haired girl aged about thirteen spoke to the governor in a loud voice that carried to all onlookers: "Why are you planning to kill us? Haven't our doctors come from far-off lands to give their lives to your people? Many with hopeless diseases have been healed; some who were blind have received their sight, and health and happiness have been brought into thousands of your homes because of what our doctors have done. Is it because of this good that has been done that you are going to kill us?"

Yu Xian looked down as the truthful words of the little girl shamed him. He had nothing to say. She continued, "Governor, you talk a lot about filial piety. It is your claim, is it not, that among the hundred virtues filial piety takes the highest place. But you have hundreds of young men in this province who are opium sots and gamblers. Can they exercise filial piety? Can they love their parents and obey their will? Our missionaries have come from foreign lands and have preached Jesus to them, and he has saved them and has given them power to live rightly and to love and obey their parents. Is it then, perhaps, because of this good that has been done that we are to be killed?"

By this time the governor was humiliated, having been rebuked in front of his officials by a little foreign girl. Each word seemed to be backed by the authority of the Almighty God, and cut to the heart of Yu Xian and all present. God could have chosen an aged and wise missionary to rebuke the evil governor, but instead he chose an innocent child to do so. The moment did not last long. A soldier, standing near the girl, grabbed her hair, and with one blow of his sword severed her head from her body. That was the signal for the massacre to begin.

Some of the executioners were skilled at killing and required only one attempt to decapitate their victims, but the soldiers were clumsy, and some of the victims suffered several cuts before death. The bodies were left where they had fallen for the night, and robbers stripped the corpses of their clothes, watches and rings. The next day the heads were placed in cages for a grotesque display on the city wall. Yu Xian was without remorse and later crowed to the empress, "Your Majesty's slave caught them as in a net and allowed neither chicken nor dog to escape." The old woman replied, "You have done splendidly."

Twenty-four Protestant missionaries and nine children, associated with the Baptist Missionary Society of England, the China Inland Mission, and the small Shouyang mission were cruelly put to death.

The Farthing family

The three Farthing children spitefully
killed by the Boxers

George Farthing was a British missionary who travelled around China, evaluating missionaries' progress in the language. The Farthing family lived in their own house in

Taiyuan. George had met and married Catharine before coming to China. God blessed their union with three beautiful children – Ruth (ten), Guy (eight) and Betty (three). On 21 June, after hearing that the empress had given permission to the governor of Shanxi to exterminate all foreigners, Farthing wrote, "I do not know whether this is true or not, but if it is true, I am ready, and do not fear; if such be God's will, I can even rejoice to die."

The Farthings were among more than 30 missionaries who barricaded themselves inside the grounds of the Boys' School in Taiyuan. Day and night bricks and stones smashed against the roof and walls of the buildings. On 5 July the magistrate ordered the missionaries to leave their homes and come to the compound connected to the governor's palace in the middle of the city, where they "could be better protected". The missionaries were highly suspicious of the offer, but felt they had little choice. George Farthing told the officials, "If you order us to go, we will go; and if you mean to kill us we must still go." The officials replied, "Oh, no, that is not our intention. We really mean to protect you."

On 9 July soldiers arrived at the school and roughly took the missionaries to the palace a short distance away. As they waited for the governor to appear they still held on to a glimmer of hope that all would end well, but when he stormed out of the palace brandishing his sword and screaming "Kill! Kill!" they knew they would soon see Jesus face to face.

A Christian named Yongzheng who witnessed the massacre said,

> Immediately Pastor Farthing stepped out. His wife clung to him, but he gently put her aside, and going in front of the soldiers knelt down without saying a word, and his head was struck off by one blow of the executioner's knife. When the men were finished the ladies were taken. Mrs. Farthing had hold of the

hands of her children, who clung to her, but the soldiers parted them, and with one blow beheaded their mother. The executioner beheaded all the children skilfully, requiring only one blow.

The Wilson family

Millar and Christine Wilson, missionary doctors at Taiyuan

Among the martyrs were Dr Millar Wilson of Scotland, his wife Christine, and their small son Alexander. The Wilsons joined the China Inland Mission in the 1880s, travelling to Shanxi Province where they operated a medical clinic for opium addicts, using their own funds to finance the treatments. Hundreds of men and women benefited from the Wilsons' sacrificial service.

At the time of the Boxer upheaval the Wilsons were due to return home on furlough. A terrible famine was plaguing north China, so they decided to stay and help famine victims. During this time Dr Wilson was afflicted with peritonitis. His symptoms worsening, Wilson finally told the local believers that he was unable to continue his work, and preparations were made for his family's trip home. The Christians presented him with a large satin sash, with the words "God's

Faithful Servant" inscribed on it. On the way to Taiyuan, Wilson wrote to a fellow missionary: "It's all fog, but I think, old chap, that we are on the edge of a volcano, and I fear Taiyuan is the inner edge." His prediction proved accurate.

Jane Stevens and Mildred Clarke

Jane Stevens   Mildred Clarke

Two single women, Jane Stevens and Mildred Clarke, were visiting Taiyuan and staying with the Farthing family when the massacre commenced.

Stevens worked as a nurse in England for five years before she sailed for the Orient in 1885. For much of her fifteen years in China she battled illness and loneliness. As a nurse she was accustomed to helping people regain their health, but she herself was frail and frequently sick. When a friend suggested that she might consider returning to the gentler climate of her home country, Stevens replied, "I don't feel I have yet finished the work God has for me in China. Perhaps – who knows? – I may be among those allowed to give their lives for the people." On many occasions Stevens asked God to send her a close friend that she could work with. After returning to China after a furlough in 1893 Stevens was paired together with a new missionary recruit, Mildred Clarke. The two became best friends, and Jane's prayers were answered. Although neither of them enjoyed robust health, they continually encouraged and spurred one another on to good works.

Mildred Clarke was the daughter of a British army colonel. A short time after arriving in China she wrote home, "Pray that God would be sanctified in my life, and in the lives of all His children here. I long to live a poured-out life unto Him among these Chinese, and to enter into the fellowship of His sufferings for souls, who poured out His life unto death for us."

In the summer of 1900 the two friends made the five-day journey north to Taiyuan, where they were savagely and callously hacked to pieces at the order of the governor, Yu Xian.

The Lovitt family

Arnold and Mrs Lovitt

The son of a prominent lawyer, Arnold Lovitt received his medical degree from the London Hospital and spurned the chance of an attractive income and comfortable lifestyle to serve Christ in China for little more than his board and daily necessities. Lovitt and his wife arrived in Taiyuan in the autumn of 1897, not expecting the Boxer storm that so suddenly broke upon them and the other missionaries in Taiyuan. In 1900, after hearing of Christians being massacred in the countryside, Lovitt wrote home, "We are being marvellously sustained by the Lord. He is precious to each of us. The children seem to have no fear. We cannot but hope for deliverance. Our trust is in Him entirely and alone. There is not much time. We are ready."

The hospital was burned to the ground by the Boxers, and the 31-year-old doctor and his wife were seized. Moments before their deaths, Mrs Lovitt was permitted to hold the hand of her little son. She boldly declared in a loud voice, "We all came to China to bring you the good news of salvation by Jesus Christ. We have done you no harm, only good. Why do you treat us so?" In a strange act of gentleness, a soldier stepped forward and carefully removed her spectacles before the devoted mother and her son were decapitated.

The Pigott family

Thomas Pigott   Jessie Pigott

Thomas Pigott was born in 1847 at Leixlip, a town on the banks of the picturesque Liffey River in County Kildare,

Ireland. As a young boy he often helped his father, William, present the gospel to the poorest people in the region. During the great Irish revival of 1862 the Pigott home was opened wide to all visiting preachers. Thomas was an impressionable fifteen-year-old boy at the time and the stories he heard shaped his young life and persuaded him to become a whole-hearted disciple of Christ.

After obtaining a Bachelor of Arts degree, Pigott travelled to China in 1879, settling in Shanxi Province, which was to remain his home for the rest of his life. On one occasion he was stabbed in his home by an intruder. While recovering in hospital, Pigott got to know a young English nurse named Jessie. They fell in love and were married.

In 1887 the Pigotts welcomed an adorable son, Wellesley, into the world. The golden-haired boy was deeply loved by the Chinese. Once, during a furlough in England, Wellesley told a friend, "We can't be martyrs in England, but my father and mother and I might be in China." His mother also expressed similar sentiments after hearing of the 1895 massacre of

Wellesley Pigott with his donkey and friends

missionaries at Gutian. She said, "It makes one feel how short our time for work in this land may be, and long to be filled with God's Holy Spirit that we may be faithful to the end."

As the Boxer troubles approached, the Pigotts tried to flee their hometown of Shouyang to nearby Taiyuan. They were captured near the gate and taken to the courtyard of the governor's palace where, unbeknown to the Pigotts, all their missionary friends had been slaughtered less than an hour before. The ground was soaked in blood, and displayed all around the courtyard were the severed heads of their friends.

Thomas Pigott was beheaded with one blow. Jessie stepped forward holding her son's hand. As each head fell, the soldiers showed their contempt by kicking them along the street.

Catholics

The Catholic Church throughout Shanxi Province experienced explosive growth at the end of the 19th century, with the capital city Taiyuan home to about 15,000 believers. The first sign of trouble appeared in the month of June 1900, with believers being harassed and threatened. The full force of the storm broke on 9 July, when twelve priests including Bishop Gregory Grassi and Bishop Franciscus Fogolla were brutally beheaded.

Bishop Franciscus Fogolla, an Italian, had worked in Shanxi Province since 1866. He travelled widely, preaching the gospel and instructing believers. He also found time to study the Chinese classics in order to better understand the people he was called to minister to. Fogolla's knowledge of the classics won him the respect of scholars and officials. Over time, Fogolla became deeply concerned at the abuse of power he saw in the Chinese church. He determined to rid the congregations of abusive and controlling leaders, and also decided the Catholic Church should defend its members against attacks and false accusations brought by non-believers.

Franciscus Fogolla

Fogolla was hauled before the governor of Shanxi. The white-bearded bishop asked the governor, "Why are you doing this wicked deed?" Yu Xian answered by drawing his sword and slashing him across the face. The Boxers then forced the

61-year-old Italian to the ground and hacked his head off with their swords. The other Catholics were then decapitated one by one.

Gregorius Grassi

Born in Italy in 1833, Gregorius Grassi had spent 40 years in China at the time of his martyrdom. On the eve of his arrest on 5 July some of the bishop's co-workers suggested he go into hiding. Grassi replied, "Ever since I was twelve, I have desired and also asked God for martyrdom. Now that this longed-for hour has come, must I run away?" The next day soldiers arrived at the cathedral. One of the men grabbed Grassi by the throat and struck him with a weapon while delivering a message from the governor: If the foreigners were willing to forsake their religion, their lives would be spared. Grassi calmly responded, "Long years ago I gave up all, I came here to save souls and lead them to God, at no price will I apostatize." Grassi was bound and taken into custody, and was one of the victims of the Taiyuan massacre.

The Italian priest Elias Facchini seemed to anticipate his imminent martyrdom. In early 1900 he told his colleagues, "If they kill me, I will get to heaven all the sooner. My body is already worn out. I will thank the Lord if I have to die for the faith." When the Boxers threatened Facchini with death unless he renounced Christ, he defiantly declared, "My faith is of steel; it may bend, but it does not break." When the soldiers began their slaughter, Facchini received more than 100 sword cuts and at each lifted his eyes to heaven and shouted, "I go to heaven!"

At the start of the 20th century the 33-year-old French missionary Andreas Bauer wrote to his brother, "We are at the dawn of a new century. I do not know what is in store for us. Oh! If only I too, like the good thief, could reach Paradise!" On 9 July a soldier ordered Bauer to stretch out his hands so he could bind them. The Frenchman knelt down, kissed the chains that bound him, and went singing to the place of execution.

Among the 46 Protestant and Catholic missionaries massacred at Taiyuan on 9 July 1900 were seven nuns associated with the Franciscan Missionaries of Mary. Their work included running hospitals and orphanages, organizing work centres, and training women to sew and embroider. Within a short time of their arrival the seven sisters had won the hearts of the people they had come to serve. When the carnage commenced the sisters chanted the *Te Deum*, the hymn of thanksgiving. To frighten them and prolong their torture, the soldiers attacked the seven nuns last so that they could witness the agonizing deaths of their companions. They prayed on their knees until a soldier struck down Clelia Nanetti. The others then calmly lifted their veils to receive the blow of the sword.

Irma Grivot was appointed superior of the Taiyuan nuns because of her deep devotion to Christ, and the other sisters loved her gentleness and meekness. When the Boxer attack was about to begin, the bishop ordered the seven nuns to don normal Chinese clothes and be taken to a remote location for their own safety. Grivot strongly protested, telling Bishop Fogolla, "For the love of God, do not prevent us from dying

Irma Grivot

with you. If we are naturally weak, believe me that God who sends the test will give us strength to meet it bravely. We fear neither death nor torments nor the rage of the governor. We came here to exercise charity and to shed our blood for the love of Jesus Christ if need be. We beg you not to take from us this palm which divine mercy extends."

Just prior to the Boxer attack Pauline Jeurise wrote to her loved ones back in Belgium,

The news is not good, danger is approaching, but we are peaceful. We are in God's hands. May His Holy Will be done. When this letter reaches you, perhaps we may already be dead. But rest assured that before we go, we have already offered our lives and our health for the non-Christians. When we came, we knew we would have to suffer. I am neither worried nor sad. I confide myself to God's care and I pray Him to console and fortify the martyrs and those who have to suffer for His Name.

God answered her prayer, and it was with great calmness of heart that she faced decapitation by a Boxer. Jeurise was 27 years old.

A group of Chinese workers and students at Taiyuan chose to embrace martyrdom rather than deny Christ. They were among those slaughtered at Taiyuan on 9 July. Among them was John Zhang Jingguang. When the threat of persecution approached in 1900, Zhang prepared himself and encouraged his fellow students to accept martyrdom. The seminarians were instructed to return home, but Zhang decided his life could better glorify God by staying. He was arrested with the foreign missionaries and a number of his fellow students. At the time one of the missionaries noticed that Zhang played around the prison yard as though he was enjoying a vacation. He sternly told him, "John, remember this is not the time for amusement." Zhang replied, "Why not? If we are put to death shall we not go to heaven?" He was brutally put to death a few days later.

John Zhang Jingguang

CHAPTER 27   SHOUYANG

The Girls' School at Shouyang in 1899. Edith Coombs is at the back. Many of these young girls were raped and sold into slavery during the Boxer Rebellion.

The missionaries and Chinese believers at Shouyang in eastern Shanxi Province nervously waited throughout the month of June as rumours that the Boxers were coming to slaughter them circulated throughout the town. In late June it was announced that a reward of 100 *taels* (worth approximately US$80 at the time) would be given for the head of any foreigner, and 25 *taels* ($20) for the head of each Chinese Christian.

On 3 July the Boxers rounded up a large group of church members and took them to the west gate of the city. Seventy-one Chinese Christians, including 18 women and eleven children, were slain that day – husbands in the presence of their wives, and children in their mothers' arms. One woman was buried alive.

Yan Laibao and his family were key members of the church in Shouyang. When the missionaries made plans to flee into the mountains, Yan offered his home for them to hide in. A few days later neighbours reported what was taking place. The Boxers were summoned, so Yan and his extended family, 20 people in all, fled into the mountains. The next day their home was burned to the ground, and the furious Boxers made plans to track the Yans down no matter how long it would take. During the day the Yans sheltered in ravines as the fierce sun beat down on them, while at night they hid in caves. Dozens of Boxers combed the mountains, searching out every possible hiding place.

Yan Laibao was the first to be discovered and was ruthlessly hacked to death. A short time later one of Yan's sons was also captured. The young man was told to divulge where the others were hiding. When he failed to do so, his feet and hands were bound together behind his back and he was suspended from a pole. Tortured with pain, he still refused to reveal the hiding-place. The Boxers placed burning incense on his back and crushed him with a heavy stone. He suffered in silence, faithfully enduring until the end. By the end of the carnage fourteen members of the Yan family had laid down their lives for Jesus Christ.

For several years Wang Tianren was the closest Chinese co-worker of Thomas Pigott. Just before the Pigott family were bound and taken to Taiyuan for execution, Wang was

Wang Tianren and his bride at their wedding
ceremony, presided over by fellow martyrs
Thomas and Jessie Pigott

captured by the Boxers and dragged before a magistrate and a
Boxer chief. A circle was drawn on the floor with a cross in the
middle. Wang was ordered to show his contempt for the cross
by urinating on it. He refused and was swiftly executed.

Zai Jingyang was a house painter by trade. Before his conversion he had painted idols for a living. On one occasion Zai
fell ill, and while recovering in the hospital he heard the
gospel for the first time and surrendered to the claims of
Christ. Upon returning home to Shidie village, Zai used part
of his house as a chapel. He fearlessly preached the good news
everywhere, even going into Buddhist temples to share his
faith with the monks. When the Boxers arrested Zai, he was
bound and beaten half to death. While lying on the ground
battered and bruised, some bystanders mockingly asked him,
"Does it hurt, teacher?" Zai was condemned to death and
beheaded outside the city, his head being hung on a tree. It
later emerged that 36 of the 40 church members at Shidie had
laid down their lives for the gospel.

Edith Coombs

Edith Coombs

Edith Coombs was born in Edinburgh, Scotland, in 1862. She was an outstanding student, graduating from college with a degree in literature. After taking up a teaching post at the Edgbaston High School for Girls, Edith adopted a motto: "Spend and be spent for Jesus Christ." The claims of the mission field were impressed upon her, and in 1898 Coombs joined the Shouyang mission in China's Shanxi Province. Before leaving home she spoke to the girls at her school, telling them, "You have many to love you, but the poor little girls in China hardly know what love means."

When the Boxers attacked the mission premises on the night of 27 June, Coombs' first concern was for the welfare of her beloved students. As each building was set on fire, the missionaries finally attempted to escape. On reaching the street, Coombs found that two of her students had been left behind. She immediately went back to try to save the little girls. One was found and put in a place of safety. The other girl was brought out on to the street, but Coombs was struck on the head with a brick, and both she and the student fell. She told the girl, "Don't be afraid; we shall soon see Jesus." Coombs begged her attackers to spare the girl's life, and someone led her away. The mob then threw Coombs on the fire in the gateway, heaping a door and tables on top of her to prevent her escape as she was burned alive. The next day only a few charred bones were to be found.

Two Christians watched the martyrdom of Edith Coombs from the rooftop of a neighbouring house. They later testified that they saw the heavens opened just above the fire, and a beautiful face looked down to receive Edith Coombs into her heavenly abode.

By the time the Boxers had completed their carnage, 71 Chinese Christians from the Shouyang area had lost their lives, many in a gruesome manner.

CHAPTER 28

TROUBLE AT THE GREAT WALL

The Soping slaughter

On 24 June 1900, ten missionaries associated with the Swedish Holiness Union gathered for their annual mission conference at the remote Soping station in the northernmost part of Shanxi, just inside the Great Wall that separated China from the vast Mongol steppes beyond. Two families, the Forsbergs and the Blombergs, also attended the meetings as guest teachers.

Before the meetings commenced, Boxer agitators were saying that the missionaries had swept away approaching rain clouds with a yellow paper broom and that the foreigners were praying to their God that it might not rain.

A mob converged on the house where the missionaries were meeting on 29 June. As the mob attempted to smash down the front door, the Christians rushed out the back of the house and ran to the magistrate's headquarters, where they pleaded for protection. The Boxers gave chase, but the magistrate refused to hand the missionaries over to them. Instead, he bound five of the men with leg irons to placate the Boxers, and promised that the missionaries would be sent to Beijing to be executed. This seemed to please the bloodthirsty mob and they slowly drifted away. Later that night, however, the mob returned with soldiers sympathetic to their cause. Sparing no one, they stoned to death all the missionaries and

A Boxer standard-bearer, armed with spear and shield

their children along with Chinese Christians who had sought refuge. Their heads were hung on the city wall.

A Chinese evangelist named Wang Lanbu managed to escape the slaughter when he fainted while being questioned. Wang later reported the grim circumstances of the slaughter of his family and other Christians at Soping:

> My mother, brother, sister, my little child, and an old lady named Wu were burned alive. Not only this, the cart was burned, the mule killed and thrown into the flames, also the dog and chickens in our yard. People were not tied, but were just thrown into the fire and driven back whenever they tried to get out. It was a slow and bitter death.

Nathanael Carleson

The leader of the Swedish Holiness Union was 33-year-old Nathanael Carleson, who grew up in the Swedish province of Nerike. Carleson was deeply loved by the Chinese Christians, who often quoted John 1:47 when introducing him: "Here is a true Israelite, in whom there is nothing false." The Carlesons had two children. When they travelled home on furlough Mrs Carleson and the children remained in Sweden while Nathanael returned to China alone. Three lives were thus spared from the Boxer cruelty, but a heartbroken family had to face life without their beloved husband and father.

Other Swedish missionaries killed at Soping included Sven and Emma Persson, Gustaf Karlberg and Oscar Larsson, who wrote just before his death, "Let us pray that the present trouble may afterwards gain a glorious victory for the Gospel." Ernst Pettersson was the youngest of the martyrs, having arrived in China just five months before his death. The other slain missionaries included four single women, each aged about 30 years old. One of them, Mina Hedlund, came to China in 1894. She spent much time in prayer and intercession, and in her last letter had declared, "I don't fear if God wants me to suffer the death of a martyr." Anna Johansson received her missionary training in England before arriving in China in 1898. Jenny Lundell and Justina Engvall came to China together and were still finding their feet when the Boxers barbarously slaughtered them.

In all, thirteen Swedish missionaries were killed at Soping, three belonging to the Alliance Mission and ten to the Swedish Holiness Union, which was still in its infancy when the massacre occurred. All that remained were two missionaries working in another province and another member, Jane Sandeberg, who was making her way home for furlough when the disaster struck. She descended the ship's gangway in Stockholm to be handed a telegram, which read, "All members of the Swedish Holiness Union killed". Sandeberg wrote,

> What suffering, pain, and sorrow were represented in those few words only God knows. The memory of their lives will always remain with me as an inspiration and a call to seek those things which are above. Strong and faithful, meek and lowly, ready for any service, bright, cheerful, and shining for Jesus all the day – truly we who knew them thank God for them.

The devil's plans to totally exterminate Christianity in Soping backfired. A missionary there reported of a revival in the summer of 1908:

> The nearness of God's presence was realised in a remarkable degree. They all knelt in prayer and immediately there were confessions made such as can only be heard when the great Searcher of all hearts is at work. Even little children of seven

and eight years of age were acknowledging their sins of disobedience and asking forgiveness.

The McKee family

Stewart and Kate McKee with
their daughter Alice

The first Protestant missionary to live in the town of Datong, situated just below the Great Wall in northern Shanxi Province, arrived in 1885. A few years later Stewart and Kate McKee from Scotland took charge of the work, assisted by Charles and Florence I'Anson. The McKees and I'Ansons experienced a decade of fruitful ministry before suffering martyrdom for the sake of Christ in 1900.

In late June news reached the McKees that the Boxers were planning to slaughter them. They took refuge with a friendly local magistrate, but a mob of Boxers surrounded the house, baying for the blood of those inside. For three days the official refused to hand them over, until a command from a superior arrived, ordering the missionaries to return to their residence. The stress of the ordeal overwhelmed Kate McKee, and she gave birth prematurely. There were now four children and a newborn baby inside the small house, while outside the mobs grew larger and more violent every day. At seven o'clock in the evening of 12 July, 300 soldiers arrived on horseback in support of the Boxers. Stewart McKee went out and tried to reason with them. Instead of listening, they hacked him to pieces with their swords and knives, and then set fire to the house. In the flames and chaos, only little Alice McKee managed to escape. In the morning the mob discovered her in a cowshed and slashed the defenceless child to death.

The I'Anson family

Charles I'Anson, his wife Florence, and three children Dora, Arthur and Eva were butchered together at Datong on 12 July.

Charles I'Anson grew up in the city of London, and came to faith in Christ when a friend took him to an evangelistic meeting. From the outset he desired to be a true disciple, preaching the gospel with great enthusiasm. He sailed for China in 1887, where five years later he met and married Florence. Their union produced three children. Dora was born first, followed a few years later by Arthur. For eight blessed years the I'Ansons worked in Shanxi Province, assisting Stewart and Kate McKee at Datong. Several single women also arrived to lend a hand. Together they had the joy of seeing a small church of faithful converts emerge in the town.

Two single English women, Maria Aspden and Margaret

The I'Anson family

Smith, were also slain at Datong, along with a number of Chinese Christians in the town. Because of the isolation of the Datong mission, it was an agonizing eight months before the missionaries' families back home received confirmation of their deaths.

TAIGU

At Taigu in central Shanxi Province an announcement was made that the missionaries were to be slaughtered on 28 June, but the day passed without any disturbance. Four days earlier there had been a riot in the streets surrounding the mission station. An angry crowd threw bricks and rocks and screamed, "Kill! Kill!" The missionaries were shocked at the sudden and dramatic change in the locals, many of whom had been kind to them just a few days before. They tried to diffuse the tense situation by calmly opening the gates, inviting the crowd in as they stood by nervously smiling. The mob crowded into the chapel and other buildings and did not leave until the evening.

Howard and Jennie Clapp

Howard and Jennie Clapp

Howard Clapp headed up the literature work of the American Board mission, distributing thousands of gospel tracts, calendars, hymnals and books over a widespread area. In June 1900 the missionaries at Taigu paid little attention to rumours of impending death, considering it "foolish talk" and unlikely to materialize. All this changed when news arrived of the 9 July slaughter of missionaries at Taiyuan.

For approximately three weeks the Taigu missionaries nervously waited for the Boxers to attack them. During this time a sharp debate arose between those missionaries who had armed themselves with revolvers and planned to defend their lives should the Boxers attack, and those missionaries, including Howard Clapp, who strongly believed Christians should never take up arms under any circumstance. Clapp declared, "We who believe in the Lord ought not to put our trust in arms, but we should meet death trusting in the Lord." The debate raged back and forth, putting everyone on edge.

The Clapps reluctantly agreed to try to flee to the mountains with the other missionaries. Howard had argued against the plan, telling his colleagues, "It will be no harder to die here on our premises than in the hills." Before they had the chance to leave the city, the magistrate locked the gates and ordered the missionaries to remain where they were. Howard Clapp's diary was later recovered. His last entry was dated 15 July:

We still live. I have never enjoyed such peace at a time of anxiety and trial. The Lord is very good to us. I am anxious now to keep my heart stayed on Christ. He is our help and our shield. This very likely is the last I can write unless the Lord should see fit to deliver us in a miraculous way.

The tide of hatred was too strong, and the missionaries were soon overpowered. One by one they were beheaded as the spiteful mobs bayed for their blood.

Rowena Bird

Rowena Bird was born at Sandoval, Illinois, in 1865. As a child she was frail and subsequently was unable to attend school regularly. Many people, including Rowena herself, feared she was too physically weak to be a missionary. She pushed on, however, and learned that God can take the weak and use them for his glory. Soon after arriving in China in 1890, Bird found the struggles of life overwhelming. There was no privacy, with people continually interrupting her and peering through her window. Her room had wide cracks in the walls, and the main entrance overlooked an open sewer.

Rowena Bird

Slowly, by persevering, Rowena Bird blossomed into an effective worker. The local people warmed to her, and she was a great help in the opium refuge. Initially, she didn't take the Boxer threat too seriously, but on 13 July 1900 she wrote to her mother, "I must say good-bye to you all, dear mother and all of you. Our people are scattering. We cannot wonder. I think some of them would die for us if they could thus save us. Poor people, these are dreadful times for them!"

The expected slaughter of the missionaries at Taigu occurred on 31 July. Rowena Bird was martyred on her 35th birthday.

Louise Partridge

Louise Partridge and her assistant, Guo Xiaoxian,
departing on an evangelistic trip in 1898

Louise Partridge was a native of Stockholm, New York. Her parents were devoted Christians who dedicated her to the Lord on her first birthday. By the time she was six she was already telling people that God had called her to be a missionary.

In many ways Louise Partridge was strangely similar to her co-worker and fellow martyr Rowena Bird. She was the same age, the daughter of a minister, and also insisted on being called by her middle name. In other ways, however, the two women were poles apart in their views and personalities. While Rowena spent much time on her appearance, Louise cared little about the way she looked. She came from a rural background and was more used to rough living. The biggest obstacle blocking Partridge from becoming a missionary was her poor academic record. The mission decided her good character outweighed her academic failures, and they accepted her. Their bold decision proved correct. From the time she first arrived in Shanxi in 1893, Partridge built many strong friendships among both Christian and non-Christian women, who warmed to her kind personality.

After Partridge heard about the murder in 1900 of Belgian and French engineers who were fleeing to the coast, she wrote, "I feel there is no hope for us. A horrible fear shook me for a minute." On 14 July she wrote her final letter, saying, "We have nothing to do now but to wait for death, or deliverance which seems to be impossible except by a miracle. I've sent letters to all my friends. Excuse all mistakes – we are all more or less stunned and stupid."

On 31 July Louise Partridge's head was severed from her body, and in an instant she was safe in the arms of the Lover of her soul.

Francis Davis

Francis Davis was not alarmed by rumours that hundreds of Boxers were planning to exterminate the Christians in Shanxi. In early June he expressed his opinion that the people of the province were not going to "change the custom of centuries and begin to row and fight". His wife, Lydia, was spared martyrdom on account of being home in America at the time of the violence.

Francis Davis

When it became apparent that the Boxer chaos was no

idle threat, Davis tried to remain at his isolated mission station and fight it out. In the end he fled to Taigu and joined the other missionaries.

The last letter Francis Davis was able to send out was penned on 28 May, addressed to his wife Lydia. He concluded it with these words, "With love unbounded and full of joy in your sweet and precious love and love to all the folks. God be with thee till we meet again." On 31 July hundreds of Boxers and soldiers stormed the mission compound. Davis and about a dozen other believers fled to a small windowless shed at the back of the mission compound, where they sat as still as possible. A Boxer climbed onto the roof, perhaps hoping to look over the wall. His weight caused the roof to cave in, right on top of Francis Davis. Dozens of Boxers swarmed to the shed, where they rained bricks and rocks down upon the heads of the penned-in missionaries and their Chinese friends. The Boxers then filled the shed with straw and set it alight. The flames flushed the Christians out into the open where their heads were cut off.

The next day the Boxers triumphantly hung Francis Davis' head on the north gate of the city. Many hard-hearted people came and laughed at it, throwing dirt at the head and shouting insults.

Chinese martyrs

The missionaries massacred at Taigu did not die alone. The Chinese believers in the town loved them so much that they willingly laid down their lives alongside those who had sacrificially travelled from their own countries to bring the Good News to them. The first Chinese Protestant martyr in the Taigu region was a shepherd named An. While out tending his sheep, 30 men and boys pounced on him, tied him up, and cut him to pieces. Later they burned his body.

Liang Xidai had been saved from addiction to opium and had given his life wholeheartedly to the cause of Christ. He gave up a profitable business in order to live on the mission compound at Taigu, so he could better grow in his faith. When the Boxers captured Liang and ordered him to denounce Jesus Christ he replied, "I am a disciple of Jesus; I cannot worship your gods. If you want to kill me, do it, for you can only kill my body; you cannot hurt my soul, and I do not fear you." He was viciously hacked to death just moments later.

Wu Sanyuan was an old man when he first heard the gospel, but he wasted no time in making the remainder of his life count for God. He once told the missionaries of his deepest desire: "I want to see the face of Jesus." When the Boxers came to Taigu, Wu left his home and moved into the mission compound. Some well-meaning people from his village wrote a statement on Wu's behalf, claiming he had denounced Christ. They brought the certificate to the mission gates, telling Wu that it was now safe to come home. The old Christian rebuked his friends for their misguided efforts and announced that he would stay with the missionaries regardless of the consequences. When the Boxers broke into the compound they launched themselves at Wu, slicing him with their razor-sharp swords. In the twinkling of an eye Wu Sanyuan saw the face of Jesus.

Cheng Zhongren found Christ after receiving help from the missionaries for his addiction to opium. When the compound was attacked he managed to escape over a back wall and hid in grain fields nearby. When darkness fell he rushed to the house of an uncle, where the Boxers captured him. They told him, "If you are a church member we will kill you." Cheng replied, "Then kill me." His body was cut into fragments.

Lin Zhen came from a wealthy family. Before meeting Christ he was a successful merchant. After his conversion Lin was so hungry to know God that he entrusted his business into the hands of others and moved into the mission compound so that he could attend all the services and prayer meetings. When the Boxers began their murderous spree, Lin Zhen refused to leave the town while his missionary friends were in danger. He told a colleague, "Our enemies can kill the body, but they cannot kill the soul. Why should we fear them? Why have we followed Jesus? Was it not to bear the cross and suffer with him? Then see these missionaries; they have loved ones across the sea, whom they left for our sakes, and now they are suffering because they came to save us. They trust in God, and are not afraid. And I am not afraid."

Guo Weihua was a teenage boy who tasted death for the sake of the gospel. Aged 18 at the time of his martyrdom, the missionaries pleaded with Guo to go home and preserve his life, but he refused, telling a friend, "Though it is so dangerous here, I cannot think of leaving. How these teachers have loved us! Can I leave them now in their extremity? This is our opportunity for showing them that they have not loved us in vain."

Deacon Liu and family

Liu Fengshi was one of the best-loved Chinese church leaders in Shanxi Province at the time of his martyrdom. Better known simply as "Deacon Liu", he was a huge man for a Chinese, standing well over six feet tall and strongly built. Liu was the firstfruits of the missionary work at Taigu. Prior to his conversion he had been addicted to opium and gambling, and was renowned for his hot temper.

At the age of 47, with his wealth gone because of drug addiction, he humbled himself by going to Taigu and asking for help from Dr Atwood, who ran an opium clinic. The missionaries relied on prayer and the power of God to bring deliverance to the addicts' lives. They also used a little psychology.

Deacon Liu and his family, martyrs for Jesus Christ

All new patients were given a weak dose of morphine to help them through the initial stages of withdrawal. As the treatment continued, the missionaries injected only water into their patients, who believed they were still being given morphine. During his first stay of 40 days, Liu heard the gospel for the first time. He gradually opened up his heart to let the Saviour in. He later testified, "This repentance of mine gave me true peace of mind. I knew that the truth in Christ leads to the right way, saves men's souls, ensures heaven and eternal life. This is true joy, and from this time I had true peace of heart."

When Liu first put his trust in Christ many of his friends and relatives thought it was a joke. When they saw he was serious they became angry and thought he had been put under some kind of magic spell by the foreigners. Liu was baptized in 1891, and matured into a Bible scholar, studying God's Word for hours every day.

The people of Taigu hated Deacon Liu even more than

they despised the missionaries. Liu's preaching always probed the wounds of sin, and his messages brought discomfort to their consciences. Hundreds earnestly joined the cry, "Kill Liu Fengshi!" Liu declared, "I have hoped to shed my blood for the Lord. Flight for me is useless; wherever I go I shall be recognized. If it is the Lord's will that I die, and he lets the Boxers come, I will die here. I shall not go a step from the mission."

On the morning of 31 July Liu led the service inside the mission compound. For an hour he spoke passionately on martyrdom and the need to endure to the very end. When the Boxers stormed into the mission compound that same afternoon, Liu sat motionless in his room, drinking tea and fanning himself. He slowly came outside to meet the Boxers, saying, "If you have come to kill, kill me first." With perfect calmness he went to meet his Redeemer. Liu's wife was also a Christian. She was a hunchback, crippled over by disease. Liu's wife and daughter-in-law were beheaded with a straw-knife and their heads thrown into a gully.

Before the Boxer carnage there were 120 Chinese Protestant Christians in Taigu and surrounding villages. By the end of the summer, 80 had been spitefully murdered and just 40 remained alive.

CHAPTER 30 PETER OGREN – THE MAN WHO WOULDN'T DIE

Peter Ogren was born in 1874 on a little farm near Jonköping, Sweden. After leaving school, he took an apprenticeship in carpentry. During those years he was a member of the YMCA. Although busy with his work, he found time for much prayer and Bible study and never missed a meeting.

Olivia Ogren and children after the death of her husband. A Chinese friend is holding Samuel.

In 1892 the famous preacher Frederik Franson visited Jonköping and appealed for people to give their lives as missionaries. Ogren responded, and after training he moved to Yongning in Shanxi Province, with his wife Olivia and son Samuel.

When the Boxer troubles began the magistrate at Yongning said he could no longer guarantee the missionaries' safety, so on 13 July the Ogrens attempted to flee to the coast. They started for the Yellow River, hoping it would carry them to safety. The pregnant Olivia, their little son Samuel and eight-month-old baby daughter survived after experiencing great hardship and suffering, but Peter Ogren finally died from horrendous injuries sustained at the hands of the Boxers.

The Ogrens managed to escape across the Yellow River into Shaanxi Province, but after being attacked by evil men they were compelled to re-cross the river near Daning. There they were seized and taken before the Boxer chief, who condemned Peter Ogren to death. Although he was terribly wounded with a sword cut to the head, the Swede managed in his agony to spring from the hands of his would-be murderers, jump into the river, and escape under the cover of darkness.

The next morning the bleeding missionary was found by church leader Deacon Wang, who lovingly bound up his wounds. Barely conscious, Ogren heard that his beloved wife and children had been cast into prison and somehow dragged himself to his feet and returned to the place of his persecution. The Boxers were shocked, both that Ogren was still alive and that he had bravely returned to their midst unafraid. His wife, grief-stricken and detained in a filthy cell, later told of her astonishment at her husband's return:

> Just as day began to break I was falling into a doze when I seemed to hear someone call my name. Soon waking, I ran out into the courtyard and looked up to the hill over-shadowing the prison. My heart was beating wildly, thinking, "Is it possible that my beloved is still alive and calling down to me?" Again that longed-for, tender voice – Olivia! oh, Olivia!

The courageous Peter Ogren was thrown into the same cell as his family. His serious injuries and the lack of medical care caused him to become delirious, and his heartbroken wife could only cry out to God for help. Olivia's description of her husband's injuries leaves little to the imagination: "A great piece of the scalp hung down loose; one ear was crushed and swollen; his neck bore two sword gashes; near the shoulder were two spear cuts, one very deep." She later wrote,

> God only knows the horror and the misery of those hours. Here lay my poor husband, who had lately been so strong and cheerful, there was our baby, the picture of health and the admiration of all when we left our home, now a living skeleton, and I – well

was it for me that I could not see my own face, for surely there
would have been little comfort in the sight. My cup of suffering
was now full to overflowing.

During one moment when Peter Ogren was calm, he told his
wife what had happened when the Boxers attacked him. His
remarkable testimony is worth repeating at length:

> The Boxer General ordered me down on my knees. He asked me
> how many people I had misled and ruined. I assured him, I had
> never in my life harmed any one. He would not listen to such
> talk, and had my hands tied behind my back, and I was bound to
> a block of wood, when all the crowd began to kick and beat me.
> As I lay there bound to the block they said jeeringly, "Now ask
> your Jesus to deliver you." I began fervently to pray, "Jesus, for-
> give them, for they know not what they do. But show forth Thy
> great power, that Thy name may be glorified."
>
> After a little while they loosed me from the block and led
> me to the river side, to kill me with my hands still bound behind
> my back. When we came to the river, they forced me down on
> my knees and set upon me from all sides, but as their weapons
> clashed one on another they did not kill me at once. Loss of
> blood soon made me feel faint, but I was so happy! The sweet-
> ness of His presence filled me as never before. Cutting and stab-
> bing were as nothing, and I felt no pain. To my inward vision
> heaven seemed open, and one step would take me there. I
> longed for deliverance.
>
> Then came to me suddenly as a flash of lightning the
> thought of my wife and children. I asked myself whether you
> were still alive and whether we should not die together. Roused
> by the thought, I suddenly leaped from the midst of the crowd
> into the water. Thirty or forty men were standing round me,
> Boxers and helpers. Two started to follow, but feared the deep
> water. The others cried, "Good! Good! He will die in the water."
> I managed to get to the other side, and with my hands still
> bound behind my back, started to run up the steep hillside.

Then there was a great hubbub; but under cover of darkness I got out of sight.

God had answered his servant's prayer as a witness to the astounded Boxers, miraculously preserving Peter Ogren's life and enabling him to see his beloved family again.

Finally, after weeks of suffering in prison, the Ogrens were allowed to travel to the coast. The bumpy roads and summer heat immediately made Peter's condition worse. On 12 October they stopped at Linfen. He fell into a delirious fever, and screamed with terror as he imagined the Boxers were chasing him. Olivia Ogren wrote,

> A terrible fear seized me, and I almost seemed to lose my senses. For the first time I realized that he was dying. I begged him to speak, but he was unable. Oh, how I cried out to God in the anguish of my soul! A few minutes later I rose to look at him. A single glance revealed the truth. The weary, suffering pilgrim had gone into the presence of the King, to receive the martyr's crown.

The wounded warrior passed away on 15 October 1900, but the lives of his longsuffering wife and children were saved.

CHAPTER 31 # LETTERS OF FAITH AND COURAGE

As the slaughter of missionaries continued throughout Shanxi Province many wrote emotional and stirring letters home to their loved ones. These precious documents provide a glimpse into the unwavering commitment to Christ these missionaries possessed, as well as the grace God provided to help his servants endure these dark times.

Edith and May Nathan

Two sisters, Edith and May Nathan, were killed at Daning. On 12 July they fled with Mary Heaysman into the mountains. For several weeks the trio lodged in small villages, and other times in remote caves and ravines. Edith Nathan penned a long letter, which she managed to send to her loved ones back home:

Edith Nathan

> One knows not what may come, and our hearts are sick and sad; but we know "Our God is able to deliver," and He has given us promises from His Word, "I will save thee." Here all is peace, but all know of troubles, and any day we have to go farther away. Truly these "Child Boxers" are devilish, and a device of the devil. We in England know little of what the power of Satan can do over the mind of a child. God deliver us from a like fate.

May Nathan also wrote a farewell letter to her mother in England, telling her,

> Darling Mother, don't be anxious, whatever news you may hear of me. It will seem useless in the eyes of the world to come out here for a year, to be just getting on with the language, then to be cut off. Many will say, "Why did she go? – wasted life." God does His very best, and never makes mistakes. We are called to suffer with Jesus. Very literally one takes the Scriptures nowadays, just as the first Christians did; they endured physical suffering for Jesus. We often endure mental and spiritual, and now we are called to endure, perhaps, extreme bodily suffering. But, darlings, death is but the gate of life, we shall see His face, and, darling Mother, I'll wait and long for you there!

On 24 September confirmation was received of the deaths of the Nathan sisters and Mary Heaysman. Pastor Zhang Qiben wrote to the parents of the three martyrs, lamenting, "The three ladies were seized, dragged to the outside of the city to a temple where it was difficult to either stand, sit, or lie down, hungry and thirsty, with no one to look after them, and surrounded by a gang of evil men. At early dawn on the morning of 13 August the three were killed."

The Price family

Charles and Eva Price

When the persecution commenced at Fenyang, Charles Price and the other men took turns guarding the mission compound, although they knew full well if the Boxers launched an attack they would have no trouble gaining access. Charles and Eva Price were respected workers with the American Board. They had operated a successful mission in Fenyang for a number of years. Dozens of people in the city and surrounding countryside had experienced the saving grace of God, and a small yet healthy church had emerged. Charles Price declared, "Though I know that we are now in the greatest danger, I am glad that God has used me in his holy work here. I am not sorry that I came as a missionary to China."

Of all who died for Christ during the Boxer Rebellion of 1900, perhaps nobody documented their experiences as much as Charles and Eva Price. Both of them kept detailed diaries telling of the stress they endured. Eva Price seems to have accepted her imminent death long before it finally took place. On 30 June she wrote her last letter to her family:

If we are to be murdered, one can but pray that it may come quickly and end our terrible suspense. Our friends at home will have suspense, but not such as ours, when the heart refuses to act properly, and knees and legs shake in spite of all efforts to be brave and quiet, trusting alone in God. We do trust in Him. That is our witness. No matter what comes, we are trusting Him, believing firmly that all this tumult and alarm and real danger, rumours of wars and terrible evil, are only working out His infinite purpose for good to come to China. Each day we live we feel it a deeper truth that man proposes and God disposes. Fear not, it is all right. God is watching and waiting. If we die, we die in peace.

William and Clara McCurrach

William and Clara McCurrach

From Aberdeen in Scotland, William McCurrach and his English wife Clara met in China and were married at Shanghai in 1898. On 3 July, with the Boxer threat imminent, William wrote to his mother,

> This is a sad time for China. If all missionaries are murdered, it will move the Church in a remarkable way. If it is God's way of evangelising China, then surely we ought to be ready to die for the Gospel's sake. None of us want to die, but we all want to say, "Thy will be done." It may be my last message to you all. Clara and I have been praying for you all one by one. I want to meet you all in heaven. Sorrow not for us, dearest mother. If we die, I trust it is together, and then we shall enter heaven and together receive our crowns.

The McCurrachs received their crowns on 9 August.

Bessie Renaut, from the English town of Leytonstone, arrived in China just nine months before her death. In her last letter to her family on 3 July she wrote, "Dear father and all loved ones, We do not know today whether we shall be in glory; if we are we are ready. Do not grieve. God has and is being good to us. Love, Bessie."

Sydney Ennals was a 27-year-old from Lewisham in England. Soon after arriving in China the young missionary was caught up in the cauldron of Boxer violence, enduring terrible hardship as he and the other missionaries hid from their pursuers. On 4 July he wrote to his family:

Sydney Ennals

> One feels quite unable to say much in a letter under these sad circumstances; we one and all, however, have been wonderfully calm, trusting in God. I do not regret coming to China, and although my life will have been short, it will in some way have fulfilled the Master's will. May the Lord's will be done! I pray earnestly for His deliverance, and feel we shall have it, but after all we may glorify Him better by passing through a deep persecution. Good-bye, dearest ones; may the Lord take all the future in His hands, and grant us all to meet in Jesus' presence.

When the carts Ennals and the other missionaries were travelling in were ambushed, the occupants were dragged out, stripped naked, and their heads were cut off. The bodies were then thrown into a nearby river. The remains were later fished out of the water and tossed onto a garbage dump outside the city, but a resident of Xinzhou paid some beggars to wrap the bodies in mats and bury them near the city wall.

The Atwater family

Ernest Atwater was an American Congregationalist missionary and a scholar. During his time at seminary he met and married Jennie Pond, a pretty 22-year-old preacher's daughter. God soon blessed them with four girls under the age of seven. The last birth had been a very difficult one for Jennie, and she died on 25 November 1896 after developing a fever of 104° F (40° C).

The Atwater children – four innocent martyrs. Left to right: Mary, Bertha, Ernestine and Celia

Ernest soon remarried; his new wife was an Irish missionary-schoolteacher named Lizzie. When the Boxers launched their attacks, Lizzie was in the ninth month of her pregnancy, and was so distraught she couldn't sleep. In her last letter to her family, dated 3 August, an emotional Lizzie Atwater wrote,

> Dear ones, I long for a sight of your dear faces, but I fear we shall not meet on earth. I am preparing for the end very quietly and calmly. The Lord is wonderfully near, and He will not fail me. I was always restless and excited while there seemed a chance of life, but God has taken away that feeling, and now I just pray for grace to meet the terrible end bravely. The pain will soon be over, and oh the sweetness of the welcome above!
>
> My little baby will go with me. I think God will give it to me in Heaven, and my dear mother will be so glad to see us. I cannot imagine the Saviour's welcome. Oh, that will compensate for

all of these days of suspense. Dear ones, live near to God and cling less closely to earth. There is no other way by which we can receive that peace from God which passeth understanding. I must keep calm and still these hours. I do not regret coming to China, but am sorry I have done so little. My married life, two precious years, has been so very full of happiness. We will die together, my dear husband and I.

I used to dread separation. If we escape now it will be a miracle. I send my love to you all, and the dear friends who remember me.

The Kay family

The Kay family

A colourful Scottish evangelist, Duncan Kay, was stationed with his wife Caroline and daughter Jennie at Quwo in south-west Shanxi Province. Caroline Kay was a gifted speaker who had encountered much success in women's ministry.

When the Boxers launched their attack a Chinese friend whisked the Kay family and three single women missionaries into the mountains, where some caves had been carefully selected to offer the best chance for the missionaries to evade their bloodthirsty pursuers. From the cave, Caroline Kay was able to send a final heartfelt letter to her elder children, who were attending boarding school in Shandong Province:

> My Dearest Children –
>
> We came up here to get away from the Boxers, thinking it was out of the way, and we might be able to stay over this time of difficulty and go back in two months. But we are molested every day by bands of bad men who want money from us. Now our money is all gone we feel there is nothing for us but to try and get back to the city; this is no easy matter, and the roads are full of these bad people who seek our lives.
>
> I am writing this as it may be my last to you. Who knows but we may be with Jesus very soon. This is only a wee note to send our dear love to you all, and to ask you not to feel too sad when you know we have been killed. We have committed you all into God's hands. He will make a way for you all. Try and be good children. Love God. Give your hearts to Jesus. This is your dear parents' last request.
>
> Your loving papa, mama, and wee Jennie.

Soon after this letter was sent, Duncan and Caroline Kay and Jennie were seized by the Boxers and ferociously butchered.

The Boxer Rebellion concluded with a total of between 30,000 and 40,000 Christians being martyred for their faith across China, including more than 300 Protestant and

Catholic missionaries. For many Chinese people today, the Boxer Rebellion is remembered fondly as a time when heroic forces rose up against their foreign oppressors. To the Chinese Christians, the Boxer Rebellion is remembered as the time when the fledgling Chinese church became the church triumphant.

Many house church leaders in China today believe the tremendous example of radical faith, sacrifice and courage displayed by so many thousands of Christians during the Boxer Rebellion, even in the face of horrible death, acted as a clear example of how the Chinese church should conduct itself during the later decades of brutal Communist persecution.

The tremendous revival throughout China in the past three decades, when tens of millions of people have been swept into the kingdom of God, is one fruit that has sprung from the fertile soil soaked by the blood of thousands of martyrs in 1900.

PART THREE

Bandits and Communists

CHAPTER 32   1901 TO 1948 –
MARTYRS OF THE
BANDIT YEARS

Although the influence of the Boxers largely subsided after 1900, small pockets of rebels persisted throughout the countryside for years to come. Bandits took the opportunity to exploit the power vacuum caused by China's political instability and wreaked widespread havoc. Thousands of impoverished people joined the gangs, more out of a sense of desperation than one of wilful violence. The economy in China collapsed, and by the late 1920s and early 1930s things had become so bad that reports emerged from one region of parents eating their children. Faced with such dire conditions, gangs found recruiting new members an easy task. The choices available to many peasants were starvation, cannibalism or banditry.

Reports of bandits attacking missionaries and Chinese Christians became a common occurrence throughout China in the first half of the 20th century, especially during the 1920s, '30s and '40s when lawlessness plagued the land. In 1930 it was estimated that more than 500,000 people operated in bandit gangs throughout the country, in groups ranging in size from 100 to 10,000 people.

1900s

In many places the local Christians showed tremendous courage in the face of great adversity. Itinerant evangelists were easy targets for bandits and other anti-Christian factions. One preacher in Jiangxi Province was seized and his hands bound. He was ordered to run through the streets shouting, "I am an imperialist, a slave dog of the foreigners." Instead, he proclaimed at the top of his lungs, "I am a slave of Jesus Christ!"

The bloodbath of the Boxer Rebellion had hardly ended when more killings occurred in various parts of China. In 1902 the 27-year-old French Catholic Hippolyte Julien was murdered at his home in Guangdong Province along with his catechist and cook. In Sichuan Province an offshoot of the Boxers called the Red Lantern Society massacred a Catholic community, cutting the throats of men, women and children and burning down their homes.

James Bruce

James Bruce from Australia and Englishman Henry Lowis served with the China Inland Mission in the southern province of Hunan until they were cruelly beaten to death at Chenzhou. Earlier in the year the town was swept by a cholera epidemic and many people died. The local rumour-mill claimed the epidemic was caused by poison the two missionaries had given to people as medicine. Another rumour stated that Bruce and Lowis had been seen poisoning the freshwater spring that served as the town's water supply. The hostility reached its climax on 15 August 1902 when hundreds of angry people stormed the house where they lived. Bruce and Lowis were stabbed and beaten to death.

The following year a Chinese priest and several other Christians were killed by bandits in Zhejiang Province. A young 18-year-old named Andrew Zu was torn to pieces by an angry mob, and his chest was sliced open in the shape of a cross.

Eleanor Chestnut

Over the centuries tens of thousands of foreign missionaries have followed God to China. A few became famous, but the vast majority quietly and faithfully served their Lord without any fanfare in lonely places far beyond the attention of the rest of the world. One such faith-filled missionary was Dr Eleanor Chestnut, an orphan from Waterloo, Iowa. Although she was raised in extreme poverty by an aunt, the living God who said he was the "Father to the fatherless" formed in this young girl a rich and generous spirit. From an early age all she desired to be was a missionary-doctor. While attending medical school in Chicago she saved money by living in an attic and eating oatmeal for most of her meals.

Chestnut went to China with the American Presbyterian Mission in 1893, and soon found her niche ministering the love of God through her medical work at Lianzhou in northwest Guangdong Province. Soon after arriving, Chestnut saw the need to build a small hospital. The mission did not have enough money to help, so she built it herself, somehow living on just $1.50 per month so she could spend the rest of her salary to purchase bricks. Her mission board learned what she was doing and offered to reimburse her, but Chestnut refused, saying, "It will spoil all my fun."

There were so many sick people needing help that Chestnut could not wait for the completion of the hospital, so she started performing surgeries in the bathroom of her home. The selfless spirit of this young woman knew no limit and there was no sacrifice too great for her to make. One day a poor unskilled labourer was brought to her door for help. The locals looked down on the man, despising him as a "good-for-nothing coolie". The man's leg had been crushed and there was no alternative except to amputate it. The surgery was successful, except that the skin did not grow together correctly. Some time later the problem was fixed and the man was able to walk with the aid of crutches. The next day someone noticed that Eleanor Chestnut was limping. When asked why, she replied, "Oh, it's nothing." It later emerged that the doctor had taken skin from her own leg and transplanted it on to the leg of the man whom the nurses saw little value in.

On 28 October 1905, Eleanor Chestnut, along with John Peale, his wife, and two others, were killed by an angry mob in Lianzhou. They were working at the hospital when the mob suddenly stormed the building. Chestnut managed to escape and alerted the authorities. She could have escaped death if she had remained at the police station, but she decided to return to the hospital to help her colleagues. When she arrived she found her four countrymen already dead, but some of the patients needed her help. The bandits returned and killed her. Chestnut died inside the hospital that had been built with her own money and sweat, helping the Chinese people she loved so deeply.

1910s

The 1911 Revolution, which hastened the fall of the Qing Dynasty and the eventual establishment of the Republic of China, was a time of grave danger for missionaries and Chinese believers. Many people blamed the foreigners for propping up the corrupt Qing rulers, and when the tide turned against them many missionaries were also targeted. In Hebei Province a Catholic priest was murdered, while a Catholic school in Shaanxi Province was destroyed and 40 Catholics were slaughtered.

W. E. McChesney joined the roll of China martyrs in July 1914 when he was shot in the head by bandits in southern China. His travelling companion, H. V. Noyes, survived the attack and recalled the events that led to McChesney's death:

I anchored one peaceful night, under the bright stars at Kam-kai, but was roused at midnight by the alarm of robbers, and my travelling companion, Rev. W. E. McChesney, struck by a stray bullet, fell bleeding and dying by my side. He could not have been conscious of pain, for the bullet had struck him just above the right ear, but his strong frame shuddered as it struggled with death. He soon became quiet, however, and my fingers felt his pulse grow weaker and weaker until it stopped, and left me wondering where now in the wide universe was the real Mr. McChesney, who, in the vigour of health, had been talking with me, only a few minutes before.

Christine Villadsen – murdered
by bandits in 1918

On the morning of 4 January 1918 the Swedish Missionary Alliance's Christine Villadsen was killed by bandits while trying to protect Chinese believers from gangs of robbers in Shaanxi Province. Villadsen's last letter home excitedly mentioned that 73 Chinese women had recently made commitments to Christ.

1920s

A new anti-Christian movement, which appeared in the 1920s, caused trouble for Christians for years to come. It flamed the old coals of anti-foreign resentment that had surfaced during the Boxer Rebellion, only this time the leaders were generally better-educated people – politicians, writers and students. Occasionally their protests spilled over into murder. In many places, especially in the countryside where government troops were small in number, bandits wreaked havoc on the church.

Civil unrest grew with each passing year throughout China. In October 1920 military action resulted in a great trial for the Christians in Weizhou, Guangdong Province. The small town witnessed the destruction of six church buildings, three schools and several missionaries' homes, and the murder of a number of Christians.

In 1923 Angelicus Melotto, a Franciscan missionary, was captured by bandits in Hubei Province. He was held for almost three months, and then, in a moribund condition, was abandoned and picked up by troops. He died a few days after arriving at a hospital. In August of the same year, F. J. Watts and E. A. Whiteside of the English Church Missionary Society were murdered by bandits in Sichuan Province. A few months later four missionaries were captured in Hubei Province. The four were finally released, but B. A. Hoff was badly injured and died soon after.

Acholle Soenen was martyred in Inner Mongolia on Christmas Day 1923. He had spoken out against a secret society that was gaining popularity in the area, and it is believed he was killed by the sect in retaliation. At the time of Soenen's death another Catholic missionary named Van Praet was being held by bandits in Inner Mongolia. He had not been seen alive for six months, when suddenly he was released because of his dire physical condition. In early 1924 he died from the torments he had received during those cruel six months in captivity.

In the summer of 1924, a Canadian Methodist, Mrs Sibley, was kidnapped by the Red Lantern Society who murdered her on the streets of Chengdu. Several Chinese colporteurs who worked for the Bible societies were martyred by bandits. The whole atmosphere in China seemed to reach a dangerous fever-pitch of lawlessness. In 1924 the China Inland Mission reported that an evangelist named Zhang Suoluobabai was killed by bandits in Guizhou Province. At Dading, also in Guizhou, a church member was hung by his wrists and burned to death because the church refused to pay the bandits' ransom demand of $600.

In 1928 banditry spilled over in Jiangsu Province. An elderly Catholic priest in his seventies was dragged behind a horse for miles and then cruelly tortured until he expired. The following year three American Passionist priests, Walter Coveyou, Godfrey Holbein and Clement Seybold, were murdered. They had been part of a Catholic mission attempting to reach the Miao minority people in the mountains of western Hunan. The following year the Belgian priest Tiburce Cloodts was killed at his mission by three bandits, enraged because the missionary only had $15 in his possession. A week later Bishop Trudo Jans, and the priests Bruno Van Weert and Rupert Fynaerts were ruthlessly clubbed to death.

1930 and '40s

By the 1930s the Communists had begun to enlist bandits into their ranks, and the line between the two blurred.

On 4 October 1930 missionaries Eleanor Harrison and Edith Nettleton were beheaded by bandits. They had been abducted three months earlier. The duo's ransom was originally set at US$500,000. When it was not forthcoming, the bandits cut off one of Nettleton's fingers and sent it with a new ransom demand to the provincial authorities. The Church Missionary Society paid US$10,000 in gold for the women's release. The bandits received the money, but when government troops attempted to secure the missionaries' release the bandits thought they had been betrayed and beheaded the two women. Before her kidnapping, Eleanor Harrison had composed a poem about an earlier martyr:

> Angel-faced and lion-hearted
>   See Christ's servant stand.
> Fill'd with grace he saw the vision,
>   Not the howling band.
> Saw his Lord and saw His glory
>   Not the hurtling stones.
> Heard his voice – and not mad gnashing,
>   Answered not with moans.
> Like his Master soft he pleaded
>   "Oh, forgive their sin"
> Then the heavens already open'd
>   Let the Martyr in.
> "Fell asleep" tho' crowds were raging,
>   Working deadliest harm
> "Fell asleep" in happiest resting,
>   On his Master's arm.

Perhaps the worst year of violence against Christians in China since the Boxer Rebellion occurred in 1938. The Communists had gained control of large areas of the country, and thousands of believers were caught up in the fighting between the Reds and the Nationalists. The Japanese military was also trying to seize control of China in a prelude to their World War II efforts, and hordes of murderous bandits roamed the countryside, taking advantage of the chaos to kill, steal and destroy. Somehow, in the midst of these trials the kingdom of God continued to grow.

By the start of World War II China had plunged into anarchy, with bandits, the Communists and the Japanese all indiscriminately killing Christians. One Chinese woman defiantly told a missionary, "My house has been burned twice and nothing is left. Four of six relatives there are dead, including my brother who was branded with a hot iron. My daughter-in-law was shot before my eyes and my only grandson has died from exposure, but I will not let go of Jesus Christ."

In 1949 the People's Republic of China was founded and banditry gradually faded as the new government exerted its authoritarian rule throughout the nation. Any hope Christians had that the new regime would bring peace to the church was soon crushed, as the Communists launched the most diabolical and concerted effort to crush Christianity in China's history.

CHAPTER 33

BLOODBATH
IN XI'AN

E. R. Beckman and family in 1904

The Scandinavian Alliance Mission quickly grew from humble beginnings in 1890 to become one of the largest Protestant organizations working in north China. In 1909 the work in the west suburb of China's ancient capital of Xi'an was taken over by E. R. and Ida Beckman. They constructed a school for the purpose of offering a Christian-based education to the children of missionaries. Unfortunately the school was not destined to operate for very long. The 1911 Revolution, which expedited the end of the Qing Dynasty, also brought tragic results for this mission.

For decades a growing resentment against the Manchu rulers had festered among the Han Chinese. Strangely, China had been controlled by two minority dynasties – the Yuan Dynasty of the Mongols from 1271 to 1368 and the Qing from 1368 to 1911 – a total period of 640 years. The emperor and empress of China had both died in 1908 and left their two-year-old son on the throne. The Chinese seized the opportunity to bring about a revolution that resulted in China becoming a republic. Manchu people throughout China were slaughtered by angry mobs, and those considered friends of the Manchus also found themselves also in grave danger.

Xi'an had long been a centre of Manchu power. An anti-Manchu and anti-foreign sect called the Ancient Society of Elder Brothers had hundreds of secret members in the city. The Manchu quarter in the northeast corner of Xi'an contained the imperial troops and their families, some 20,000 people in all. A stash of new weapons and ammunition had recently been delivered for their use, but these were carelessly stored in the southern part of the city. The Elder Brothers seized the weapons before the Manchus had time to respond.

On the night of 23 October 1911 a mob rushed into the missionary school, setting fire to the gate and breaking down the wall. The missionaries and the children were huddled together on the second floor of the school building. E. R.

Beckman and a young teacher named Wilheim Vatne fetched a rope and a wheelbarrow to help the children escape over a back wall. Vatne went over first, and Beckman had just helped his eldest daughter Selma over when shots rang out. Beckman, his wife Ida and six remaining children tried to hide in a small room of an outbuilding. E. R. Beckman later wrote,

> I sat down and took our smallest girl in my arms. We began praying, and asked God to prevent the mob discovering where we were, if it was His will to deliver us. At the same time we committed ourselves into His hand, to live or to die. My wife took our youngest girl from me for a moment, pressed her to her bosom, and kissing her tenderly said, "I must say goodbye to you, my darling.

Moments later their hiding place was discovered. They all ran out of the room and tried to get through the crowd. Beckman, who was carrying his little daughter Thyra, became separated from the others. Seemingly oblivious to the punches and blows hitting him, he ran through the gate and hid in a row of trees surrounding a large pond. Minutes later Beckman heard people coming, so he jumped into the water and waded into the middle of the pond, where he and his daughter huddled amid some thick vegetation. For hours mobs of bloodthirsty pursuers crowded around the pond waiting for the prey to emerge from the dark. Beckman recalled, "I sat there for an hour or more until my arms were numb from exhaustion, and the little girl's legs dropped into the water, still she did not cry or make a noise."

Just before daybreak the two carefully made their way out of the pond and back to the mission station, where they were told that the beloved mother of the family, Ida Beckman, and five children had been killed by the mob. The murdered

Ruth Beckman (at back) with
her sister Thyra

children were Ruth Beckman (aged eight), George Ahlstrand (ten), Hilda Nelson (fifteen), Hulda Bergström (twelve), and Oscar Bergström (thirteen). Apart from the Beckman girl, the youngsters were the children of missionaries stationed in other parts of the province.

Ida Beckman (née Klint) was born in Sweden in 1865. She was converted at a Salvation Army meeting, and afterwards became an active Christian worker on the streets of Stockholm. After emigrating to the United States in 1888 she settled in the city of Brooklyn. Ida felt called to go to China, where she married E. R. Beckman on Christmas Eve 1896.

E. R. Beckman painfully recalled how he felt when he heard the news:

> Behind me lay our own place a prey to the dying flames, and there lay my wife and little Ruth, as well as the other dear children, slain! How the hearts of the parents of these children would bleed, as well as mine, when they should learn to know what had happened – the thought of this called forth deep pain.

With the addition of the uncertainty concerning Mr Vatne and Selma, I was nearly overcome.

A Chinese seminary student told Beckman that his wife and the children had pressed through the gateway, but had not gone far before they were slain. Hilda Nelson had run a short distance, seeking refuge among some graves. Oscar Bergström had reached halfway to the pond. George Ahlstrand had fallen in the road a short distance from the gate, where his pet dog remained, keeping watch. One of the boys had been shot.

E. R. Beckman was in a state of shock at the death of his wife and daughter, but wanted to know what had happened to his thirteen-year-old daughter Selma and the 21-year-old teacher, Wilheim Vatne, both of whom had scaled the wall before the mob broke down the gate. Three days later it was learned the pair had escaped into the night and taken shelter with a Chinese family. The townspeople heard about it and constantly pelted them with broken bricks and hard lumps of earth. Vatne, taking hold of Selma's hand, was occasionally knocked to the ground, but sprang to his feet again, still holding her fast. About noon they were separated. They were cruelly tortured and then put out of their misery, their abused bodies being left to rot in a field.

Wilheim Vatne

Wilheim Vatne was born in America to Norwegian parents. He grew up in Cooperstown, North Dakota, placing his trust in Jesus Christ at a young age. After graduating from high school early, Vatne became a schoolteacher himself at the age of just 18. A few years later the mission school in Xi'an was looking for a consecrated Christian to teach the missionary children. Vatne wilfully accepted the call, arriving in China in September 1910. After hearing of his son's martyrdom, Vatne's aged father wrote,

> You can hardly believe how we feel these days. It was a hard stroke when we heard that our beloved Wilheim has already been taken away from us. How strange that his day of work should be so short! Oh, Wilheim was a dear son to us! I am weak and weary, and this heavy sorrow is weighing me down, but sweeter will be the rest when I reach Home. I could have written this letter with my tears! Yet, the Lord had the greatest claim to him: He gave him to us, and He took him. Blessed be the name of the Lord!

The mob thoroughly destroyed the new school and all the adjoining buildings at the Xi'an mission. On the days following the bloodbath, Beckman replayed the terrible events over and over in his mind. When Beckman told his little daughter that her mother and sisters had gone to be with Jesus, she asked, "Did they go to *our* Jesus?" When her father replied "Yes", she said, "Then I am glad, for I can go to them."

The mission school in Xi'an was rebuilt in 1915 on the same spot where the martyrs had spilled their blood. The missionaries returned and went bravely on with their work, preaching the good news of Christ's salvation.

E. R. Beckman and Thyra returned to Sweden to recover from the ordeal. Years later Thyra married a missionary and returned to serve in China, the land that had taken her mother and sisters from her. Such an act of grace and forgiveness amazed everyone who heard about it.

CHAPTER 34 ALPHONSO ARGENTO – THE LAST BOXER MARTYR

Alphonso Argento and his family,
a short time before his death in 1917

Alphonso Argento is somewhat unique in the list of China's martyrs in that he survived death during the Boxer Rebellion in 1900, yet carried the pain of his ordeal for another 17 years – many of which were spent in service in China – before finally succumbing to his injuries in 1917. Despite the long lapse between the time he sustained the injuries and his death, all the missionary publications at the time considered Argento a true martyr of the faith.

Argento was born in Italy in 1873. At the age of 18 he met Christ and felt deeply burdened for missionary work in China. He dedicated his life to serve God in the Orient, and applied to join the China Inland Mission. At the interview Argento was warned of the possibility of danger, to which he boldly replied,

"I am not afraid even to die for Christ and the gospel. I was led to take this step after having known Christ's promise, 'Blessed are they which are persecuted for righteousness' sake, for theirs is the kingdom of heaven.'"

In the autumn of 1895 Argento left his home in Sicily and made his way to London, where he undertook training for a year. Argento was fluent in English, French and German. He learned Mandarin soon after arriving in China in October 1896. Within three years he had established the first mission station at Guangshan in Henan Province.

During the Boxer Rebellion in 1900 the mission station was attacked on the evening of 8 July when a large crowd of people armed with swords and knives rushed into the chapel. As the murderers pressed in to kill Argento, someone knocked the lamp over and the chapel was plunged into darkness. The besieged Italian crawled into a corner and hid under some rubble as the Boxers, presuming the Italian had managed to escape, plundered everything they could. Argento was discovered after managing to crawl upstairs and hide beneath a table. He later described the distress of the occasion:

> With a rush they got hold of me and dragged me from under the table and on to the pile of wood with which they planned to burn the building down. Others took up the benches and struck me with them. They poured kerosene on my clothes and set them on fire. Friendly neighbours, however, quickly quenched the flames, tearing off the burning part of the garment. I was lying with my face to the ground. The rioters, seeing these neighbours wanted to save me, got hold of a pole, and began to strike me on the head and all over my body. I tried to protect my head with my hands, but had not reached the doorsteps when a very heavy blow inflicted on my head caused me to lose consciousness.

For two days Alphonso Argento lay unconscious. Some of the Boxers dragged his body into the street outside the chapel, wanting to decapitate him, but sympathetic locals convinced them the missionary was already dead. After Argento regained consciousness the local magistrate was afraid he would die within his jurisdiction and so ordered the missionary to be carried by stretcher to a town 140 miles (227 kilometres) to the north. All along the route people came to stare at the half-naked Italian, who was covered in terrible bruises and lying in a pool of his own blood. Many people urged the stretcher-carriers to put him out of his misery. At one location Argento said, "They thought I was dead, for I did not move or make a sound, although they pinched me, pulled my hair, and knocked me about – an ordeal which lasted an hour long." At one town he was treated like an animal, being made to lie outside in the rain all night. After two weeks of misery, Argento was carried back to Guangshan where the ordeal had begun. The locals were astonished to see him still alive, yet they still had the audacity to mock his God. A large crowd gathered around him, saying, "God has brought you back safely, has he? Your God cannot save you. Jesus is dead; he is not in this world. He cannot give real help. Our god of war is much stronger; he protects us, and he has sent the Boxers to pull down your house and kill you."

The cowardly Guangshan magistrate, again afraid the people would kill the missionary in his jurisdiction, ordered Argento's journey to recommence, this time in a sedan chair. As they travelled westward to Xinyang a group of 30 armed Boxers pursued the Italian, determined to slaughter him once and for all. By obeying the inner promptings of the Holy Spirit, Argento managed to evade his pursuers and was finally delivered to safety.

The people of Guangshan thought they had finally seen the back of the stubborn missionary, but after a year recuperating in Europe, Argento returned to Guangshan, to the amazement of the town's inhabitants. Here was a man who had learned to overcome fear and intimidation. He wrote, "It was the greatest joy I have ever experienced in my life to see the Christians again, and hear what the Lord has been doing during my absence." For the next seven years the Italian continued to serve the Lord boldly in Guangshan, and the church grew steadily.

In 1905 Argento married Miss Bjorgum of the Norwegian Mission. Together they raised two fine boys. The injuries to Argento's head continued to cause him much pain, but he carried on regardless. His deteriorating health finally caused him to leave China in 1908. Up to that time 385 baptisms had resulted from his fruitful ministry. After returning to Europe, Argento gradually became blind, then lost his memory and the use of his limbs. His interest in the work in China never flagged, and in May 1917 he wrote, "I will use my strength in prayer and in intercession for China."

Finally, in the Norwegian city of Trondheim on 3 July 1917, Alphonso Argento was released from the pain of this life and went to be with Jesus. He was 44 years old. God cannot be mocked. In the Guangshan area, where evil men once said, "Jesus is dead; he is not in this world. He cannot give real help", there are approximately 120,000 Christians today – following the example of the pioneer missionary Alphonso Argento.

CHAPTER 35   TROUBLE AMONG
THE TRIBES

A group of tribal Christians on Hainan Island.
Faithful missionaries helped establish the gospel among
dozens of China's ethnic minorities.

The majority of people in China belong to the Han Chinese ethnicity, the largest people group in the world. Approximately eight per cent of the country's inhabitants, however, are members of nearly 500 distinct ethnic minority groups. Some, such as the Tibetans and Mongols, are well known to the outside world, but many hundreds of small tribes live scattered throughout the isolated mountains and deep valleys of southwest China. Many minority areas were virtually inaccessible until the 20th century, and the existence of some remote groups has only been discovered in recent years.

Christian work among China's tribes grew throughout the 20th century, and a number of martyrdoms occurred as men and women bravely laboured among these forgotten people.

Hainan Island

Hainan Island is located at the southern tip of China. Originally the lush island was occupied exclusively by the Li and Miao tribes. Frank Gilman was one of the first missionaries sent out by the United States Presbyterian Mission Board, arriving on Hainan in 1886. After losing his first wife Marion and two daughters to disease, Gilman remarried in 1903, and he and his wife Mary enjoyed fourteen years together on Hainan Island until she died in 1917. Less than a year after he tearfully buried his second wife, violence broke out on the island as rival warlords fought each other. Gilman and another missionary sought to disarm soldiers who were hiding in the hospital. In the confusion, Gilman fell and was seriously injured. He died two weeks later.

George Byers arrived in Hainan in 1906. For 18 years he laboured on the remote island, faithfully sharing the gospel with the Li and Miao tribal groups in the mountainous interior. Byers came to be called "the spiritual father of the Miao people". On 24 June 1924 he was attacked as he walked home after attending an evening worship service at the Jiaji Hospital. Four armed men were waiting in the shadows and seized Byers near his home. A rope was fastened around the American's neck and he was dragged down the street. When Byers' ten-year-old son, Robert, heard the incessant barking of his dog he went out to investigate. Fearing the commotion would bring the police, the bandits began firing. A bullet grazed young Robert Byers' leg, but he managed to escape and sound the alarm. By the time the authorities arrived George Byers was already dead, shot through the abdomen.

Although there were relatively few Christians on Hainan at the time of George Byers' death, missionaries continued to sow the Word of God, paving the way for a tremendous revival that has impacted the island's house churches in recent years.

Albert Shelton

Albert Shelton

Albert Shelton is remembered as the prince of Protestant missionaries among the Tibetans in the 20th century. Shelton's dream was to establish a hospital in Lhasa, the capital and spiritual stronghold of the Tibetan Buddhist world. For years he tried to secure permission from the Dalai Lama to travel to Lhasa. The Dalai Lama responded, "I know of your work and that you have come a long way to do good. I will put no straw in your way." Before he could start out for Lhasa the political situation in Tibet deteriorated and bandits ruled the countryside. In 1920, while travelling from Batang to Kunming with his wife and two daughters, Shelton was kidnapped by bandits who demanded a ransom of $25,000 for his release. The rest of his family, although badly shaken, were allowed to go free. Hauled off into the mountains, Shelton was held for 72 days. During the whole time he refused to cooperate with his captors' demands, telling them, "You can kill me or whatever you wish but I will not be ransomed." At the same time Shelton lovingly treated the sick and wounded bandits, and gradually they came to view him as their friend. After more than ten weeks in captivity, Shelton's body was so emaciated that he was unable to stand up. The bandits left him by the side of the road where he was found by government troops.

After being reunited with his grateful wife and daughters, Shelton again started to plan the long and dangerous journey to Lhasa. The bandits who had kidnapped him one year before heard about the missionary's intended journey and devised plans to kidnap him again. This time their intention was to keep him as their doctor. In February 1922 Shelton started on the trip with three Tibetan companions. On 16 February they were ambushed and shot just six miles (10 kilometres) from Batang. Albert Shelton's colleagues did all they could to revive him, but at 12:45 in the morning of 17 February he passed to glory.

Among the Zhuang

The Zhuang are the largest ethnic minority group in China, with approximately 18 million people dispersed throughout several provinces of south China. They speak a language from the Tai group, making them the distant relatives of those living in Thailand, Laos and other Southeast Asian nations today.

The success of the Protestant missionary efforts in rural China was largely due to the work of thousands of colporteurs

– Chinese Christians who preached the gospel and distributed evangelistic material to people. The southern province of Guangxi was overrun with bandits and disease in the 1920s, and many of these faithful workers succumbed to these dual dangers. In 1926 two colporteurs, Tang and Pan, were murdered by bandits.

Tang had set out on a journey which was expected to take two or three weeks. As the weeks passed by and no word was heard from him, men were sent to trace his steps to discover what had happened. For the first few days it was easy to see Tang's progress, as there was a steady flow of gospel tracts that he had distributed to families along the way. An inn was found where he had spent the first night, but from that point on no clues could be found as to his whereabouts. In one village the people obviously knew something about his fate, but nobody was willing to help with the investigation. The men believed that Tang had been martyred in that location and his body thoroughly disposed of.

The second colporteur, Pan, was murdered a few months later. He left the mission station in Liuzhou in late November 1926, planning to walk through Zhuang villages before returning home by Christmas. When he failed to return a search party was dispatched, but the Zhuang tribespeople were determined not to assist the Chinese in their enquiries. It was surmised that Pan, too, had been killed by bandits somewhere in the rugged mountains of Guangxi.

Many months later a Zhuang man named Wei from a remote mountain village visited the church in Liuzhou. He said that some time before a colporteur had visited his village and left some books with him. As a result, a small group of believers had emerged in that isolated place. It was later found that the colporteur who had left a good spiritual deposit in that village was the slain Brother Pan. Missionaries visited the village and found two men wearing bamboo

The two Zhuang tribesmen who wore bamboo crosses on their backs

crosses on their back, believing they were obeying the Saviour's command to take up the cross and follow him. The missionaries stayed with these simple-hearted tribesmen and patiently instructed them in biblical truths, establishing them in the faith.

George King

Dr George King served in remote Gansu Province. He was the director of Borden Memorial Hospital, and was described as "the only physician for a thousand miles". The Borden hospital had been established after a young millionaire, William Borden, died after contracting spinal meningitis in 1913 while studying Arabic in Egypt en route to a life of missionary work among the Muslims of northwest China. When the young Borden, who was educated at both Princeton and Yale universities, announced his intention to leave his

George King

family's wealth and spend his life serving Christ in one of the most isolated places on earth there was widespread astonishment – thanksgiving from Christians, and ridicule from unbelievers. After Borden's early death a gift of $250,000 – representing one quarter of his estate – was made to the China Inland Mission. This amount of money at the time was worth much more than today. It was used to establish the Borden Memorial Hospital in Lanzhou. Thousands of needy people – Chinese, Tibetan Buddhists and Turkic-speaking Muslims – came for treatment and heard the gospel.

During a Muslim uprising in 1927, it was decided that 37 missionaries and their twelve children would be evacuated from Lanzhou to a safer place until the fighting subsided. George King decided to remain at his post, but being a strong swimmer, his help was needed to evacuate the missionaries by goatskin raft down the Yellow River. As they made their escape they were attacked by bandits. They were able to flee, but a few miles further down the river they became stuck on a sandbar. While trying to free the rafts, King fell into the swift current. A fellow missionary asked, "Can you make it?" George King replied, "I don't know", and slipped under, never to be seen again.

Teacher Yang

A man with severe sword cuts to his head brought to the mission for medical treatment

One of the more intrepid and fearless Christians to ever walk on China's soil was the American Assemblies of God missionary Victor Plymire. Through decades of danger the American toiled away in one of the most remote corners of the earth, faithfully proclaiming the gospel to Tibetan nomads from his base in Qinghai Province. With tears streaming down his cheeks he buried his wife Grace and little son John on a lonely mountain after they both died suddenly from smallpox in 1927. Inwardly devastated, Plymire refused to bow to the devil's attacks and continued to obey the call that God had placed on his life.

During the early months of 1929 the fledgling church at

Huangyuan was endangered by banditry, which was rampant throughout the province. One group roamed around the countryside, killing and looting. Its ranks swelled until it resembled a small army of about 20,000 men.

On 14 February news arrived that the bandit army was a short distance from Huangyuan. The gates of the town were locked and the residents prepared to defend themselves. The murderers finally gained access by burning down the west gate. They rushed through the town, butchering innocent people right and left. Plymire later said of the satanically inspired attack, "Children were hung up by the feet and cut in half or pulled apart. Some were carried about on spears." Expecting to die, Plymire and the gathered Chinese and Tibetan Christians readied themselves to meet the Lord. When all the homes in Huangyuan had been looted, hundreds of people lay dead, their bodies strewn about the streets in pools of blood. Government troops arrived and chased the bandits into the mountains, leaving hundreds of severely wounded people within the town. Many were brought to the church in the hope the Christians might be able to help them.

One man who was carried to the church on top of a door panel was a young schoolteacher named Yang, who had only recently believed in Jesus. Plymire looked at Yang's injuries to see what could be done to help, but the Christian teacher protested, "I do not have long to live, pastor. I want to die here because this is where I found Christ. So I asked my friends to bring me." Then in a feeble voice he began to sing, "Take the name of Jesus with you". His faith grew stronger as death drew near. Addressing his grieving family, Yang exhorted them to put their trust in Christ so that they might meet him in heaven. He then committed his spirit into the care of the Lord and went to be with him forever.

No Ga

No Ga

One of Victor Plymire's earliest Tibetan converts was a young man named No Ga, who had accompanied Plymire on one of his trans-Tibet evangelistic expeditions where dozens of yaks laden down with thousands of Tibetan gospel booklets made their way across vast, sparsely populated regions. No Ga first believed in God because of the strange and unusual incidents that transpired during the long trek. The most remarkable occurrence came when No Ga, his brother Ka Zong and Plymire were sentenced to death by a chief in a remote part of Tibet. At the very moment the executioner's sword was being placed on their necks, a messenger burst in with a letter from the Dalai Lama granting permission for the trio to proceed. A few seconds later and three heads would have been severed from their bodies.

In a culture steeped in secret magical arts and demonism, strong opposition to Christians was to be expected. When No Ga's family heard about his conversion they were infuriated, but none of their threats of violence moved him. No Ga's own brother-in-law threatened to kill him unless he agreed to participate in the building of a shrine. No Ga replied, "I am not afraid. I know Jesus will be with me." Several days later he became sick with a cold. His brother-in-law left the village and was seen in a fur trapper's supply store buying a packet of animal poison. That evening he called on No Ga and feigned concern. He went to the kitchen and prepared some hot tea, into which he placed the poison. The unsuspecting Christian thanked his brother-in-law and drank every drop. In a few moments faithful No Ga lay still in death. He had paid the supreme price for his faith in Christ.

William Simpson

William Simpson

William Simpson, the son of missionary parents, had grown up among Tibetans since he was one year old. Living in a remote area along the China–Tibet border, the rugged life was the only one he had ever known. At a young age William Simpson faced tragedy when his baby sister died, followed by the loss of his beloved mother during a trip home. While studying in the United States, Simpson longed to return to Tibet, despite knowing that growing lawlessness would place him at risk. Whereas other foreigners struggled greatly with the culture and conditions in this primitive part of the world, Simpson felt at home. He spoke several dialects of Tibetan fluently. After one lonely and exhausting trip, Simpson wrote to the Assemblies of God Foreign Mission Department:

> All the trials, the loneliness, the heartache, the weariness and pain, the cold and fatigue of the long road, the darkness and discouragements, and all the bereavements, temptations and testings, seemed not worthy to be compared with the glory and joy of witnessing to this "glad tidings of great joy."

William Simpson was attacked by a horde of Muslim army deserters who swooped down on him near Xiahe on 25 June 1932. He was killed instantly. Simpson's father went and recovered his son's mutilated body, when he noticed a paper smeared with blood lying nearby. The words, "In remembrance of me", were an apt tribute to the reasons Simpson had died.

The Great Cold Mountains

The Nosu tribes living in the remote Daliangshan ("Great Cold Mountains") in southern Sichuan Province had lived for centuries outside of the control of the Chinese, who feared entering their domain. In the 1920s French Catholic missionaries bravely commenced a work in the mountains of Mabian County, and it was there that Baptistin Biron was killed in 1935.

During his itineration around the district, Biron came into contact with Nosu tribesmen from the nearby mountains. These fierce and proud people fascinated Biron. They appeared to come from a thousand years back in time, and had little or no knowledge of Chinese customs or language. In 1934 the Nosu from one tribe proposed giving Biron a piece of land to build a mission. The Chinese authorities, however, were strongly opposed to the idea. Rumours abounded that the Frenchman was going to be proclaimed "king of the Nosu". Consequently, the Chinese military launched a punitive strike into the mountains.

Nosu from another area blamed the problems solely on the presence of the French priest. Unexpectedly, at nine o'clock in the morning of 20 August 1935, a Nosu man and his slave appeared at the house where Biron was staying and acted as if they were selling musk. About 100 Nosu warriors suddenly emerged from the forest with wild screams and cries. They placed a rope around the Frenchman's neck while others punched him and plucked out chunks of his beard. He soon perished, while his torturers celebrated by singing a victory song. They dragged Biron's lifeless body along a path before stripping him of his clothing and departing into the mountains.

Maurice Tornay

A native of Valais, Switzerland, Maurice Tornay attended the seminary of Grand St Bernard after graduating from high school. This order was well known for their work in the Swiss Alps, where they had built a monastery along the Swiss–Italian border in the eleventh century. In order to rescue snowbound travellers the monks bred dogs, later known as St Bernards, which were specially trained to dig buried travellers out of avalanches. The Order of St Bernard sent Tornay to the town of Yanjing in Tibet, where a strong Christian work had been established. After he had been in Yanjing just a few months the local Buddhist lamas broke into Tornay's home and demolished it, as they did the church and rectory.

Maurice Tornay

In 1949, after years of harassment from the lamas, the Swiss missionary decided to make the long journey to Lhasa, the capital of Tibet, to personally petition the Dalai Lama to protect the Tibetan Christians and allow them to practise their religion freely. Tornay and several travelling companions departed on the morning of 10 July. To avoid detection, Tornay shaved off his beard and disguised himself as a Tibetan. For 17 days they progressed deep inside Tibet, experiencing no problems until they were halfway to their destination. On 27 July a group of Tibetans rode up and surrounded the unsuspecting travellers. Tornay was instructed to return home. On 11 August, as they descended the west slope of the Chula Pass, four lamas suddenly rose out of the forest and shot Tornay and a Tibetan convert, Dossy, to death. The Swiss priest who had given thirteen years of his life for the salvation of Tibet sealed his sacrifice with his own blood.

CHAPTER 36   CAUGHT IN THE CROSSFIRE

Carnage after a Japanese air raid in 1938

During the first half of the 20th century war raged through-out China. The Japanese and Russians vied for control of the northeast region of Manchuria, and the Communists and Nationalists staged a long and bitter civil war. Missionaries and Chinese Christians were often caught up in the fighting. Many were inadvertently killed as part of the chaos, but some were specifically targeted for destruction because of their faith in Christ.

The 1919 Norabawie massacre

More than three million ethnic Koreans live in northeast China today, concentrated in areas near the North Korean border. In 1905 China's vast northeast region was divided between the Japanese and the Russians, who vied with one another to plunder the rich natural resources. Korean Christians were especially hated by the Japanese because of their unwillingness to worship the Japanese emperor as a deity. Intense persecution resulted. Entire Korean villages were obliterated by the Japanese military. The attacks escalated in 1919 after popular uprisings in Korean communities against the Japanese occupation. Many churches were taken over or burned to the ground. Christians' homes were demolished, and 33 church leaders in Manchuria lost their lives.

The worst incident occurred in the Christian village of Norabawie. A Canadian Presbyterian missionary, S. H. Martin, filed the following sickening report:

> At daybreak Japanese infantry surrounded the main Christian village, and starting at the head of the valley, ordered the people to vacate their homes. As each son and father stepped forth he was shot, and though perhaps not dead, heaps of burning straw were placed over them. If they struggled to escape the flames, they were bayoneted. The Japanese soldiers then set fire to the houses. I have names of, and accurate reports of, 32 villages where fire and wilful murder were used – in one village the dead numbering 145. I saw the ruins of a house which was burned with women and children inside. At Sonoyung four men were stood up near an open grave and shot.

Because of the geographical isolation of the villages attacked by the Japanese, little has ever been written about the slaughter. The Korean Christians in Manchuria later again came under brutal attack from the Japanese throughout the 1930s and '40s.

Morris and Ruth Slichter

In 1927 the Slichter family, who worked with the China Inland Mission at Anshun in Guizhou Province, decided the situation had deteriorated to such an extent that they could no longer remain at their post. Morris Slichter, his wife and their two children John (six) and Ruth (three), and a single female missionary May Craig, set out from Anshun with plans to reach the coast. Their journey appeared to be progressing well as they made their way into Yunnan, travelling under military guard. After passing the town of Luoping a band of robbers suddenly attacked them. As the first shots were fired the guards suddenly fled, leaving the missionaries unprotected in a rice field. Ignoring their cries for mercy, one bandit fired at Mrs Slichter who was holding little Ruth in her arms. The bullet passed through the child's head and ripped a gash across the mother's left wrist. Another robber stabbed Morris Slichter in the back. He immediately fell to the ground dead.

Struck with grief and anguish, the two helpless women and six-year-old John sat there dazed. About 30 minutes later the bandits returned and decided to take the two women and child captive, adding more pain to their already horrific ordeal. For more than a week they scrambled over the hills, "terrible days filled with suspense and terror", as May Craig later described them. They were finally released.

Luigi Versiglia and Callisto Caravario

Italians Luigi Versiglia and Callisto Caravario,
martyred together in 1930

Luigi Versiglia, a 56-year-old Catholic bishop, and Callisto Caravario, a 26-year-old priest, were members of the Salesian Congregation. On 25 February 1930 the two Italians set out from their mission station for the town of Linzhou in Guangdong Province. The journey in a small Chinese junk along a tributary of the North River was through pirate-infested territory, but the pair was travelling in a group with two other missionaries, two Chinese catechists, some Catholic schoolteachers with their students, and the pastor of the Linzhou parish. They believed that by increasing their numbers they faced less danger of being attacked by pirates. Just after noon, as they neared the village of Litaoqui, they suddenly heard a shout from the riverbank, "Halt, or we fire!" They looked up to see 20 ruffians with their rifles trained on the little boat. Versiglia realized they had no choice. "Push ashore," he said to the boys. "They will only shoot us down if we refuse."

The pirates demanded a payment of $500. While the two missionaries were trying to reason with their attackers, the thugs noticed the pretty schoolgirls on board and, with lust-filled eyes, tried to carry them away to do whatever they pleased with them. The bishop firmly stated, "Not in my lifetime, you won't. Hands off!"

As the evil men tried to board the boat, one girl jumped into the river to try to drown herself but the attackers yanked her out by the hair. Two other girls desperately clung to Versiglia. The bandits knocked the bishop senseless while Caravario was pinned to the ground. The two Italians were dragged to the shore and moments later shots rang out. They had been martyred while trying to protect the lives and dignity of the young women.

Herman Liu

Herman Liu was one of the most notable Christian leaders in Shanghai during the 1930s. He was the first Chinese president of the Baptist University of Shanghai, and he held a PhD degree from Columbia University. This link to the West made Liu an enemy of the Japanese, and they constantly threatened him and disrupted his work of helping the thousands of refugees who had flooded into Shanghai from the war-torn countryside.

Seeing that Liu would not bow to their wishes, the Japanese placed him on their blacklist. Numerous attempts were made on his life. The gate leading to his home was blown up with dynamite as an apparent warning, and on another occasion a basket of poisoned fruit was sent to his home. Liu discovered the poison just in time. Concerned friends urged him to flee Shanghai, but he refused, declaring, "I will remain as the Lord can use me here. I will not desert." On the morning of 8 April 1938, Japanese soldiers shot Herman Liu dead in front of his home, while he was waiting with his son for a bus.

Harry Wyatt, Beulah Glasby and Hu Shifu

Dr Harry Wyatt

In 1938 a group of British Baptist missionaries in Shanxi Province became caught up in the three-way war between the Japanese, the Nationalists and the Communists as they travelled towards the town of Dai Xian. The victims, Dr Harry Wyatt and Miss Beulah Glasby, were shot dead along with their Chinese Christian driver, Hu Shifu.

Harry Wyatt was born in the English community of Blisworth, Northamptonshire, and had spent ten years leading the medical mission at Taiyuan. Wyatt came to be loved and respected by thousands of people who benefited from his labours. When the Japanese military reached Taiyuan in November 1937 Wyatt moved his wife and children to a safer location away from the war zone. After spending Christmas with his family, Wyatt returned to Taiyuan intending to only be there a short time before he was replaced by new recruits coming from England.

On 5 May 1938, Wyatt caught a ride in a lorry loaded with

goods. His fellow passengers included missionaries Mr and Mrs Vincent Jasper and Beulah Glasby, who had been working in China for fourteen years, most of it taking care of 20 abandoned children. The journey progressed smoothly until a shot rang out and the driver, Hu Shifu, was wounded in the arm. He managed to bring the lorry to a stop. The tall and athletic Dr Wyatt immediately leaped out of his seat and dragged Hu to the opposite side of the road from where the shot had originated. Mrs Jasper had recently suffered an injury to her hand. She quickly unravelled the bandage and gave it to Wyatt, who used it to try to stem the bleeding from the driver's arm as a hail of bullets was fired at them. The Jaspers and Wyatt motioned for Glasby to join them under the vehicle, but she said she felt safer where she was, crouched down in the front seat.

While the shooting continued, Wyatt decided to make an attempt to save the life of his friends. He grabbed the Union Jack from the rear of the lorry and waved it above his head as he started out in the direction from where the firing was coming. It had no effect. The shots continued, and when a hand grenade was lobbed in his direction, Wyatt returned to the shelter of the vehicle. A few minutes later Beulah Glasby, still sheltering inside the lorry, was hit by a bullet and killed. Wyatt, dragging the badly injured driver, attempted to climb into a ditch but was struck by a bullet just before reaching it. He passed into eternity while continuing to wave the Union Jack.

Evangelist Kim

In the mid-1930s a rumour circulated among missionaries in Manchuria that the Japanese army was determined to destroy the Korean Christians because they refused to accept the doctrine that the emperor of Japan was the Son of Heaven. This infuriated the Japanese.

One Korean preacher, Evangelist Kim, endured intense

suffering for his faith. Because of his God-given ability to win souls for Christ he was a constant target of the Japanese and was tortured for his refusal to stop preaching the gospel. Kim strongly objected when the Japanese insisted that all churches install a small shrine in honour of the emperor. He preached that Christians could not serve two masters. They had to decide to worship either Jesus or the emperor. Kim was arrested, tortured and released on seven different occasions. On the eighth time he was stretched out on a bench with his head forced back, and water was poured from a kettle down his nostrils. Choking and half insane, he finally consented to sign a paper signifying his approval of shrine worship.

Soon after his release, Kim became wracked with feelings of remorse. He wrote a letter to the Japanese authorities again voicing his disapproval of shrine worship, even though he knew that by so doing he would be subjected to more deprivation. Within days Kim was rearrested and diabolically tortured in a tiny cell until he could not stand it any more. The Japanese believed Kim was about to die, so they called in one of his friends to collect the body. The friend took him to the home of Presbyterian missionary Roy Byram and his wife. They lovingly treated him, and the bold evangelist gradually recovered his strength and continued to preach the gospel and exhort believers. Kim was again subjected to barbaric cruelties and perished in 1943.

Other Korean Christian martyrs in Manchuria include a Sunday School teacher named An. In the spring of 1940 she went to the police station to try to secure the release of a friend. Instead, she was arrested and imprisoned. By November An had become critically ill. She was released and taken to the mission dispensary, jaundiced and little more than skin and bones. A few days later An suddenly rose up and declared, "I go into the presence of my Father." Then she fell backwards on her bed and died.

John Botton

John Botton

John Botton was born in 1908 near the Italian city of Padua. When John departed for China, his father was unable to see him off as he was suffering a fever. John's mother also stayed at home to take care of her husband. She went as far as the doorway with her son, kissed him and burst into tears. After closing the door she went back inside to her sick husband who whispered, "My dearest, we will never see him again." Botton enthusiastically joined the work in Henan Province. In 1904 the mission had consisted of just 600 Catholics. Thirty years later they numbered more than 20,000.

On 30 April 1944, Japanese troops approached Xuzhou and fierce fighting ensued. A few low-flying aircraft appeared and fired upon the mission buildings. All of the Christians rushed into the cellar. At about 5 p.m., Japanese soldiers arrived outside. Botton said, "They are coming! I am going out; if not they will bomb and kill us all!" He went up the wooden steps with a white handkerchief in his hand. In the doorway he was confronted by two Japanese with their bayonets drawn. Botton called out: "Italy! Italy!" then he cried out and rolled back down the stairs. The soldiers had stabbed him with their bayonets.

Botton was bleeding badly, but told the Chinese Christians, "Do not cry for me. I am happy it happened this way." Then, with a sigh, he said, "Lord, come and take me. I am suffering greatly. I offer my life for China." Throughout the evening the 35-year-old Italian slowly slipped towards death. Just before midnight he breathed his last. The Chinese Christians were deeply moved by John Botton's sacrifice, saying he had given his life to save theirs. They lovingly buried him in the garden of the mission.

John Birch

Many people have presumed that John Birch died for his involvement in secret military operations rather than for the cause of Christ, but a thorough examination of his life and motives reveals a different story.

At the time of his death, Birch was not a famous personality. It was not until 1958 – thirteen years after Birch was slain – that Robert Welch founded the John Birch Society, a radical right-wing political group. Welch declared Birch a Cold War martyr, and ever since, his name has become synonymous with politics, a label that he would never have desired for himself. One historian has described John Birch as "a missionary who has long been lost to the political cause that was unfortunately named after him".

Birch was born in India to American missionary parents and grew up in a devout Southern Baptist home in Macon, Georgia. It became apparent while Birch was at college that he was extremely intelligent, even bordering on genius. He graduated top of his class and enrolled in the Bible Baptist Seminary at Fort Worth, Texas, where he completed a two-year curriculum in a single year. Birch applied to be a missionary to China and was accepted. In the summer of 1939 he sailed for the Orient, aged just 21. Birch displayed such extraordinary progress in the Chinese language that he was speaking fluently within a few months. For two years he travelled widely throughout China, sharing the gospel and developing a wide network of friends and contacts that would later prove crucial.

An evening in April 1942 changed Birch's life forever. He was eating at a riverside restaurant in a remote village in Zhejiang Province when a Chinese man approached him and quietly asked Birch if he was an American. The missionary was then led to a boat in which were concealed several American military personnel. He was shocked to discover the leader of the group was the famous Colonel James Doolittle, who had just parachuted into China after bombing Tokyo in retaliation for the Japanese bombing of Pearl Harbor. The bombers did not have enough fuel capacity to return to a safe base after the offensive, so they decided to fly towards the Chinese coast and parachute out before ditching their planes. This was an extremely risky plan as many parts of China were under Japanese control at the time. Birch led Doolittle and his men out to safety. He was deeply affected by his time with the soldiers, and a short time later accepted a new assignment: to help locate the whereabouts of the other fifteen planes that had crashed after the Tokyo raid. Birch used his network of contacts and was able to rescue most of the men.

Although John Birch later became an intelligence officer for the United States Army, he never lost sight of his call to serve Jesus Christ and the Chinese people. In fact, Birch came to believe that by helping to fight against the insidious threat of Communism he was doing the best thing he could to help the Chinese church in the long term. He wrote, "I know the big enemy is Communism, but the Lord has called me. My life is in his hands, and I am not turning back." Between 1943 and

1945 Birch became involved in evacuating missionaries and Chinese evangelists from the war zone. In one operation called "Harvey's Restaurant" he arranged for 60 missionaries and their children to be flown to safety. During these years he often longed for the day when the war would end and he could return to his normal work of preaching the gospel and establishing churches.

Birch was taken prisoner by the Communists on 25 August 1945 near the city of Suzhou in Jiangsu Province. His hands were tied behind his back and he was shot in cold blood. His body was later recovered and revealed a bullet hole in the skull, and multiple wounds in his face where he had been bayoneted. Chinese friends lovingly wrapped the body in white silk and several missionaries and pastors attended John Birch's funeral. Just four months before his death, Birch had composed the following prose, entitled "The War Weary Farmer", which expressed his deep longings for a peaceful and simple life:

I should like to find the existence of what my father called "Plain living and high thinking."

I want some fields and hills, woodlands and streams I can call my own. I want to spend my strength in making fields green, and the cattle fat, so that I may give sustenance to my loved ones, and aid to those neighbours who suffer misfortune.

I want to live slowly, to relax with my family before a glowing fireplace, to welcome the visits of my neighbours, to worship God, to enjoy a book, to lie on a shaded grassy bank and watch the clouds sail across the blue.

I want to love a wife who prefers rural peace to urban excitement, one who would rather climb a hilltop to watch a sunset with me than to take a taxi to any Broadway play.

I want of government only protection against the violence and injustices of evil or selfish men.

I want to reach the sunset of life sound in body and mind,

flanked by strong sons and grandsons, enjoying the friendship and respect of neighbors, surrounded by fertile lands and sleek cattle, and retaining my boyhood faith in Him who promised a life to come.

CHAPTER 37   1925 TO 1953 – THE
EARLY YEARS OF
COMMUNISM

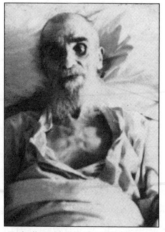

To hell and back: The condition of
Catholic bishop Alfonso Ferroni
after 31 months in a Hubei prison

Thousands of Christians throughout China have been butchered by the Communists during the 20th century. Using farcical public trials to intimidate and mock Christians, the Communists showed the masses that any effort to resist their authority was futile. No details remain this side of eternity of the sufferings of the vast majority of Chinese martyrs. The accounts listed here offer just a small glimpse into the mayhem and carnage witnessed throughout China.

Christians were just one segment of society massacred by the Communists. According to one estimate, during the year 1930 the Communists killed an estimated 150,000 people in

Jiangxi Province and burned 100,000 homes. The carnage was so extensive that it shocked even some of the Communist leaders. In 1931 Mao Zedong, the orchestrator of the violence, was temporarily removed from leadership and reprimanded due to the excesses, which had alienated the population against the Communists. Some villagers even called openly for Mao's death.

The persecution of Christians by the Communists started long before they officially seized power in 1949. In 1927 – just two years after the Chinese Communist Party was established – approximately 600 Catholics at Haifeng in Guangdong Province were massacred by the Communists, angered because many people in the town opposed their message and aims. The bloodbath was carried out on 20 November by 300 soldiers and a motley crowd of farmers armed with hatchets, crowbars and farm implements. One report said the Communists inserted iron wires through the ears and noses of the village leaders and dragged them through the streets of the city until they bled to death. The rampaging crowd threw others alive into a pool and when they surfaced shot them to death. Many more were bound together, doused with gasoline and burned alive, amid shouts of joy from the persecutors.

The Long March

As the Communists grew in size and influence across China in the late 1920s and '30s they came to areas where foreign missionaries and many Chinese Christians lived. Thousands were slaughtered by the merciless Reds. Others were taken hostage in the hope of receiving ransom payments. On 3 February 1930, three women working with the Finnish Free Mission Society were kidnapped by Communist bandits in Jiangxi Province. Ili Cajander (aged 66), Edith Ingman (56) and Agnes Hedengren (49) were captured and cruelly murdered.

The Communists' Long March brought untold misery to the areas it passed through as Mao Zedong and his forces fled from the pursuing Nationalist armies. Today's Communist propaganda paints the Long March in glorious light, telling how the liberated masses warmly welcomed the Reds as they marched through their regions. The reality is markedly different. As they made their way through areas of western Sichuan Province in 1935, the Communists killed thousands of people, among them hundreds of Christians who were members of fledgling churches along the route. Many of the martyred Christians were from small minority groups such as the Qiang, where Christianity had only recently begun to gain a foothold. Tragically, all Qiang pastors and most of their families were executed by Mao's men. The Communists tried to burn all Bibles and New Testaments, and even destroyed the Christians' grain, so as to inflict as much misery as possible. The believers saved some of their Bibles by hiding them in caves.

Between 1925 and 1941, 312 Catholic missionaries were captured and 71 of them murdered by the Communist forces. A diocesan priest named Laurent Chen and his catechist were buried alive at Gaocheng in Hebei Province in 1940 after being captured as they walked along a street. They were killed because the priest had just rebuked a Catholic woman for committing sexual sin with the Communist soldiers. In the same year two Chinese priests, Pierre-Marie Fan and Paul Liu, were killed at Baoding in Hebei Province. Fan was shot while travelling along the road, while Liu was wounded and taken into captivity, where he died four days later.

John Fu, a Chinese priest, was killed in Jiangxi Province in May 1942, while missionary Humbert Verdini and 30 Chinese Catholics were cruelly burned to death in July of the same year.

Christians on trial

A marked increase in Communist aggression against Christians was seen in 1946. Dozens were slaughtered for their faith in God. In December the Communists descended on the village of Shunde in Hebei Province. The bishop and 20 priests, nuns and believers were stripped naked and beaten with gun butts. One of the missionaries, Casimir Skowyra, was burned alive in a pool of gasoline. In countless other locations across China, Catholic priests simply "disappeared" and were never seen again.

By 1947 the frequency of reports of believers being killed had risen, and less outrage was expressed from around the world as helpless governments grew immune to news of Communist bloodletting. During one large public "trial" in Beijing, a Polish nun and her Chinese assistant were tried as "Japanese spies" before 10,000 spectators. The Red guards flew at the defenceless women, clubbing them with their rifles, tossing them to the ground and crushing their faces. As they were marched back to prison, bloody and half naked, they worshipped God, and the people along the route were heard to murmur, "It is impossible to destroy the church. Be of good heart."

The Communists made strong progress in their long war against the Nationalists. Buoyed by their success, a series of systematic persecutions was launched against Christians throughout China, resulting in numerous martyrdoms. Among the worst accounts was that of the martyrdoms of two Chinese priests, Zheng Xinhua and Chen Yueshi, who were beaten to death in Shandong Province in July 1947. The official published account of the public rally dryly stated,

> A man named Wong rose with a hatchet and struck Chen on the back of the head. The priest immediately fell unconscious. At

that, several men used clubs to beat the priest to death. His companion, Li Dongming, was taken back to jail for several months. In September 1947 he was removed from prison and flogged with thorn-imbedded scourges and then, half-conscious, dragged over the fields until he died. His last words were, "Jesus, help me!"

In addition to the terrible toll on human life, the Communists tried to ensure the Catholic Church would never rise again by destroying or seizing all church and mission buildings. They failed to realize that the kingdom of God lives in the hearts of obedient followers of Christ, and not in buildings made by human hands. In the six northern provinces of Manchuria, Inner Mongolia, Hebei, Shaanxi, Shandong and Ningxia, during 1946–47, 183 churches were turned into offices and 123 into theatres and cinemas, 166 were plundered, 25 destroyed, 101 closed, and twelve burned to the ground. During the same period at least 57 Catholic priests, including 16 foreigners, were killed. Some were shot, others were beaten or burned to death, while some were cruelly dragged along by horses until they died. An American Jesuit, Calvert Alexander, travelled throughout north China in early 1948 and heard so many horrendous accounts of what was happening to believers that he decided he could not remain silent any longer. His account of Communist persecution caused a sensation in both the religious and secular press of the United States. Alexander documented that forms of diabolical torture included

> Pushing bamboo slivers under the prisoner's fingernails, forcing the victim to kneel on chains with the board spread on the calves of his legs, on which his torturers jumped until his shinbones broke in two; the Tapestry Chair torture, in which the victim is placed, naked, in a large basket lined with thorns and carried through the streets, with the carriers bumping it on the ground at every few steps. One torture gaining rapidly in

popularity is known as the Dragon Lantern; in this, the back of the priest is slashed open, cotton saturated with gasoline is inserted in the wound, and the cotton is ignited. One Catholic layman had holes drilled in his back, the holes filled with gasoline and then set on fire.

For a start the Communist attacks against Christians were confined to rural areas, but in 1948 the oppressors grew more confident and shifted their energies to congregations in cities like Beijing and Shanghai. In Hebei Province, Li Wanfu, the leader of one Catholic village, was hauled before a Communist court and mockingly told, "Chant your prayers aloud to entertain us." Li refused, so the Communists commanded him to pull out his beard, hair by hair. When he took too long to start doing this, they made a crude torch and burned his face. After hours of being tortured, the old man was asked, "Will you still persist in being a Christian after this?" He answered, "Yes, as long as I breathe." He was immediately shot through the head.

The *China Missionary Bulletin* in 1948 listed the names of 100 Catholic priests who had been killed during the previous two years alone, while *Les Missions Catholiques* lamented that in one year more than 82 priests, nuns or laypeople had fallen victim to the Communists.

The People's Republic of China

The Communists finally gained control of China. On 1 October 1949 Mao announced the founding of the People's Republic of China and a new era was launched. If Christians needed any clearer indication that they were facing their darkest hour it came when Mao Zedong's book, *New Democracy*, was published in 1949. In it Mao clearly stated, "Whoever chooses to oppose Communism must be prepared to be mauled and torn to pieces by the people. If you have not yet made up your mind

The Catholic bishop of Ningxia, Carlo Van
Melckebeke, at forced labour after the
Communist takeover in 1949

about being mauled and smashed to smithereens, it would be wise of you not to oppose Communism. Let the anti-Communist heroes therefore accept this piece of sincere advice from me."

In August 1950 a Chinese priest named Paul Jia made a trip of 50 days' duration to various Catholic villages in the Baoding area of Hebei Province. Before he had finished his circuit the authorities seized him. He was never seen again. Archbishop Ignatius Bi Xushi of Liaoning Province had been held in prison without charge since October of the previous year. When his health began to deteriorate he was denied medical care, and soon died for his faith in Jesus Christ. He was the first Catholic bishop martyred by the Communists.

In 1951 persecution intensified as the Communists attempted to obliterate the church with an intense fury. At the same time the entire nation was groaning under the weight of Mao Zedong's bloodshed. In December 1951 the Hong Kong *Shui Pao* newspaper, citing official government statistics, reported that 250,000 people in Guangdong Province had been executed during the second half of the year. It was said of the Chinese pastors and priests at the time, "Having lost all their own, they are the envy of no one. Their dedication to the apostolate is complete, lacking only the sacrifice of their own lives."

A hundred lepers burned alive

Of all the cruel and inhumane acts perpetrated against the children of God in China throughout history, perhaps none is as evil as that inflicted on approximately 100 lepers in April 1951.

Near the town of Yongren, located alongside a deep ravine formed by the Yangtze River in Yunnan Province, a Catholic work had been underway for some years, aiding the many victims of leprosy who lived in the area. Lacking funds, the mission was only able to construct two huts for the lepers to live in, with roofs of dried grass and walls made of earth. Despite the humble facilities this most despised section of Chinese society was attracted to the warmth and love of the Christians, and by 1950 more than 80 lepers had moved into the community. Most if not all of the lepers believed in God, and the atmosphere of rejection they had lived in for so long was gradually replaced by God's grace and love.

In April 1951 the Communists told the lepers that they needed thatch to cover the two houses, and asked them to go to the mountains and cut grass. The unsuspecting lepers did as they were told. The bundles of dry grass were carried back and placed against the walls of the huts. Six Communist soldiers then told the lepers to go inside, and they blocked all the exits. Diabolically, the soldiers used the grass to set the huts ablaze. All the lepers were burned alive, with the exception of three who miraculously escaped to tell the story.

In 1952 a French–Canadian Franciscan missionary from

Quebec, Didace Arcand, was dragged through the streets, beaten by crowds and subjected to other tortures at Yantai in Shangdong Province. As a result of blows received, he fell unconscious in the street and died. On 29 March Antonio Shen was suspended by his hands and beaten to death because of loyalty to his bishop. The bishop was Italian Alfonso Ferroni (whose picture appears at the start of this chapter). Although Ferroni survived 31 months of prison and torture, he came out of China in such a traumatized and skeletal state that death soon overtook him.

In the early 1950s the Communists used their boundless energy and resources to try to gain control of the church. They launched the Three-Self Patriotic Movement (TSPM), for Protestants, and the Catholic Patriotic Association (CPA), organizations that continue to the present day. The government hoped these institutions would allow them to control, manipulate and ultimately destroy the effectiveness of the church in China. Most of the foreign missionaries remaining in China at the time gave stern warnings to the Chinese leadership and believers not to join these organizations, calling them the "harlot church". Thousands of Chinese pastors and priests stood up in their churches and warned the people not to compromise. Other church leaders could not understand the need for such alarm and willingly registered themselves and their congregations with the government. The issue became a huge dividing line which continues today. Those leaders who stubbornly refused to join the TSPM or CPA were branded "counter-revolutionaries" by the Communists and harshly treated. Hundreds died in prison, while many spent over 20 years locked away for their faith.

The Communists, eager to exert their authority, resorted to making many ridiculous charges against Christians that only made themselves look silly. One of their favourite accusations against priests and nuns was that they operated orphanages so they could murder the babies and young children entrusted to their care. There was a belief among some Chinese that missionaries stole the eyes of babies to use in their medicine. The rumours were exacerbated by the fact that most of the children delivered to the orphanages were extremely sick or injured to begin with, and many soon died. The Communists could not believe the motives of the missionaries could be anything but impure, so they set out to "prove" their crimes. In Wuhu, Anhui Province, the Spanish Sisters of Mercy were charged with the murders of 80 Chinese orphans. In preparation for their trial, the Communists constructed 80 small coffins and dug up the orphanage cemetery in search of small corpses. They found the bodies of only five children; but since the accusations printed in the newspapers mentioned 80 "murders", these bones were distributed among all the dirt-filled coffins. When members of the public passed by the exhibit, they murmured, "Only one bone to a coffin? Where are the skulls?" The nuns, nevertheless, were sent to prison.

As the red tide of Communism swept across China, the world was unaware of the extent of death and destruction it would bring to the country. The church, in all its various forms, has suffered horrifically in China to the present day. There is no way of making any accurate estimate of how many Chinese Christians have lost their lives at the hands of the Communists. What is known is that the number is massive. One historian, John Young, compared the legacy of Mao Zedong with that of Tamerlane, saying, "It was not until the modern ruler of China, Mao Zedong, with his estimated 45 million executions, including 200,000 Christians, appeared in history that anyone was again responsible for a comparable slaughter of his fellow man."

CHAPTER 38

THE FATHER AND SON MARTYRS

Daniel Nelson

Daniel Nelson

Daniel Nelson was born in the Norwegian town of Søndhorland, near Bergen, in 1853. He married Anna in 1878, and four years later the couple migrated to America, where they bought and operated a farm in Eagle Grove, Iowa. Their lives were hardworking yet peaceful. They loved Jesus Christ and raised their four children in the fear of the Lord.

Many missionaries to China throughout history went through an elaborate and lengthy process to discern the call of God. Daniel Nelson, on the other hand, said that while he was laying shingles on the roof of his house in 1889, the call of God suddenly came upon him to go to China. He got up, put down his hammer, climbed down the ladder and told his wife his experience of the unmistakable call of God to become a missionary to China. Anna answered, "I'll go where you want me to go."

Their call to China was simple, but the process of getting there was anything but. Their pastor told Nelson he was foolish and advised him to return to his farm. He was reminded of his responsibility to his family, and told there were enough heathens in America so he should forget about faraway China. Daniel Nelson was also reminded that he lacked the proper training, that he was not an ordained minister, and that no church had called him, and nobody would support him. Some of his friends thought he had lost his mind. The future looked bleak.

Nelson applied to a missionary organization, only to be turned down. Countless reasons for him not to go were placed in the way, but Nelson was sure of his call from God and refused to lose heart. Deciding to obey God at all costs, the Nelson family sold their farm and all their worldly possessions and booked passage on a ship to China. When church and mission leaders saw that the Nelsons were determined to go with or without their blessings, they let Daniel attend Augsburg Seminary from 1889–90, after which they were appointed to work with the Lutheran United Mission. After tearful farewells, Daniel and Anna Nelson and their four children set sail for China, arriving at Shanghai in November 1890. They purchased provisions and set out on the 600-mile (972 kilometre) trip up the Yangtze River to their new home in Wuhan.

Life was difficult for the new missionaries. They succeeded in renting a small one-room mud house in Wuchang, across the river from Wuhan. In this room a fifth child, whom they named John, was born. The summers were terribly hot and their humble home filled with mosquitoes, while in winter icy winds howled through the cracks in the roof and walls. Deep sorrow soon came to the Nelsons. Two of their missionary colleagues died of disease. They then lost their fourteen-year-old daughter, Nora. A few months later the Nelsons' infant daughter also died. This was the darkest moment, when all the forces of hell seemed to be attacking them.

After six years of travelling and preaching with little rest, Daniel Nelson suffered a physical and emotional breakdown. The Lutheran Mission sent the exhausted missionary back to America for eight months in the hope he would recover. Funds were not available to send the whole family, so Anna had to remain in Wuhan with the children. Daniel returned to China with improved health and threw himself into the work with fresh zeal and enthusiasm. He fixed his sights on southern Henan Province, but he soon suffered another breakdown. This time money were found for the whole Nelson family to return to America. They arrived at Portland, Oregon, in 1899, thus missing the Boxer persecution of the following year.

Three years later the Nelsons returned to China, and they continued to minister in Henan Province for many years. From 1911–17 Daniel Nelson served as the superintendent of the American Lutheran Mission, a startling achievement considering he had been mocked and rejected when he first applied to become a missionary. Nelson had laboured for the Lord for 36 years when he was killed in his own home at Xinyang, Henan Province, on 8 February 1926. A large group of bandits had laid siege to Xinyang for a month. Government troops stoutly defended the city, but one evening a bullet struck the pioneer missionary in the head and he died three hours later.

Because of the fighting, Daniel Nelson's funeral could not be held for a month. Their son Bert rushed from his home in Luoshan to comfort his grieving mother. When the funeral was finally able to take place the overwhelming response from the local people showed the measure of respect Nelson had gained. Hundreds of Chinese followed the casket as the procession slowly wound its way to the cemetery. Anna was calm and brave. When asked how she felt, she answered, "I can only thank God for giving us so many happy years of friendship together."

Bert Nelson

Bert Nelson was just two years old when his father Daniel received his sudden call to become a missionary, so he spent most of his childhood growing up in China.

When it came time for Bert to attend high school he was sent back to the United States. He attended Waldorf College, followed by three years at seminary. During this time Bert longed for

Bert Nelson

the day he would return to China to be with his family and among the people he had grown up with. After graduating from seminary Bert Nelson was ordained by the Lutheran United Mission. He reached China in 1917 and was appointed to Luoshan in Henan Province. There was a great deal of rejoicing in the Nelson household when Bert arrived back in China. His father had often told his children that he would rather they be missionaries than become the president of the United States.

In 1918 Bert attended a missionary conference where he met and befriended Marie Pillskog. They fell deeply in love and were married the following year. Bert wrote that he had never been happier, but his joy was to be short-lived. Soon after the newlyweds returned to Luoshan, Marie became seriously ill. They were the only foreigners in the city and it was an arduous two-day journey to the nearest doctor. Bert sent an urgent message for help but before the doctor arrived Marie had passed away. Bert's brother later wrote,

> Those were dark days. He had no one to help him in his deep bereavement. But God gave him strength to carry on. He prepared his wife for the coffin, and placed her tenderly in the

casket with his own hands. It was heart-breaking to part with his loved one. They carried her to the Chinese cemetery and there by the pine trees she was laid to rest. In later years he spent many long and lonely hours at that grave and wept many bitter tears. This loss made his coming years lonely, but undoubtedly strengthened his spiritual fibres for the stony road which lay ahead – the road of death and martyrdom.

In 1926 another deep sorrow cut into Bert Nelson's heart when he received news of his father's death. Bert rushed to his mother's side and found her in deep shock. The following year the Nationalists launched systematic offensives against the Communist forces which, fuelled by help from the Soviet Union, had quickly grown in popularity. On 5 October 1930, Bert Nelson was with Christians at Guangshan when a large Communist contingent attacked the town, raping and pillaging as they went door to door. Nelson was captured, and for the first few days was treated well.

As soon as the superintendent of the American Lutheran Mission heard about the capture of Bert Nelson, and the similar fate of Kristofer Tvedt at Luoshan, action was initiated in a bid to secure their release. The Nationalist army then pushed the Communists back into their mountain hideouts, and Nelson was taken on a long and arduous hike into the mountains as a prisoner of war.

Contact was made with the Communist leaders, who demanded a ransom of US$30,000 for Nelson's and Tvedt's release. Neither the mission nor the US Consulate replied to the ransom note, which angered the Communists. Finally, other Lutheran missionaries decided they could not wait any longer, and between them they raised the amount. They sent two Chinese workers – with wads of cash sewn into the linings of their winter coats – into the mountains to pay the captors. Unfortunately they entered a military zone where intense fighting was taking place, and the government troops would not allow them to go any further. They returned with the money still inside their coats.

On 22 February 1931 a letter from Bert Nelson suddenly appeared at the mission headquarters. It said, "We have been tied and beaten with bamboo poles and told to write and tell you to hasten with money or worse things will follow for us. Cannot you do something to save us?" In April enough ransom was paid for the release of one man. The Communists chose Tvedt, who was married with six children, but continued to hold Bert Nelson. Attempts to send money and provisions to Nelson proved increasingly difficult. Christmas came and went, and 1932 arrived without celebration. Despite frequent illness, filthy conditions and the stress of his ongoing ordeal, Nelson continued to hope for a miracle from the Lord and constantly shared the gospel with his captors. He was allowed to write letters from time to time. One revealed the deep level of spiritual surrender that he had achieved:

> If it is God's will not to be without a witness in this "Babylonian Captivity," you, my dear brothers and sisters and Mother and friends, must yield as well as I. Your prayers will be necessary until the end. Without the intercession of the dear ones of the Home Church and the tender mercies of God I should not now be in the land of the living. I know how you suffer on my behalf. I no more plead for my own sake but for the sake of my dear ones.

In the summer of 1932 Bert Nelson's position became more perilous when a split within the Communist camp led to two of their officers being executed. By now Nelson was so feeble that he had to be carried around on a stretcher. His captors finally decided the burden of keeping him alive outweighed the prospect of having him dead. A Chinese messenger came with news that the missionary had been killed. He had been taken to an ancestral temple and cruelly executed.

Bert Nelson, whose body was never found, had been held captive by the Communists for 22 months. His friends in China honoured him with the nickname, "The Apostle to the Communists". Many of Nelson's 44 years on earth had been filled with pain and suffering. He had endured great hardship, living through the deaths of two of his siblings, his beloved bride and his father. Despite all of this, he remained true and steadfast in his commitment to Christ.

Apart from Christian families massacred together, Daniel and Bert Nelson are probably the only father-and-son missionary martyrs in the history of Chinese Christianity. The sacrifice of the Nelson family was not in vain. Luoshan and Xinyang, where they laboured for so long, lie in one of the strongest Christian areas in all of China. Today approximately 100,000 of Luoshan's 600,000 people are professing Christians, while in Xinyang around ten per cent of the population follow Jesus Christ.

CHAPTER 39   SADHU SUNDAR
SINGH

Sadhu Sundar Singh

373

Sundar Singh, the son of a wealthy Sikh landowner, was born in north India in 1889. Considering his background, nobody would have guessed that this man would one day be remembered as the most famous Indian evangelist of the early 20th century. As a young man, Sundar's mother took him every week to sit at the feet of a *sadhu* – an ascetic Hindu holy man – who lived in a remote forest. When their son was old enough, Sundar's parents wanted the best for him so he was sent to a Christian school run by missionaries so he could learn English.

When Singh was fourteen his mother suddenly died. This tragedy plunged the teenager into deep despair and he became violent against anything to do with religion. He began to hate the missionaries, persecuted the Christians he knew, and ridiculed their faith. He bought a Bible and burned it page by page while his friends watched. He decided to commit suicide by throwing himself in front of a train. That night he went to bed hardened against God, but Christ stepped in and introduced himself to the troubled young man. Before dawn he woke his father and announced that he had seen Jesus Christ in a vision and heard his voice. Singh declared that for the rest of his life on earth he would follow Jesus and seek to make him known. Singh later shared what happened on that night when he decided to kill himself:

> Jesus came into my room. As I was praying for the last time a bright cloud of light suddenly filled the room, and out of the brightness came the face and figure of Jesus. He spoke to me, "How long will you persecute Me? I have come to save you. You were praying to know the right way; why do you not take it? I am the Way." He spoke in Hindustani, and He spoke to me.

Sundar Singh's family did not share the excitement of his newfound faith. His enraged father, Sher Singh, held a "farewell feast" where he publicly disowned his son, pronouncing him "dead". Several hours after the feast Sundar was violently ill and realized he had been poisoned by his own family. He rushed to a nearby Christian hospital and his life was spared.

On his 16th birthday Singh was publicly baptized at Simla in north India. A year later, in October 1906, he shocked everyone by appearing in a yellow robe and turban – the dress of a *sadhu*. He declared, "I am not worthy to follow in the steps of my Lord, but, like him, I want no home or possessions. Like him I will belong to the road, sharing the sufferings of my people, eating with those who will give me shelter, and telling all men of the love of God."

Sundar Singh's zeal for the things of God soon became legendary. He was known to pray several hours each day and to fast for weeks at a time. He took a vow of poverty and decided to hold nothing back from the cause of Christ. His travels not only took him to Hindu, Muslim and Buddhist settlements throughout the Himalayas, but also to Europe, America, Australia and various Asian countries where he spoke to large audiences. On one trip, while still a teenager, Singh walked barefoot through fanatical Muslim territories in the Punjab, Kashmir, Afghanistan, and through parts of present-day Pakistan. In all the places Singh went, he wore the garments of a *sadhu*. Soon after the start of his ministry, Christians gave Singh the nickname, "The Apostle with the Bleeding Feet". On a number of occasions he reported being helped by angels, and the only word to describe some of his escapes from death is miraculous.

He was often arrested, beaten and stoned. He faced incredible hardship, yet he carried on, a trophy of God's grace in one of the harshest spiritual climates in the world. There were many admirers of Sadhu Sundar Singh, but also many critics. For many of the missionaries in India, Singh's ways were just too radical to embrace. Those who enjoyed safe Christianity felt threatened by the intensity of his commitment and his methods of operation. Missionaries persuaded Singh to enrol at a Bible college in Lahore so that he would be "equipped for the ministry". He graduated and was ordained, but in 1911 he had a change of heart. He handed back his preacher's licence and returned to the simple life of a *sadhu*.

The mysterious land of Tibet had attracted Singh since he was a young boy, and he made his first preaching trip there in 1908. In 1912 he decided to preach the gospel for several months each summer in Tibet, Nepal and areas along the north India border. He encountered much opposition in these dark places, and many attempts were made on his life. The methods of torture he endured included being sewn into a wet yak skin and left in the sun to be squeezed to death as the skin tightened; being smothered with cloth filled with leeches and scorpions to sting him and suck his blood; and being tied to a tree overnight as bait for wild animals. On one occasion Singh reached a Tibetan town called Razar. He was arrested for illegally entering the country, and the head lama sentenced him to death. Buddhists are forbidden to take life, so the lama had Singh cast into a well, and the iron cover locked until he had perished. The smell of the putrid water made the evangelist recoil, for the bottom of the well was full of dead men's bones and rotting flesh. He was in the well for two days and nights, almost passing out from the stench. On the third day he heard a sound up above. The cover of the well was removed and a rope was lowered down. Someone told Singh to take hold of it. He was pulled to the surface and immediately felt revived by the fresh air. He turned to thank his rescuer but strangely nobody was there.

The following day news reached the head lama that the *sadhu* who had been thrown down the well was free and had recommenced preaching. Again Sundar was brought before him. The lama demanded to know how he had escaped, but all Sundar could tell him was what had happened, and that he had seen no one. Furiously the lama asserted that someone must have stolen the key to the well, and ordered that a search be made for it. No one was more taken aback than he when it was eventually found on his own belt.

By the early 1920s Singh's health was beginning to deteriorate from the hardships he had endured, even though he was only in his early thirties. He made another trip to Tibetan areas in 1923 and came back exhausted. For the next several years he continued to minister, refusing to belong to any denomination or to start one himself. During these years he turned his hand to writing books. These encountered great success, and were translated into numerous languages. In 1927 Singh again attempted to enter Tibet, but was forced to return due to illness.

Finally, in June 1929, he disappeared while inside Tibet and was never seen again. He had told friends of his intention to go back to the Mount Kailash area, and possibly to visit Razar, the town east of Lake Manasarowar where he had been thrown into the well years before. Singh had heard there were a few Christians living there, and he wanted to go and see if it were true.

Just how Sadhu Sundar Singh died remains a mystery, but rumours circulated that he had been put to death by enraged Buddhist monks.

CHAPTER 40   IN THE LAND OF MOHAMMED

Christians leaving church in Kashgar in happier times.
The church was destroyed in 1933.

The vast desert expanses of northwest China's Xinjiang Region are home to more than ten million Muslims belonging to a host of different ethnic minority groups including the Uygur, Kazak, Kirgiz, Uzbek, Tajik and Hui. Xinjiang is much more historically, culturally and linguistically akin to nearby Central Asia than to China.

One of the greatest mission figures of the 19th century is a name few Christians in the English-speaking world are familiar with. Nils Fredrik Höijer travelled through Russia, the Middle East and Central Asia in the 1870s and 1880s, preaching the gospel in spite of tremendous opposition and difficulties. Through Höijer's tremendous courage and persistence the Swedish Missionary Society was founded in 1878. Dozens of pioneer missionaries were sent out over the following decades. Wherever the Swedes went they seemed to encounter more success than other Protestant missionaries working in similar areas. In 1892 they established a work at the strategic city of Kashgar in western Xinjiang. For the first two years the mission had just one worker – Mehmed Shukri, the son of a Muslim mullah from Turkey. Shukri, who changed his name to Aveteranian after his conversion to Christ, proved to be a highly effective evangelist in Kashgar. In 1894 four Swedish missionaries joined him, and a mission base was established. Within a few years they had established Christian bases at several other towns. The presence of Christians in the midst of fanatical Muslims was not without trouble. Over the years several riots occurred, and on one occasion a Swedish missionary and his converts were beaten and dragged through the streets of Yarkant.

The Swedes overcame incessant opposition and succeeded where no other Protestant mission had done so before. Dozens of Muslims gave their lives to Jesus Christ. The Swedes gradually won over many of the local people with their godly lives and sacrificial service. By 1926 more than 28,000 people had received treatment at the various medical centres established throughout the region. The missionaries fed the hungry, clothed the poor, ran orphanages and established ten schools. The Bible was translated into Uygur, and the missionaries printed and distributed copious amounts of Christian literature, boldly handing some of it to mullahs and other Islamic clerics. By the 1930s the total Christian community numbered over 500, all of them converts from Islam.

In April 1933 an armed Muslim faction from Khotan took control of Kashgar, Yarkant and the other towns south of the Taklimakan Desert. Hundreds of Chinese were massacred in the assault, while their wives and daughters were captured and used as sex-slaves by the deviant attackers, who had as one of their first objectives to get rid of the Christian church in Xinjiang.

On 27 April the rebel leader, Abdullah Khan, ordered the Swedish missionary Nyström to appear before him. Nyström went to see Abdullah with his colleagues Arell and Hermansson. After being forced to wait a long time at the governor's mansion, Abdullah entered the room, holding a handkerchief to his nose (to filter the air contaminated by Christian breath). He yelled, "It is my duty, according to our law, to put you to death because by your preaching you have destroyed the faith of some of us! Out with you – bind them." The missionaries escaped death but were expelled from Xinjiang and returned to Sweden.

After dealing with the missionaries, the cruel tyrant focused his energies on the local Christians, demonstrating a particular hatred towards all who had turned their backs on Islam.

The female Christians (including girls as young as eleven) were forced to become wives of Muslim men. The male Christians were beaten and thrown into prison at Yarkant and Kashgar. Some were beheaded, while others perished under the terrible tortures. None of the girls denounced their faith. At least 100 Christian men suffered martyrdom for Jesus Christ between 1933 and 1939. Numbered among those who paid the ultimate price for their faith was 20-year-old Hassan Akhond of Yarkant. A Muslim friend of his was later released from prison and told how Hassan's soothing voice had often calmed the nerves of the prisoners at night as he sang hymns to his Saviour. Some nights later they heard him faintly singing, "Loved with everlasting love". Just a few days later Hassan died of starvation.

The Christians were herded into groups and then crammed into small, unventilated cells not large enough for each man to even sit down. This forced them to spend day and night in a crouching position. The few who survived suffered from swelling in their knees and in the upper part of the calves and in the thighs. Mortification usually set in and death followed. The unheated cells were bitterly cold, especially for prisoners who had only been allowed to take the clothes they were wearing when arrested. A number had been sent to prison only half clad. Many perished after suffering unmentionable tortures. The list of martyrs included an evangelist from Yengisar named Khelil Akhond, and Liu Losi, the principal of the Hancheng school.

Ali Akhond

Ali Akhond grew up a dedicated Muslim. He faced Mecca and prayed at the five prescribed times each day, and was careful to obey the teaching of the Muslim clerics. One day Ali rode his horse into the market at Kashgar. While there he overheard an old man in a dusty grey cloak telling a group of students that he would never die. Ali thought the man, a Swedish missionary, was crazy, but he was strangely drawn to his claim that he would never die, and thought about it often.

Some time later Ali obtained work at Kashgar, leaving his wife back on the farm with his elderly father. Ali intended to use his time in the city to hear lectures on Islam, but instead he came into contact with the Swedish mission and he often went to listen to their singing and preaching. One night a missionary stood up and read the words of Jesus from the Bible, "I tell you the truth, if anyone keeps my word, he will never see death" (John 8:51). Ali remembered the time he had

Ali Akhond (left) with another Uygur Christian

heard the old man say the same thing at the market, and he decided to find out what the Christians meant by this saying. Ali accepted some gospel literature and took it home to read, but a friend threw it into the fire, warning Ali that if he read it he would become an infidel. Ali returned to the mission and was given the same books, but this time another friend ripped them up before he had a chance to read them.

Undeterred, Ali Akhond secured yet more Christian literature and over the coming months closely observed the lives of the missionaries and their converts. What he saw impressed him. Whereas many marriages among the Uygur people ended in divorce or discontent, the missionaries seemed to have genuine love and trust in their families. All of the Christians seemed to have an inner calm and joy that he longed for, and which Islam was unable to provide. A few years passed, and by this time Ali had taken a second wife. He struggled to support both wives in this polygamous arrangement. One day, Ali Akhond thought about the Swedes' successful married lives, and their honesty and unselfishness. He concluded that their character might be due to their obedience to the teachings of Christ, so he decided to follow Jesus for himself. About a year later it dawned on him that he too had become a true believer in God. He left his second wife, providing for her and their little son.

After his public baptism, everybody in Kashgar knew that Ali Akhond had turned his back on Islam and embraced the "religion of the Crusaders". Ali returned to his first wife, and after a few years she also repented and became a new creation in Christ. The transformation in Ali's life was startling, and he could not keep the good news to himself. In the mid-1920s he was appointed as a full-time evangelist by the church in Kashgar, and he led many Muslims to faith in Jesus Christ. These advances came at great cost for the gifted preacher. He was constantly harassed and threatened by his fellow countrymen, who considered him an infidel.

When the persecution of 1933 came, there was nowhere to hide for the Christians, and certainly not for someone with such a high public profile as Ali Akhond. He was one of those who gained a martyr's crown at Kashgar.

The honest Ali Akhond, who had found God after seeking for him with all his heart, finally discovered the true meaning of what the missionaries had taught years before. He had kept

Habil and his sister Hava at Yarkant in 1932

the words of Jesus, and as a result never experienced spiritual death.

Habil and Hava

Habil (Abel in English) and his sister Hava (Eva) lived next door to a school run by the Swedish missionaries in Yarkant, Xinjiang. Their father, Tokht Akhond, was a carpenter by trade. When Habil was ten years old and Hava four, their mother suddenly died. This sad event threw the family into turmoil. The father went into serious debt to a Chinese opium smuggler. Two years later, in 1926, more heartache was added to the children when their father died. That same night the opium smuggler came to take Habil and his sister into slavery as payment for their father's debts. The children ran to the school and begged the missionaries to save them. The Swedes did not have the kind of money owed to the creditor, but they devised a plan to protect and keep Habil and Hava. Habil had attended classes at the mission school for a number of years, but his father had not been able to pay the fees. The missionaries used this as a way to claim the children. They lodged a legal paper claiming the mission was owed a sum of money for unpaid fees. In return, they had accepted guardianship of Habil and his sister, and considered the debt paid in full. Because of his illegal dealings, the opium smuggler did not dare contest the claim in court. The children were saved.

Gradually the grief-stricken children grew to love the Swedish missionaries. Habil enjoyed playing soccer, and proved better at the sport than other boys much older and larger than himself. He also enjoyed bird-watching. Little Hava came to love Gerda Andersson, who was in charge of the Girls' Home. In 1931 a great evangelist named Yusuf Ryekhan came to live in Yarkant and revival broke out among the Muslim population. Several of the young men connected to the mission put their faith in Christ and were baptized. Habil was one of them. In a Muslim society baptism is the point of no return for someone interested in Christianity. Habil knew it would cost him his friends, reputation and possibly his life, but he did not care. All he wanted was to follow Jesus. The missionaries were greatly impressed by Habil's zeal and hunger for God, and at the end of 1932 he was asked to be the assistant principal of the mission school at Kashgar, even though he had only just turned 19.

Yarkant was overrun by the Khotan rebels on 11 April 1933. Just before the road between Kashgar and Yarkant was cut off, Habil returned to Yarkant so he could take care of his sister. Hava was then thirteen, and many young girls and women were being raped and carried off by the rebels. The Swedish missionaries were rounded up and eventually expelled from Xinjiang, and then the rebels turned their attention to those people who had deserted Islam. Sensing the storm that was about to break, Habil drew a cross on the mud wall, and asked a Christian friend, "Do you see that?" Then he drew a crown. "And do you see that? You see the cross comes first and then the crown."

That afternoon Habil and the other Christian boys prayed together, asking God to strengthen them for the ordeal ahead. Suddenly, while they sang a hymn, a shout went up to run. Soldiers surrounded the building and only one boy managed to escape. The Christians were roped together and taken to the governor's house, where Abdullah Khan had taken residence. Abdullah struck Habil over the head and yelled, "Shoot them all!" At the same time the wicked man signalled to a soldier that Habil should be separated from the others and untied. Habil knelt down and looked up to heaven with a peaceful face. The order to shoot was given, and Habil fell to the ground dead.

The Muslims then began to thrash the other prisoners until they called out, "Shoot us, too, and put us out of our pain!" After he had finished inflicting his anger on them, Abdullah Khan sent the Christians to prison, and ordered that Habil's body be thrown out for the dogs to eat. When it had remained untouched for three days, some kindly Muslims buried it, believing that Habil must have been a holy man of God.

About a week later Abdullah Khan ordered Hava to come to the governor's mansion. The believers prayed for her, afraid the wicked man planned to vent his lust on the pretty thirteen-year-old girl's body. Just after sunrise the next morning Hava returned to the school and sank down on the floor. After wiping the tears from her eyes, she bravely recounted what had happened the previous night. The evil man had locked the door and told Hava, "Now, you shall be mine!" Hava begged to be killed, so she could join her brother in heaven. Abdullah Khan was surprised to hear that the young girl was the sister of the man he had shot dead. Somehow this plea managed to touch even Abdullah's hard heart, and he allowed her to go free as long as he was provided another Christian girl in her place. That dreadful experience fell to a young woman named Buve Khan, who was engaged to Habil at the time of his martyrdom. She was forced to become Abdullah Khan's wife.

Hava and the other Christian girls were later forced to marry Muslim men. The man Hava was made to wed suffered from syphilis and she soon contracted the disease and also fell pregnant. The baby died at birth. Missionary Gerda Andersson was still in Yarkant at the time, and she heard what had happened to the beloved girl. Andersson sent a cart to Hava's house and collected her at the point of death, and lovingly nursed her day and night until she recovered.

The Khotan rebels were later defeated, and Hava's husband fled from Yarkant with them. He later sent her a letter of divorce. Having suffered the deaths of her mother, father, brother and newborn baby, young Hava's heart was crushed by the evil she had endured. Through the love and tears of the other Christians who survived, Hava continued to walk with the Lord, but several years later she died from all the strain. She had not yet turned 20.

CHAPTER 41

JOHN AND BETTY STAM

John and Betty Stam

One of the most well-known martyrdoms in the history of Christianity in China occurred in December 1934, when a young American missionary couple, John and Betty Stam, were beheaded in Anhui Province.

John Stam was of Dutch ancestry. His family had settled in New Jersey, but from an early age he had felt burdened for China, a land in which he often reminded people, "a million a month pass into Christless graves". The early 1930s were a difficult time both sides of the Pacific Ocean. In America the Great Depression was wreaking havoc with the economy, and great hardship was felt by all. In China the rise of the Communists was seriously disrupting missionary work. The Red Army seemed to be growing daily in size and strength. Numerous missionary bases were forced to close, and workers were being evacuated from areas near the Communist forces. Stam considered these events mere distractions to God's work, and nothing that could force him to alter his commitment to Christ and to China. When he was asked to speak to the Moody Bible Institute class of 1932, Stam gave the following stirring challenge: "Shall we beat a retreat, and turn back from our high calling in Christ Jesus, or dare we advance at God's command in the face of the impossible? Let us remind ourselves that the Great Commission was never qualified by clauses calling for advance only if funds were plentiful and no hardship or self-denial was involved. On the contrary, we are told to expect tribulation and even persecution, but with it victory in Christ."

Betty was the daughter of missionary parents in China, and so grew up familiar with Oriental languages and culture. While she was attending school in America, everyone expected her to return to China to start her own career as a missionary. Before she was appointed for service, Betty wrote,

> I want something really worth while to live for. Like most young people, I want to invest this one life of mine as wisely as possible, in the place that yields richest profits to the world and to me. I want it to be God's choice for me and not my own. There must be no self-interest at all, or I do not believe God can reveal

His will clearly. I know very well that I can never realize the richest, most satisfying, life Christ meant for me, if I am not giving my own life unselfishly for others. Christ said: "He that would find his life shall lose it," and proved the truth of this divine paradox at Calvary. I want Him to lead, and His Spirit to fill me. And then, only then, will I feel that my life is justifying its existence and realizing the maturity in Him that Christ meant for all men, in all parts of the world.

John and Betty first met at the Moody Bible Institute in Chicago. Betty was a year ahead of John, so after graduating she made her way to China first, living in Shanghai. John arrived and a year later they were married on 25 October 1933. Soon after, joyous news came that Betty was pregnant. In September 1934 Helen Priscilla was born in a Methodist mission hospital. The Stams were assigned to Jingde in southern Anhui Province. They arrived at their new home after many weeks of arduous travel by boat and over land. Communist activity in this part of Anhui had lessened in the preceding years, and both the Stams and their mission leaders felt the risk of an insurgency in Jingde was small. The Jingde city magistrate welcomed the Stams and gave a personal assurance that they would be safe from the Communists.

Almost as soon as they had settled in, the Stams started to hear rumours of the Red Army nearing Jingde. It was impossible to tell which stories were imaginary and which contained truth, such was the frequency and inconsistencies of the information reaching their ears. Suddenly, on the morning of 6 December 1934 a letter was rushed to the Stams' house from the city magistrate, informing them that 2,000 Communist insurgents were just four miles from the city. The Stams were advised to flee. The magistrate, who just a few weeks before had personally guaranteed the Stams' safety, was one of the first to flee Jingde. While the insurgents entered through the east gate of the city the magistrate and other officials escaped through the west gate.

The Communist soldiers made their way directly to the mission compound. They broke open the lock on the gate and rushed to the front door of the house. John Stam calmly opened the door and welcomed the men inside. Betty served them tea and cakes while John attempted to explain their reasons for coming to China. When they finished their tea, the soldiers politely said, "You will go with us." John pleaded with the soldiers to let his wife and baby daughter remain behind, but his request was refused. The Stams were held in Jingde Prison for the remainder of the day. The soldiers forced John to write a letter to the China Inland Mission headquarters in Shanghai, outlining their ransom demand. Stam knew the request would not be considered, as it was the strict policy of the mission never to pay a ransom for a kidnapped worker, believing such an action would only encourage more kidnappings and result in a more dire situation overall. John's letter displays his faith and courage, and also reveals that he was well aware of the likely outcome of his life:

Dear Brethren,

My wife, baby and myself are to-day in the hands of the Communists in the city of Jingde. Their demand is $20,000 for our release. All our possessions and stores are in their hands, but we praise God we have peace in our hearts and we had a meal to-night. God grant you wisdom in what you do, and us fortitude, courage and peace of heart. He is able – and a wonderful friend in such a time.

Things happened so quickly this morning. They were in the city just a few hours after the ever-persistent rumours really became alarming, so that we could not prepare to leave in time. We were just too late.

The Lord bless you and guide you – and as for us – may God be glorified whether by life or death.

One man, as he was being released from Jingde Prison, over-heard the soldiers discussing what to do with the Stams' baby. The soldiers were irritated by her constant crying, and decided to kill the baby for their own convenience. The pris-oner, whose name is unknown, stepped forward and asked the Communists what the innocent baby had done to deserve death. They shouted back, "Are you a Christian?" "No, I am not," the man replied. They asked, "Are you willing to die for this foreign baby?" The man immediately answered, "I will." As the Stams hugged their baby tighter, they saw the kind man hacked to pieces before their eyes. Helen Priscilla's life was spared because a Chinese stranger sacrificed his life for her.

The next day the Communists abandoned Jingde, taking John and Betty Stam with them, along with little three-month-old baby Helen. After arriving in Miaoshou, the sol-diers made John write a second ransom note to the mission. When the postmaster was summoned to receive the letter he recognized Stam and asked, "Where are you going?" The mis-sionary replied, "We don't know where they're going, but we are going to heaven." John and Betty Stam were bound with ropes that cut deeply into their wrists, then stripped of their outer clothing, leaving them in their underwear. John was tied to a bedpost throughout the night, while Betty was allowed to attend to the needs of her baby. The next morning they were paraded through the town, with the whole population rallied to come out and witness the execution of the "foreign devils". The Communists cursed and ridiculed them as they were marched through the streets.

The procession wound its way up a small hill lined with pine trees. Miaoshou had been visited by missionaries for a number of years, so there were a small number of believers there. On their way to the execution spot the Stams saw a medicine seller named Zhang Shuisheng, who had been a rather lukewarm Christian. When he saw that the Reds were determined to behead the courageous couple, Zhang pleaded on his knees for their release. The Communists bound him, and searching his house they found both a Bible and hymn book. They needed no further proof that Zhang too belonged to this foreign group, so they took him with the Stams.

John and Betty were ordered to kneel in the dust. While John was praying he was struck to the ground, his throat having been cut so completely that his head fell beside his body. Betty trembled, and she uttered a prayer as she fell over the body of her beloved husband. In this position the blood-stained knife was inserted in the back of her neck and she fell down dead.

Remarkably, on the same day that news of the Stams' death reached America, John's father, Peter Stam, received a letter from his son that had been posted from China many weeks before. In his letter he told about the Communist threat, but reiterated his faith and commitment to serve God in China regardless of the cost. John Stam repeated the poem "Afraid?" written by E. H. Hamilton to commemorate the martyrdom of Jack Vinson in 1931:

Afraid? Of what?
To feel the spirit's glad release?
To pass from pain to perfect peace?
The strife and strain of life to cease?
Afraid? – of that?

Afraid? Of what?
Afraid to see the Saviour's face?
To hear His welcome, and to trace
The glory gleam from wounds of grace?
Afraid? – of that?

Afraid? Of what?
A flash – a crash – a pierced heart;

Darkness – light – O heaven's art!
A wound of his counterpart!
Afraid? – of that?

Afraid? Of what?
To do by death what life could not –
Baptize with blood a stony plot,
Till souls shall blossom from the spot?
Afraid? – of that?

A Chinese evangelist named Lo arrived in Miaoshou the day following the martyrdom. He wrapped the bodies in white cotton and prepared them for burial. Wanting to give the Stams the most decent burial possible, Lo lovingly sewed their heads back onto their necks so that those seeing them would not be too upset. The people of Miaoshou came out in large numbers to watch the funeral. Lo could not discover what had happened to little Helen Stam. Nobody was sure if she had also been killed or if the Communists had carried her off to their next destination. Lo searched around Miaoshou before finally an old woman pointed to an abandoned house and whispered, "The foreign baby is still alive." Lo found the Stams' daughter wrapped up in a blanket, completely oblivious to the events of the previous day. She had been left alone for more than 24 hours, but appeared none the worse for the experience. Later, Lo found a $10 bill hidden inside the baby's clothing, no doubt secretly placed there by her loving parents so that milk could be bought for her.

Helen Priscilla Stam came to be known around the world as "the miracle baby". She became the focal point of many newspaper reports, as people preferred to read about the saving of her precious life than to contemplate the awful carnage that had murdered her parents and Zhang Shuisheng. Helen was taken to her grieving grandparents, Dr and Mrs Charles

Baby Helen, the "miracle baby"

Scott, at their mission station in Shandong Province. Dr Scott announced that his daughter and son-in-law had not died in vain: "The blood of the martyrs is still the seed of the church. If we could hear our beloved children speak, we know from their convictions that they would praise God because he counted them worthy to suffer for the sake of Christ."

Little Helen remained in China in the care of her grandparents until the age of five, and was then adopted by her aunt and uncle who were missionaries in the Philippines. She grew up there before attending college in the United States. Helen decided to avoid the publicity brought about by her family's experiences, so took the last name of her uncle to obtain anonymity. When she was fourteen Helen was asked if she hated the Chinese people for all they had done to her parents. She immediately responded, "Oh, I think they are just wonderful. I love them. Just think, I am alive today because a Chinese man took my place and died for me."

The martyrdom of John and Betty Stam made a

significant impact in America and the Western world. Interest was given momentum by a biography of the Stams, which soon ran through eight reprints to meet the huge demand. Hundreds of letters, many containing large financial gifts for the work of China, were sent in from all around the world. For several years the China Inland Mission had been in a financial slump because of the Depression, but now the support they were able to send into China for their workers remained strong for years to come. Many young men and women offered to go to China to replace the Stams. One mission leader remarked, "I personally know of hundreds of volunteers of all ages who gave their lives to the Lord for missionary service because of the death of John and Betty Stam." A co-worker of the Stams wrote to Betty's grieving parents: "A life which had the longest span of years might not have been able to do one-hundredth of the work for Christ which they have done in a day."

CHAPTER 42

ERIC LIDDELL – OLYMPIC CHAMPION AND MARTYR

Eric Liddell

Perhaps the most celebrated China martyr of all time is the Scottish-born Olympic champion, Eric Liddell. Born in 1902 to missionary parents at Tianjin, China, Liddell returned to his homeland as a teenager. Even as a young man his life was marked by a deep faith and consecration to Christ, and he considered all worldly achievements nothing compared to the joy of following God.

At the age of 16 Liddell was already an outstanding athlete. He captained his school cricket team, and possessed an exceptional turn of speed. After entering Edinburgh University in 1920 his sporting career blossomed. He excelled in running events, especially the 100-metre sprint, and his speed enabled him to play international rugby for Scotland. Many athletic victories came Liddell's way, including a winning run for the British Empire team against the United States.

The 1924 Olympic Games at Paris were looming, and Britain held high hopes that the flying Scot would bring home a gold medal. Sport was not the priority in Liddell's life, however. In 1923 he had joined the Glasgow Students' Evangelistic Union, giving himself wholeheartedly to the service of God. Liddell continually asked himself, "Does this path I tread follow the Lord's will?" His devotion to Christ was complete, and he viewed his sporting ability as a God-given gift by which he could glorify Jesus Christ. An opportunity came in a unique way during the Olympics. A short time before the Games commenced, Liddell discovered that the heats for the 100-metre sprint were scheduled to be run on a Sunday. The idea of running on the Lord's Day was abhorrent to him. His withdrawal meant he gave up the almost certain prospect of winning a gold medal in his strongest event, and the hopes and aspirations of a nation were dashed. For weeks Eric Liddell's decision not to run was vehemently criticized by the press in Britain and other parts of the world. Much pressure was brought to bear on him, but nothing would alter his convictions. He later wrote,

Ask yourself: If I know something to be true, am I prepared to follow it, even though it is contrary to what I want, or to what I have personally held to be true? Will I follow it if it means being laughed at, if it means personal financial loss, or some kind of hardship?

The Olympic 100-metre competition went on without him, and a world that idolizes its sports stars was left reflecting on Eric Liddell's radical obedience to Jesus Christ. Liddell did compete in the 400 metres, which did not take place on a Sunday. He won a gold medal and set a new world record for the event, and also won a bronze in the 200 metres. Scotland loved its native son, and Liddell's countrymen paraded him around the streets of Edinburgh to the cheers and adulation of thousands of people.

Liddell had only come back to his homeland for his education. All along, his plan was to return to China as soon as he had graduated. Despite his success and popularity, Liddell shocked Scotland by returning to missionary work in 1925. Everywhere he went for the next few years people flocked to see the Olympic champion. This opened many doors for Liddell to share his faith. Twice during his missionary career he returned to Britain on furlough, and each time the intervening years seemed to have hardly dimmed the appreciation of him as large crowds flocked to his meetings and hung on his every word.

For twelve years Eric Liddell taught at the Anglo-Chinese College in Tianjin. He was an outstanding teacher and highly respected by all. He taught science and also supervised the school's sporting activities. Liddell married Florence Mackenzie in 1934. Their relationship produced three beautiful daughters. For years he had faithfully served in the school while countless missionaries passed through from far-flung fields, sharing their victories and struggles. Inwardly Liddell longed to experience such work for himself, and in 1936 he sensed the Holy Spirit was leading him to a new ministry. A vacancy opened at Xiaochang in Shandong Province, but the opportunity coincided with the arrival of the Japanese army. It was considered too dangerous for a family to live in the war zone, so to accept the appointment meant Liddell would have to spend periods of time away from his beloved wife and precious daughters. After wrestling with the decision for a year, Liddell was convinced God was calling him to accept the position.

Shandong was in chaos due to the war. Liddell spent much of his time helping wounded soldiers, knowing that if caught he would be sentenced to death by the Japanese. With the outbreak of World War II in 1939, the danger for missionaries greatly intensified. Florence and the three girls travelled to safety in Canada, but Eric decided to remain in China. In 1943 he and all his missionary colleagues were arrested and held in a Japanese internment camp at Weifang.

For Eric Liddell, being imprisoned with more than 2,000 other foreigners (including 327 children) meant an opportunity to teach and encourage the downcast, and threw all his energy into his activities. The prison camp's Employment Committee appointed him to teach mathematics and science, and to organize athletics.

After nearly two years of incarceration away from his family, Liddell's health began to break down. He battled depression, and interpreted the symptoms to mean he was wavering in his faith. He didn't realize he was suffering from a malignant brain tumour. The end came quickly, and on 21 February 1945 the missionary and Olympic champion went to be with Jesus Christ, just months before the end of the war.

The story of Eric Liddell was celebrated in the award-winning 1981 movie, *Chariots of Fire*. In 1991 a memorial stone was sent from Scotland to be placed on Liddell's unmarked grave in China. After much research the grave was located within the grounds of a school at Weifang in Shandong Province. Although he was just 42 when he died, millions have been touched by Eric Liddell's self-sacrificial life and death.

CHAPTER 43

MASSACRES IN NORTH CHINA

Xiwanzi

An underground Catholic meeting in the woods,
with approximately 1,000 believers present

By the end of 1946 it became apparent that the Communists
had gained the upper hand in the Civil War against the
Nationalists. Many considered it only a matter of time before
they gained control of the whole nation. For much of the time
prior to 1946 the Communists had been careful not to kill
Christians. Indeed, some Chinese church leaders and a few
missionaries even believed a Communist government would
be good for Christianity in China.

The village of Xiwanzi in northwest Hebei Province came
to prominence in the 1800s because it was used as a regional

base for Catholic missionaries and it was seen as the last stop before the vast Mongolian steppes. By 1946 the entire community of 3,000 people in Xiwanzi was Catholic. Xiwanzi had become the centre of activity from where 200 new converts were won to Christ and discipled each year. The village had a magnificent cathedral, a seminary, a hospital, a primary school for boys and girls, an orphanage and two convents.

A Belgian priest, Francis LeGrand, had been the pastor at Xiwanzi for five years. He was away on business on the day the Communist persecution commenced. This not only preserved his life, but enabled him to record the incident for the outside world to read about. To start with, two leading Christians were thrown into prison in a bid to intimidate the other believers. On 23 September 1946 the Chinese priest Benedict Ying was shot dead. The following month two more Chinese priests were imprisoned on trumped-up charges. They were never seen again. Then, in December, the full force of the Communist plan was unleashed. A Christian landowner was given a public "trial". He was humiliated and accused of various "crimes" before being thrown down from the platform and beaten to death in front of the terrified spectators. All the women of the village, the children, and even the mother of the victim witnessed the ghastly incident. Shortly after, the bishop was imprisoned and the Catholic mission was fined "three million pounds of flour" for their imaginary crimes. Because the mission was unable to pay, the Communists took away all its buildings and assets. The last remaining building the Catholics were forced to hand over was the cathedral. Soldiers arrived and stripped all valuables from the sanctuary.

Religious articles and Bibles were removed from every home, and any attractive Catholic girl who caught the eye of a Communist soldier was forced to marry him. This applied to the nuns as well. Next, the believers' land and farms were confiscated. Despite the tremendous pressure, not a single

Catholic at Xiwanzi denounced their faith, even after countless brainwashing meetings were held in an attempt to indoc-
trinate the believers.

On 9 December 1946 Xiwanzi was attacked by the
Communist military. The inhabitants fled to the side of a
mountain, where they were caught and brought back. One
group of believers barricaded themselves inside the seminary
and refused to surrender. The building was then set on fire,
but the Christians remained inside praying. A short time later
the flames engulfed them and they were all burned to death.

Next, the cruel Communists rounded up villagers for
interrogation. Some individuals were shot immediately, while
172 others were marched off under armed guard, many of
them stripped to their underwear. This group – which
included three priests, six women, a blind man and a cripple
– had to walk for two weeks. At the end of that time, 60 were
freed; the rest were forced to join the Communist cause or
were executed.

The Communists decided there was little reason to
remain in Xiwanzi and withdrew. Reporters arrived the next
day and found a scene of frightful carnage. In a single day the
dead totalled 250. Francis LeGrand wrote,

> Every family lamented lost members – no one knew whether
> they were dead or among the prisoners. The survivors examined
> the corpses one by one in the fields, in the wastes, in the moun-
> tains, and at the morgue we had set up to facilitate this lugubri-
> ous rummage. Cartfuls of corpses were brought in – dreadful
> remains in the most tortured positions, the trunks shrivelled,
> the frozen hands sticking out as stiff as wood. Many of the hun-
> dred bodies found that first day were naked. Some of them had
> ropes still binding the bayoneted torsos. Fifty of the victims had
> been buried alive. Others had bullet holes in their heads. Many
> of them bore marks to show they had been beaten, tortured and
> defiled.

The Christians still refused to abandon their faith, and worship services were soon held again, where the survivors poured out their grief before God. As if the villagers had not suffered enough, Xiwanzi was recaptured by the Communists in 1948 and again pillaged and persecuted. Few communities have endured as much horrific and barbaric persecution as the small village of Xiwanzi. As a testament to their faithfulness and to the grace of God, today a Christian community remains there. The darkness was not able to snuff out the light of God.

Chifeng

As the Communists gained control of the towns and villages of Inner Mongolia they launched a programme of systematic destruction and murder. Catholic missionaries had laboured in Inner Mongolia for centuries and their work was already well established in several key areas. Some of the worst carnage took place at Chifeng in the southern part of Inner Mongolia.

In October 1946 two Chinese priests, Paul Xing and Paul Liu, were murdered after being falsely accused of being spies. They were taken out of the prison where they had been mercilessly tortured and were shot on the side of the road. Their remains were left for vultures to devour.

One prominent Catholic, Zhang Yunsing, was hung up by his thumbs in an attempt to induce him to bear false witness against one of the priests. Another man, Zhang Ruixiang, had his face and body smeared with gasoline and was set on fire. He still refused to compromise.

Frightened by the events in Chifeng, a group of two priests, 20 nuns and dozens of other Catholics decided to flee the area on foot, but the severe winter temperatures soon took their toll. After travelling for nine days and nights, three of the children died from exposure to the elements.

In 1947 Paul Shi Guangjiu was stripped to his waist by the prison wardens. A large man sat on the priest's chest while others secured a rope to his feet. He was dragged over rough paths for two hours. Shi was finally put out of his misery with a bullet to the head.

Joseph Zhang was arrested and treated cruelly by his persecutors, who offered him an office job with the Communist Party if he would denounce his faith. Despite this chance to gain his freedom, Zhang refused to do so. He consequently was made to stand motionless for days and nights, and then to sit over a coil of burning cord until his skin blackened and cracked. He finally had a rope tied around his ankles and was dragged over rocky ground until he died.

Francis Zhu Yunxin, the Catholic priest of Guandi village near Chifeng, was arrested and dragged behind a horse for more than twelve hours in a failed attempt to make him deny Christ. Somehow he survived the ordeal, but was later slaughtered by the merciless Communists. Camille Xia, a 70-year-old priest, was tied to a mule and dragged around the fields in a similar manner. Witnesses said his flesh was torn and his body covered with blood by the end of the ordeal. A priest named Ho was tortured for refusing to join the Communist army. Just before he was shot dead he told his tormentors, "You are loyal to revolution, I to religion; I cannot give up my loyalty for yours."

Still the attacks continued. John Ren was dragged to death through the crowded streets as hundreds of Christians were forced to watch the spectacle. Up to his last breath Ren continued to pray for his persecutors. Joseph Liang was thrown into prison for the "crime of celibacy". His church was turned into a granary and the other mission quarters were used as barracks for the Communist soldiers. Liang was hung

mmunity to such an extent that people
om the forests around the monastery.
ar II, Japanese troops came to
e monks' grain and other food. Later
ame into the area they accused the
helped the Japanese by providing
nists' hatred for the Catholics was
e troops drew near, Communist
o give the impression the shots
eir agents also painted abusive
e monastery walls, bringing the
the monks.
equence of events that led to
astery began. On 1 July two
cows near the monastery
ppressors of the people". A
1,000 people from 30 vil-
at the "People's Court",
ere shouted at the star-
er belongings of the
accused the monks of
es" who were trucked
ry's cows and goats
e ten tons of grain
ere stolen to feed
sly the local com-
e monks, which
weighty as the

s bare of any
from books
lumes were
sants. The
any of the

from a beam almost daily for ten months and beaten until the
bones of his body stuck through his flesh. When he was
instructed to deny his faith he responded, "Even if you cut off
my head, I shall always be a Christian!" He was finally beaten
to death. In another location 300 believers who refused to
denounce their priest were locked in prison, where twelve of
them died of cold and hunger.

Leonides Bruns

On 4 October 1947, the Dutch Fransiscan priest Leonides
Bruns celebrated a feast with his fellow missionaries at
Jiangzhou in northeast China. He returned to his own mission
unaware that the Communists had already made plans to kill
him. The Dutchman was arrested and charged with being a
spy. Bruns objected, declaring he had never violated the laws
of China or his home country. The judges were unimpressed,
and had him bound and incarcerated in a small cell next to
the courtroom inside Hengshui Prison. Bruns could hear all
the court proceedings through the flimsy walls, and heard his
own death sentence announced.

From the time he was a boy back in his native
Netherlands, Leonides Bruns had put his faith in Christ and
his hope in eternal life. The news of his impending death did
not cause him any visible anxiety. The first thing he did was
to call for the boy who brought his breakfast. He ate heartily,
showing no fear. At noon Bruns' hands and feet were bound
and he was taken to the marketplace in the centre of
Hengshui. A large crowd watched as the missionary was raised
up onto a special platform. Bruns was urged to confess his
"crimes against the people". When he failed to do so, guards
beat him and stripped him nearly naked. Bruns then started
to remove his socks and shoes. The judges told him it wasn't
necessary, but the missionary replied, "I want to take them

off. I want to die as poor as my Lord upon the cross." The people near the platform were invited to beat the kneeling priest with sticks. Bruns remained in a posture of prayer until the blows forced him to collapse. He cried out, "My Lord, quickly, quickly, take my soul to you!"

The Communists assumed that the priest was dead and went on to execute six other prisoners. When it was discovered that Bruns was still breathing, he was stabbed with a bayonet and his heart was hacked out of his body and his head cut off.

Leonides Bruns went to heaven at the age of 35.

CHAPTER 44

The Cistercian
Church. Also
1098 when
remote lo
monaster
silence,
ground
the n
learr

monks, arguing that the villagers didn't wear glasses, so why should the monks?

During the looting the Trappist brothers knelt in silent prayer for their oppressors. One by one they were called into the church to stand trial, where guards armed with clubs stood by to beat them into "confessing". A young Catholic woman, Maria Chang, displayed remarkable courage and boldness. She told the judges the truth – that the monks had come to China only to share Christ and to help the poor. The beating she received was so severe that many thought she had died. Maria recovered, but was placed under arrest and held at Yangjiaping for months. The judges were embarrassed by her courage, and determined not to let anyone else make a speech to prevent a similar occurrence. The judges moved straight to announcing the verdicts, calling out names of monks and asking the mob for a decision. One by one the people shouted, "Death!" By the end of the farcical proceedings, most of the monks had been sentenced to death. They were ordered to leave the monastery with their hands tied behind their backs.

Most of the Trappist martyrs died during an exhausting death march when they were used as pack animals to move supplies from the monastery to an army battalion 100 miles (162 kilometres) away. The monks were forced to march over extreme terrain day and night. After returning to the monastery, three men, including 82-year-old priest Bruno Fou, died from the sheer physical exhaustion and mental strain of their ordeal. Fou had been due to celebrate 50 years as a priest on the very day he died. The celebrations would certainly have exceeded all his expectations as he was welcomed to heaven by Jesus, whom he had loved and served for so many years.

The monks who survived soon came to envy those who had died. Wire was tightly bound around their wrists. It remained there for months, so that when they ate they were forced to lap up the food from the ground like animals. Clement Gao, aged

75, dropped dead from exhaustion, while Philip Wang Liu, also in his seventies, fell in the doorway after reaching his beloved monastery and never recovered. For those who had survived the initial ordeal, only a short recuperation was allowed before they were ordered to do another march on the night of 28 August. Along the way they were made to sleep in pig pens. To entertain their sadistic captors, daily "trials" were held, where the "accused" were beaten for the soldiers' pleasure.

William Camborieu   Stephen Maury

On the night of 6 September 1947, as the group approached Ma Lai village, one of the younger monks carrying the 69-year-old Frenchman William Camborieu stumbled and fell on the mountain trail. The frail priest's head was cut open on a jagged rock and he bled to death. Camborieu had already endured imprisonment at the hands of the Japanese a few years earlier. After his release he could easily have returned to the comfort of his native France, but he chose to remain in Yangjiaping because of his love for China and his desire that its people might know Christ.

When the march reached the village of Dengjiayou, Albert L'Heureux felt that he had reached the end of his life. The Canadian-born priest signalled this to the other prisoners with the sign language Trappists use to communicate during the times they observe a vow of silence. That night L'Heureux passed away. His body had simply expired from the toll of inhumane torture and stress. The next morning a young soldier said, "He died very peacefully. He looked like that man on the figure-ten frame in your church." In Chinese writing, the figure ten is a cross.

Because of the incredibly filthy conditions, the stay at Dengjiayou achieved nothing but to further break down the physical and mental health of the prisoners. Those who had their hands unbound tried to help their shackled brothers remove lice and other vermin from their unwashed bodies. It was later reported that several of the monks whose hands were bound were literally eaten to death by the vermin which afflicted them.

One priest, Maurus Bougon, tried to escape from the Communists during the death march. They soon recaptured him and cut off both his feet as punishment, and later executed him to put him out of his misery. A 60-year-old French priest, Stephen Maury, had invested many years of his life in China. Unable to bear the load of the march, he was carried into Dengjiayou by four of his brethren on 8 September. As soon as they entered the village, Maury breathed his last and passed into the presence of God. Two days later Marcus Li Chang, a 62-year-old monk from Hebei Province, also surrendered his life as a result of the intense strain. During one agonizing week five more Chinese believers died. Their bodies were placed in shallow graves. Hungry dogs and wolves dug up and ate the corpses. Body parts were left strewn about the village. To the Trappists, funeral rituals are extremely elaborate and death is considered a monumental event to be cherished and honoured. To have the limbs of their beloved colleagues devoured by beasts was almost too much for the survivors to bear. More sorrow was added to the monks when they were told the Yangjiaping monastery had been destroyed. Three of the believers were allowed to return to see for themselves. The huge stone walls remained standing, but everything inside the monastery had been reduced to rubble.

The 62-year-old prior of Yangjiaping, Anthony Fan, suddenly died on 13 October. Five days later the 70-year-old Augustine Faure, who was the last remaining foreign missionary, also perished. The fact that the health of these two men had appeared to be improving led the others to suspect they were poisoned.

Before the end of 1947 eleven more Trappist monks had perished. The Communists believed Seraphim Shu was the future leader of the monastery, so he was tried and beaten more than 20 times. By the end, his thumbs were wired together behind his back, and his big toes were wired together. He could only kneel or lie on his side. On 5 February 1948, Seraphim and Chrysostom Zhang were taken out and laid on a flat stone. A large rock was then smashed against their heads, causing them to explode. Four other brothers were shot dead, including Damian Hang whose hands had been wired behind his back since July the previous year. His feet had been crippled from an earlier frostbite, and by the end he was only able to crawl.

In all, 33 of the 75 Trappists at Yangjiaping were martyred for their faith in Christ. The monks who survived the carnage realized the new China was no place for them. In addition to their physical ailments they suffered major psychological scars which most of them carried to their graves. A small group of survivors was led to the safe environment of Hong Kong by Paulinius Lee. They built a Trappist monastery on Lantau Island which continues to function to this day.

Anthony Fan   Augustine Faure

Aelred Drost

CHAPTER 45

BILL WALLACE

Bill Wallace is considered one of the greatest martyrs of America's largest Protestant denomination – the Southern Baptists. Few would have believed this would be the case when he was born in Knoxville, Tennessee, in 1908. The son of a doctor, Bill's main interest was fixing cars until the age of 17, when he dramatically heard God's call to become a medical missionary while working in his father's garage. The teenager answered "Yes" to God, and recorded his commitment on the inside cover of his Bible.

After graduating from medical college in 1935, Wallace was appointed to join the Baptist-run Stout Memorial Hospital in the south China province of Guangxi. He arrived exactly ten years after receiving his calling to missionary work. His colleagues in Wuzhou, who for years had been praying that God would send a surgeon to their midst, were immediately impressed by the young man's fervency and godliness. Wallace rebuffed all marriage prospects. One girl who had hoped for his affection finally gave up, saying, "Marriage to Bill would be bigamy. He's married to his work."

For more than fifteen years Bill Wallace remained in Wuzhou, doing good to others and sharing the aroma of Christ wherever he went. No sacrifice was too great for him to make, and once he was even found tending patients as Japanese bombs fell all around the hospital. The Catholic missionaries working in Wuzhou became close friends of Wallace. They

Bill Wallace

could not fail to be impressed by the godliness and selfless-ness of his life. One wrote,

> Dr. Wallace was famed for his surgery and medical work, but most of all for his kindness and devotion to the sick and poor. His whole life was medicine and charity. He would be called a strange fellow by the hustlers, bustlers and seekers of wealth who people the world today. They would call him stupid and impractical, for when people asked him the charge for services he would usually answer, "Forget about it." His cancelling of charges drove the treasurer's staff to despair, for he was all charity; a sort of mystic walking on clouds and looking for the stars.

Nothing could seemingly move Wallace from his calling in Christ. When bandits raided Wuzhou the other missionaries fled, but Bill Wallace remained behind and continued treating the sick. An American ship anchored in the river to rescue the missionary, but Wallace refused to board. When an officer from the ship came on shore to warn Wallace that his safety could not be guaranteed unless he boarded immediately, the intrepid doctor replied, "Tell your captain that he was not responsible for my coming here in the first place and he does not need to be responsible for my staying here." When heavy Japanese bombing raids regularly threatened to destroy the city, Wallace transferred his staff, patients and equipment onto a barge. Whenever air raid sirens sounded, he would instruct the tugboat captain to pull the floating hospital under the shelter of one of the many large caves located along the riverbank.

As Christmas of 1950 approached, Wallace's mind wandered to the memories of wonderful times he had had as a young man back in Tennessee, the excitement of opening presents and the enticing aromas of the Christmas feast lovingly prepared by his mother. Now he was in Wuzhou, faraway China, attending to the needs of the sick and dying.

Wallace was often so busy in the work that he didn't have time to contemplate what others were whispering. At the time rumours abounded that the Communists would not tolerate the Christian hospital in the midst of their newly won territory. China angrily declared war on the entire United Nations during the Korean War, and the United States was intensely hated. It seems everybody knew that Bill Wallace was in great peril except the man himself. Perhaps he believed he had won some favour with the Communists as a result of treating many of their wounded soldiers during the war against Japan.

On the night of 18 December 1950 Wallace was so exhausted after a full day's work at the hospital that he slumped into bed after a snack of six slices of buttered bread and a glass of milk. At three o'clock the next morning a squad of a dozen young Communist soldiers arrived at the gates of Stout Memorial Hospital, intent on arresting the American doctor, whom they called "President Truman's chief spy in Wuzhou". The soldiers forced Wallace into the main part of hospital, where the Chinese staff had gathered. The officer in charge shouted, "We know this is a den of spies! The People's Republic is aware that some of you are counter-revolutionaries. This will not be tolerated. You have been found out; you will no longer be able to carry on your clandestine activities."

The staff looked on aghast, but Wallace spoke in a measured tone, "We are what we seem to be. We are doctors and nurses and hospital staff engaged in healing the suffering and sick in the name of Jesus Christ. We are here for no other reason." Unimpressed, the soldiers started a search of Wallace's room, emerging triumphantly a few minutes later with a brown package containing a small pistol, which they claimed to have found under the missionary's bed. "That is not my gun. I do not own a gun, and I do not know where it came from," Wallace protested.

For weeks Wallace was held in solitary confinement as the Communists gathered "evidence" that he was a spy. Neither the American Consulate nor the Southern Baptist Foreign Mission Board could do anything to help him, and permission to visit the prisoner was denied. The hospital staff, directionless without their leader, tried to secure his release. Wallace told them, "Go on and take care of the hospital. I am ready to give my life if necessary." One night a few weeks after his arrest a public meeting was called at the Wuzhou town hall where charges of espionage were levelled at the missionary. Many believed that the Communists' intense hatred of Bill Wallace stemmed from jealousy. The people loved and respected him, and no fault could be found in his character.

Wallace was presented with a typed statement listing his name, age, length of service in China and other facts. He signed it, only to discover later that a sentence was added into a blank space on the statement saying he was a secret serviceman sent to China by the US government. Wallace was subjected to long and gruelling brainwashing sessions, with his hands tied painfully behind his back. He was a sensitive and gentle man, and the non-stop filthy accusations and intense degradation wore his mind and emotions down. Two Catholic missionaries in the same prison said that Wallace was "shaken and strained" by the interrogations. One of them managed to ask Wallace how he was holding out. He grinned weakly, and said, "All right. Trusting in the Lord."

Only those who have been subjected to a Communist brainwashing can fully understand the ordeal that Bill Wallace went through. The accusations and methods of application come from a spiritual intensity born of Satan. Wallace's biographer explained,

The battle was not whether he could out-argue his accusers. He was not even equipped to begin. It was not a battle of physical endurance, though that soon became involved. It was a battle for sanity. From his cell in the night, Bill sometimes cried out in agony after the battle was over. Delirium, crying, and blank periods came, but he fought on – clinging to his faith.

The aim of the psychological torture seems to have been to break Wallace so that he made a full "confession" of his "crimes". On the night of 10 February 1951, the guards came to the missionary's cell and jabbed him with long poles until he fell unconscious. This final attack was the "straw that broke the camel's back". His spirit quietly slipped from his torn body and went to be with the One he had so faithfully and unstintingly served. Bill Wallace was 43 years old.

The next morning the guards raced to the cell of the two Catholic missionaries, claiming Wallace had hanged himself during the night. The Catholics saw his lifeless corpse suspended by a strip of sheet that had been strung from a beam in the cell. The guards tried to get the priests to sign a statement that Wallace had committed suicide, but they refused to. It was clear to them that the façade was a staged show. The prison notified the hospital staff to come and take the doctor's body. A nurse said, "The facial characteristics of hanging were missing – bulging eyes, discoloured face, swollen tongue. Instead, the upper torso was horribly bruised. The Communists had tried to cover up one botch with another." The body was taken to the Believers' Cemetery overlooking the West River. Communist soldiers watched as Wallace was laid to rest in an unmarked grave. Later, the local Christians secretly erected a monument over the grave with the simple inscription: "Dr. William L. Wallace – 'For Me to Live is Christ'".

After news of Wallace's death reached America numerous tributes were offered to the martyred doctor. M. Theron

Rankin, the head of the Southern Baptist mission at the time, wrote, "The irrefutable quality of Dr. Wallace's love made it imperative that the Communists get rid of him. His life refuted everything the Communists said. They have tried to get rid of the witness of Bill's life. But that is precisely where they will fail. Bill Wallace's witness of God's love in Christ has been made immortal."

Everley Hayes, a missionary nurse who had worked with Wallace for years, said, "Many think of martyrs as those long-faced people. But I knew a Dr Wallace who was very much interested in everything around him. He was a martyr not because he died in service but because he so identified with the Chinese that they considered him one of them. And they loved him."

Perhaps one friend summed up Bill Wallace's life the best: "The Chinese had heard sermons before, but in Bill Wallace they began to see one, and that made the difference."

CHAPTER 46

MARTYRS AMONG
THE A-HMAO

Hundreds of A-Hmao Christians meeting on a hillside in 1948

The Miao ethnic minority group straddles the mountainous areas in southwest China. Consisting of dozens of different subgroups with their own languages and dialects, the Miao were despised and oppressed for centuries by the Chinese and other tribes.

When Samuel Pollard and other missionaries first brought the liberating message of the gospel to the A-Hmao (also known as the "Big Flowery Miao") subgroup in 1904, thousands of the poor, downtrodden tribespeople eagerly embraced the gospel. The 1917 translation of the New Testament into A-Hmao was a source of great uplift. Possessing a written script for the first time in their history, people found their worth in Christ and his Word. By the time the missionaries were expelled from China in 1950 the A-Hmao church numbered more than 80,000 Christians.

After the removal of the missionaries the A-Hmao were left to lead the church by themselves. Zhu Huanzheng was given the administrative leadership of the believers at Zhaotong in northeast Yunnan Province. A Chinese believer, Zhu Shuiguang, was also involved with the work. In 1951 they were both arrested, along with an evangelist named John Li, when the Communists captured Zhaotong. The three Christians were tortured so inhumanely that they could not stand the diabolical treatment. They all died.

In 1954 the government concocted a sinister plan to destroy the faith of the A-Hmao at Sapushan by selecting 16 young church leaders and sending them to work in 16 different locations. The authorities believed that by separating them from their Christian environment the youngsters would soon reject their faith. They were wrong. Not only did each of the 16 believers continue to follow Christ, they also influenced their workmates and in several locations small Christian fellowships started where there had previously been no knowledge of the gospel.

The Little Flock of Narrow Gate

The A-Hmao Christians living in Wuding County in northern Yunnan Province experienced intense persecution throughout the 1970s. The most barbaric treatment was meted out to the inhabitants of Xiaoshiqiao village, located on a mountaintop near Wuding town.

In the late 1960s Xiaoshiqiao (which means "Little Stone Bridge") consisted of just seven Christian households totalling about 60 people. These Christians were zealous in their faith but also model law-abiding citizens. This wasn't good enough

A-Hmao Christians from Wuding County

for the Communist authorities, and a systematic plan was launched to obliterate them. In 1969 officials came to the village and asked the family leaders whom they were loyal to. They replied, "On earth, we rely on Chairman Mao, but spiritually, we give our allegiance to God." This answer was deemed unacceptable and persecution commenced. The believers were told, "The land belongs to Mao; you cannot till it. The cattle belong to Mao; you cannot pasture them. Every blade of grass belongs to Mao." All the Christians in the village were condemned as "counter-revolutionaries". The government cut off their monthly salt rations and clothing coupons, and the village leader was cruelly tortured. Their land was confiscated and given to the people of neighbouring villages.

Now cast aside by their country, the Christians of Xiaoshiqiao tried to make ends meet. They roamed the forests eating wild herbs and fruit. Some dwelt in isolated caves. Many of them died, especially the young children and elderly who were not able to endure the hardship. All of these difficulties could not shake the Christians' resolve. They declared,

> Many years of torment have made us disillusioned with the mortal world. We are now striving for sustenance from the Scripture. We do not blame the cadres who inflicted those

sufferings on us. What was said in the Scripture has all come true. Genuine Christians are bound to bear intense sufferings. It goes without saying that the gate of heaven is very narrow indeed. In the past we believed it with some reservation. Now, we have convincing evidence to believe it is true.

Because of all their troubles, the Christians called their church "The Little Flock of Narrow Gate", seeing themselves as those who were willing to pass through the narrow gate to enter heaven. In 1978 an order was issued from Beijing to "unmask the counter-revolutionaries hiding under the cloak of religion". A fresh wave of attacks against the Little Flock of Narrow Gate was launched. The People's Liberation Army surrounded the harmless community, reacting as if they were facing a foreign army. Machine guns were positioned around the village, and loudspeakers blasted out messages ordering the Christians to abandon their faith and surrender. When this failed, more than 200 soldiers rushed up the mountain. They bound the hands and feet of adult villagers, put a wooden pole through them, and carried them down the mountain in the same way pigs are transported to market. Everyone arrested was imprisoned for two months and subjected to brutal torture. The village leader was imprisoned for seven years.

The Christians had passed from the place of selfish living to a state of wanting only to please God. Consequently, their witness was blessed in a mighty way and people repented and believed in Jesus Christ all over the county. By 1981, 34 of the 62 villages in Wuding had joined the Little Flock of Narrow Gate, totalling over 3,000 Christians. In neighbouring Luquan County the number of believers connected to this movement numbered 1,043. One of the leaders in Wuding was a Han Chinese named Li Zicheng. At the height of persecution he issued a lengthy statement of defiance to the Chinese government. After detailing all the persecutions he and his family had been forced to endure, Li concluded with these words:

> What you, the government, intend to do is your own decision. I firmly believe that Jesus will eventually remedy all the injustice imposed. What I have just said, though it might be in a fit of righteous anger, came from my deep conviction. I have nothing to fear. If you want to punish me again, go ahead, the sooner the better. You can even arrest me now. More arrests would surely accelerate the second coming of Jesus.

The worst attack against the A-Hmao Christians in southwest China came during a meeting on 28 July 1974, when many A-Hmao believers were massacred by Chinese troops as they secretly met for prayer in a cave at Xinglongchang. The church leaders had boldly and defiantly told the government:

> The more you forbid Christianity, the more we will cling to the church. If you confiscate our churches, we will worship in caves. If you announce the extermination of the church, we will develop even more secret meetings. If you attack ordained pastors, we will use even more independent house church preachers instead. If you take action against us on Sundays, we will multiply our meetings to every day of the week and into the night.

The persecution was designed to destroy the A-Hmao church, but instead it caused a doubling of the number of Christians in a short space of time.

Wang Zhiming

The village of Sapushan is located just two kilometres from the town of Wuding in northern Yunnan Province. Arthur

Nicholls from Australia first brought the gospel to Sapushan in 1908. Other missionaries joined him and Sapushan was chosen as the headquarters for Christian outreach among the Miao in the whole of Yunnan Province.

After all foreign missionaries were expelled in 1952, Wang Zhiming was elected president of the work at Sapushan. Instead of trying to destroy Wang by force, the government attempted to change him. By 1955 it was impossible for him to continue in the ministry and he was sent to Beijing where he met Mao Zedong and was exposed to Communist ideals in the hope that he would denounce his faith and join the Party. Wang, however, was a slave of Jesus Christ and wanted nothing more than to see God's kingdom come among all people. He continued to preach the gospel boldly, increasingly becoming an irritation to the authorities. In 1969 he was condemned as a counter-revolutionary and sent to prison after being opposed by Elder Long, a backslidden pastor who gave in to government pressure and declared himself an atheist.

For the next four years little was heard of Wang Zhiming's whereabouts until a four-day long "open trial" was held just after Christmas 1973. More than 10,000 spectators were forced to attend the meeting at the Wuding sports stadium. A death sentence was announced and Wang was immediately shot dead. The dire spectacle produced the opposite result of that intended. The Christians did not manifest the slightest fear. Moments after the cruel murder was committed a group of women, disregarding the consequences, rushed to the grandstand where Elder Long was sitting together with the Public Security officers. The women cried out indignantly at Long, "Dire Satan, you previously preached the gospel. Now you are committing a heinous crime in opposition to it. Dare you come down?" The courageous protest threw the whole stadium into turmoil. Following Wang's martyrdom, 34 church leaders were arrested and sent to prison labour camps.

In 1980 the government decided they had made a mistake in killing Wang Zhiming and they "rehabilitated" him. A sum of 1,300 Yuan (about US$250) was paid to his family as compensation. A statue of Wang now stands in the western façade of London's Westminster Abbey, one of ten statues honouring 20th-century martyrs.

The systematic plan to obliterate the A-Hmao church in southwest China backfired on the Communists. Today there are at least 200,000 Christians among the A-Hmao. They remain vibrant and enthusiastic followers of Christ.

CHAPTER 47

1954 TO 1982 –
BEHIND THE IRON
CURTAIN

The door closes

Catholic nuns boarding a ship after being expelled from China in the early 1950s

At the start of 1954, just 267 Catholic missionaries remained in China, 71 of whom were in Communist prisons. A total of 5,113 had been expelled in the previous four years. With the foreigners out of the way, the Communists continued their relentless pursuit of Chinese believers. The carnage was so severe that even unbelievers felt compelled to protest. During one public trial of an innocent priest, a villager stood up and boldly proclaimed, "I am poor and childless, and therefore have no fear of being killed or dispossessed. In the name of the whole population I protest against the injustice which we are being made to commit against our will. We have nothing against the church and no one has the right to plunder it. One day the King of Heaven will see that justice is done."

The leader of a well-known Christian family, a man respected for his generosity and service to the community, was tied to a mule and dragged across a field. As he lay there bleeding, at the point of death, he cried out: "My God, I thank you for having allowed me to be ill-treated as Jesus Christ was, and for his sake!"

During the 1950s thousands of Chinese Christians were sent to prison labour camps. Many died, while some survived the horrors and were released more than 20 years later. The heartache for many Christian families was overwhelming, as the authorities rarely notified the prisoners' families of their whereabouts. When the political situation in China finally started to thaw in the early 1980s hundreds of families were notified that their loved ones had perished in prison many years earlier.

By the late 1950s a real sense of doom settled upon many Christians who loved the church in China. Mao was closing China's doors to the outside world, and news about the fate of believers became increasingly scarce. Concerns were expressed as to whether Christianity would survive the onslaught it was being brutally subjected to. One report stated, "The future of the Church in China rests entirely in Chinese hands, and in the hands of God. Whether the Church will survive in that vast land is known only to God. Humanly speaking it is a disastrous state of affairs."

Henan Province was chosen as one of three experimental zones in an anti-religion drive by the extreme elements of the Communist Party, along with Zhejiang and Inner Mongolia. The ultimate aim was to eliminate Christianity once and for all, and to consign it to a curiosity section of a museum. As a result, cruel and horrific persecution was displayed by local officials. Brother Yun, in his bestselling book *The Heavenly Man*, detailed some of the events that unfolded in his hometown in southern Henan Province:

> In my home area of Nanyang believers were crucified on the walls of their churches for not denying Christ. Others were chained to vehicles and horses and dragged to their death. One pastor was bound and attached to a long rope. The authorities, enraged that the man of God would not deny his faith, used a makeshift crane to lift him high into the air. Before hundreds of witnesses, who had come to falsely accuse him of being a "counter revolutionary," the pastor was asked one last time by his persecutors if he would recant. He shouted back, "No! I will never deny the Lord who saved me!" The rope was released and the pastor crashed to the ground below. Upon inspection, the tormentors discovered the pastor was not fully dead, so they raised him up into the air for a second time, dropping the rope to finish him off for good. In this life the pastor was dead, but he lives on in heaven with the reward of one who was faithful to the end.

All across China the Communists launched a systematic plan to destroy Christianity. In Wenzhou City, 49 leading pastors were arrested and each sentenced to 20 years or more in prison labour camps near the Russian border, where winter temperatures regularly plummet to minus 30° C (–22° F). Forty-eight of the pastors died before their sentences were completed. Just one returned home alive. Today, Wenzhou has the highest number of believers of any city in China.

In northeast China a Christian leader protested against the Communists' indiscriminate killing. He was promptly arrested and dragged into court, accused of numerous "crimes against the people". The judges ordered the onlookers to march past the pastor and strike him with a club until he was beaten to death. The people refused, however, declaring "He's a good man!" The judges changed their tactics, offering to release the pastor if he would denounce Jesus. "Which do you choose – Jesus Christ or Communism?" they demanded. "Jesus! Jesus! Jesus!" he shouted back. The pastor was dragged down to the riverbank for execution. Along the way he sang "Jesus loves me" and the 23rd Psalm. A crowd of onlookers followed. When they arrived at the river he asked permission to pray. He knelt down, committing his spirit into the care of the Lord Jesus Christ. Then, as he stood up, he was shot in the back. He fell backwards, as if he was falling into the arms of Jesus.

Family or faith

The 1950s saw the family structure in China torn asunder for the first time in history, as the Communists systematically separated families. Husbands were taken from wives, and parents from children. One house church pastor named Fang Cheng was dragged into the local prison and ordered to recite the Ten Commandments. When he reached "Honour your father and mother ..." the guards interrupted him, and showed Fang Cheng his emaciated mother chained up in the corner of the cell. She had been arrested some months before, but Fang Cheng could hardly recognize her. Her hair had turned white and her body was covered with welts and bruises. The guards told Fang Cheng that he had a chance to obey his religion. If he would tell them the names of the other church leaders his mother would be released and they could be reunited at home that very day. Fang Cheng looked at his mother and asked, "What shall I do?" With a weak voice she replied, "I have taught you from childhood to love Christ and his holy church. Don't mind my suffering. Seek to remain faithful to the

Saviour and his little brothers. If you betray, you are no more my son." He never saw her again.

In the late 1950s many pastors and evangelists were slaughtered in Shanxi – the province that will always be remembered for the Boxer bloodbath in 1900. At one location a preacher was tortured by the Communists, then told he could go if he promised not to preach again. "No, I cannot do that," he replied. "I cannot obey you." The infuriated official shouted, "Then you must die, you miserable lout!" "I am not the one who is poor and miserable," the preacher replied, and he began preaching. A few moments later a shot rang out and the faithful disciple was dead.

Lepers in China were treated with abhorrence and often put to death to prevent them from having contact with other people. In some locations they were forced into the wilderness for the rest of their lives, despised and hated by all who came across them. In 1886 an Anglican missionary-doctor, E. G. Horder, established the Pu Ren Hospital at Beihai in southern Guangxi. Horder intended to operate a normal medical clinic in Beihai, but he soon found there were a large number of lepers in the area and so built a leprosarium next to the hospital. It continued to operate despite the objections of many locals. By 1949 the leprosarium had 299 inpatients. They were not only treated physically, but also taught the gospel of Jesus Christ. Most of them believed and were baptized. They also had their own church and pastor. In 1952 the hospital and leprosarium were taken over by the government. The church was occupied, and the pastor died in prison. Only 43 of the Christian lepers survived this baptism of blood and fire.

By the 1960s the Communists' attempt to obliterate Christianity from China moved into a new stage. Few visible signs of religion remained. Christians were ridiculed and all expressions of faith mocked as "superstition". Those believers who continued to follow Christ were forced to do so privately.

The church went "underground". News about the fate of Christian leaders dried up as China became increasingly xenophobic.

A 25-year-old Catholic man named Liu was working in the telephone exchange in Inner Mongolia. Although he was employed by the government, Liu never missed church on Sunday. Soon the authorities arrested him and threw him into prison. He was offered freedom if he would agree to accuse the priests of crimes against the Chinese people and promise not to go to the church again. He refused. After a month in prison without compromising his faith, the Communists became infuriated by Liu's stubbornness and sentenced him to death, with a two-year suspended sentence offered if Liu should change his stance and agree to incriminate other believers. This was a plan to pressurize the young Christian into saving his own skin by falsely accusing others. Liu was distraught at the death sentence as he was engaged to be married in two months' time, and had often prayed that God would give him a long and productive life. He spoke to a priest who was incarcerated in the same facility, sharing his personal agony at the options before him: remain steadfast and be killed, or sign a prepared statement and enjoy immediate freedom and marriage to the girl he loved. The priest simply told him, "You know what you are allowed to say. There must be no false accusations. There is nothing to fear from those who can only kill the body, but cannot touch the soul." Several days later Liu was executed. He had made his decision.

The Cultural Revolution

The Cultural Revolution of 1966–76 saw new heights of barbaric suppression for Christians in China. Mao's Red Guards wreaked havoc throughout the nation. Bibles were scarce, and to all outward appearances the church of Jesus Christ had been obliterated. Thousands of former church leaders and laypeople were imprisoned for their faith, and hundreds perished in silence and isolation. China shut itself off from the rest of the world during these dark years, so few reports emerged to the outside world.

In 1969 the Cultural Revolution was in full swing throughout China and thousands of Christians were in prison labour camps. A young girl was bound hand and foot and made to kneel in the centre of a circle of people who were commanded to stone her or be shot. Several Christians refused to participate and were immediately executed. The girl died under a hail of stones – her face shining like Stephen's when he was stoned. Later, one of those who threw the stones broke down and received Christ as Lord.

In the same prison a young man was hung on a cross for six days until he died. For the whole time he prayed out loud that his persecutors might repent and believe in Jesus Christ. Five Christian students were forced to dig five deep holes in the ground. Other prisoners were instructed to throw the five into the holes and cover them with dirt. As they were buried alive they worshipped God.

One of the most tragic martyrdoms in Chinese history is that of two girls, Jiu Jinxiu and He Xiuzi, in Jiangxi Province. The two young Christians were arrested in 1977 and sentenced to death because of their faith. Before they were taken out for execution, the duo prepared themselves to submit to death without renouncing their faith.

The executioner appeared with a revolver in his hand and slowly walked towards the bound girls, who had been ordered to stand against a wall. As he came nearer the girls were shocked and horrified to see that it was their own pastor! The Communists had tortured him and caused him to turn against his own flock in exchange for saving his own life. The girls trembled at the scene – not for their own fate, but for the soul of their beloved pastor. Jiu and He whispered to each other, then bowed respectfully before their pastor and said, "Before you shoot us, we wish to thank you heartily for what you have meant to us. You baptized us, you taught us the ways of eternal life, you gave us holy communion with the same hand in which you now hold the gun. You also taught us that Christians are sometimes weak and commit terrible sins, but they can be forgiven again. When you regret what you are about to do to us, do not despair like Judas, but repent like Peter. God bless you, and remember that our last thought was not one of indignation against your failure. May God reward you for all the good you have done to us. We die with gratitude."

The two girls bowed their heads, and two loud shots rang out. The pastor's heart had been hardened and his conscience seared. Instead of the release promised to the pastor, as soon as the bodies of the two girls had fallen to the ground, the guards put him against the wall and shot him.

Mao died and the Cultural Revolution ended in 1976. The 1980s promised a time of relative freedom for Christians in China. Although the three decades since have seen many changes and more liberal religious policies, Christians who refuse to align themselves with the wishes of the Communist authorities have soon found the full force of brutal persecution waiting just around the corner. Throughout the 1970s, '80s and '90s numerous Christians died in prison labour camps throughout China. Most of their names have never been documented on earth, but they have surely been recorded in heaven.

CHAPTER 48

ZHU YIMING

Kangding was formerly one of the most important monastery towns on the outskirts of Tibet. After the Chinese military invaded Tibet in the 1950s they redrew the maps, allocating vast tracts of land into present-day Yunnan, Sichuan, Gansu and Qinghai provinces. Kangding now finds itself located in western Sichuan Province.

Two of the first Chinese Protestant missionaries to reach out to the Tibetans in this lonely part of the country were John Ding and his wife Zhu Yiming. Ding had received a vision to serve God among the Tibetans in the border regions while studying in Chongqing. One of his teachers was a consecrated young Christian woman named Zhu Yiming. A native of Shandong Province in eastern China, she had completed a university degree in mathematics, and had held teaching positions in several different parts of the country before taking up the appointment in Chongqing.

The vision for the Chinese church to take the gospel back to Jerusalem was moving through the church in Chongqing at the time. The believers saw sharing the gospel among the Tibetans as a key part of the vision, which has been reignited among China's churches in recent years. Ding and Zhu attended "Back to Jerusalem" meetings together and got to know and appreciate one another. The more Ding thought about the call God had placed on his life, the more he felt attracted to his young teacher. Just prior to graduating he finally got up enough courage to talk with her about marriage.

He said, "Perhaps I'm not what you want in a husband. You're more like a Mary while I'd be more like a Martha. I'm a Mr Fix-it, and you are a scholar." After a pause that seemed to last a lifetime, Zhu Yiming told Ding, "Those differences could complement one another." Before long the two disciples of Christ were engaged to be married. Ding talked to Zhu about his call to minister among the Tibetans, and the deprivation and difficulties that would entail. His fiancée responded with the kind of selfless manner that characterized her life: "Well, if you are to be my husband, I'll certainly go where you go. And if that means Tibet, so be it."

The young couple arrived in Kangding and started to work alongside a small team of foreign missionaries who were attempting to establish Christianity in the far-flung town. Zhu Yiming's mother, who was a powerful and effective preacher of the gospel, came to Kangding and, with her daughter and son-in-law, influenced many for the kingdom of God. Yiming's mother passed away in 1958.

When the Communists decided to crack down on the Tibetan areas in the 1950s they did so with an iron fist. Tens of thousands of Buddhist monks were arrested and killed, and anyone suspected of anti-Communist activities was targeted for elimination. Ding and Zhu were imprisoned at Kangding on 29 November 1958. Ding was incarcerated in the men's prison while Zhu was confined in the women's. For almost three years the couple saw nothing of each other, until one day Ding was sent to gather baskets of vegetables from the hillsides surrounding the town. As he edged his way down a hill with a full basket on his back, he was overwhelmed to see his wife coming up the same trail. She too was on a work detail. He thought it was strange that nobody else was near them at the time, which gave them an opportunity to say a few words to each other. John asked his beloved wife, "How have they been treating you?"

"There have been some bad days," she replied. "I got reported for witnessing, and the guards beat me up for that. Some of the women are Christians, and I urge them to be faithful. That got me into trouble. But God has been so good all along. From time to time I heard about you." "I love you, Yiming," John whispered. "I pray for you so much!" "And I pray for you, John, that your faith will not fail." And with that they separated and moved slowly away. John Ding returned to the prison full of joy and hope, not realizing he would never see the face of his beloved wife again.

In 1960, after three years of incarceration at Kangding, John Ding and Zhu Yiming were transferred to a huge prison in Chengdu, the capital of Sichuan Province. John lost all trace of his wife, and for years the only thing that kept him going was the thought that one day he would be reunited with his sweetheart. In 1964 John was told to see the prison warden. The cruel man broke the news of Yiming's death in a heartless manner, saying, "Your old woman was just like you. She wouldn't stop praying, and we had to put her in a struggle session. She wouldn't give in, even when she was beaten. After that she died. Do you want the same? Do you want to die?"

Ding courageously looked straight into the warden's eyes and said, "Everybody dies. If my wife has died, I'm glad for her that she could leave this bitter life. Why didn't you inform me when my wife died?" The warden looked uncomfortable and told Ding, "She died in 1961. Your health was bad at that time, so we didn't tell you. You may go now!"

John Ding was later allowed to collect a box of his wife's meagre possessions. The list of contents was simple: one dress, one pair of shoes and one quilt. On the box a paper stated that Prisoner number 975 had died at 2 p.m. on 17 August 1961. It had taken the heartless authorities three years before they bothered to notify her husband. With tears in his eyes and a broken heart, Ding returned to his cell with the box of relics. He inspected Yiming's dress and found it was worn out at the knees, and her shoes were scuffed on the toes – the marks of a woman who had spent much time on her knees in prayer.

After many more years of hardship and misery, John Ding was finally released in 1981 – after 23 years of imprisonment. He returned to Christian ministry, remarried, and never lost his deep faith in God.

CHAPTER 49   MOLLY O'SULLIVAN

Molly O'Sullivan

One of the most touching accounts of martyrdoms in China is that of a plump, jovial Irish Catholic nun named Molly O'Sullivan. Although she died in September 1966, the story of her martyrdom could not be told for 20 years, for that was the length of time her co-workers in Beijing had been sentenced to prison, and it was feared that any publicity about the case might add to their suffering.

Eamonn O'Sullivan, known to everyone as Molly, was born in Cork, Ireland, in 1907. She was the oldest of ten children – a moderate number in comparison to her father Ned, who came from a family of 18 children. Raised in a devoutly Catholic home, Molly developed a strong desire to serve the Lord and help others. She offered herself for service in China, and was accepted to work at the Sacred Heart school in Beijing.

Although all other missionaries had been expelled from China during the 1950s, the Sacred Heart Catholic School continued to function as a religious institution in the heart of China's capital city right up until August 1966, in a facility housing eight Western nuns and approximately 70 Chinese nuns. Children continued to attend school every day. The foreign sisters were allowed to send and receive letters during these dark years of Communist rule, and were allowed to function relatively normally. Just why Mao Zedong decided to allow this one isolated Christian institution to function in China is unclear. For all these years the convent and school kept a low profile, shunning publicity because they feared it would disrupt their work. Perhaps the government wanted to retain this one school and convent to show it off to the world as "evidence" of religious freedom in China. Whatever their motivation, everything came to a sudden halt on 24 August 1966. The Cultural Revolution was underway and this quirky enclave of Christendom could no longer be tolerated.

A mob of fanatical Red Guards rang the doorbell. Mother

Olga Sofia answered the door and was brushed aside. A huge group of Red Guards came surging up the steps and in through the front door, shouting and screaming and brandishing knives, hatchets, scissors, hammers and whips. They stormed into every room, destroying whatever stood in their way and screaming blasphemies and obscenities.

As the nuns were dragged to the lower floor, they were struck and kicked repeatedly and insulted with vile words. An elderly nun named Mary, who was 76 years old, was attacked with a whip. She was lashed across the face with such force that her eyes were almost knocked out. The other Red Guards shouted at the man with the whip after he did this. It was apparent they had been given permission to insult and rough up the foreign women, but not to kill or seriously injure them. The Chinese nuns, however, were not subject to such protection. As the Red Guards waited for further orders they started to smash all the Catholic images in the convent with hammers and hatchets. They especially seemed to enjoy demolishing crucifixes, stomping on the image of Christ on the cross, knocking the head and arms off with great glee. They didn't understand that the Risen Christ does not live in such objects, nor in buildings made by human hands, but he resides in the spirit of every person who believes in him, in an inner place that no human being can destroy.

A few days later a mock trial was held in front of a large crowd of frenzied people, who bayed for the women's blood. After the nuns' veils and headdresses were torn off and trampled on by their persecutors, they were made to kneel with their foreheads touching the ground until their punishments were announced. The entire crowd, seemingly possessed by the Prince of Hell himself, shouted and screamed, "They are deserving of death!" Unsurprisingly, the eight foreign nuns were pronounced guilty and were labelled "counter-revolutionaries". This was the most serious charge possible in China, and almost always resulted in execution. The court delayed announcing the sentence and sent the eight nuns back to the school, where they were separated from the Chinese believers. Over the next few days the Red Guards never stopped intimidating and insulting the women. One source says,

> They would thrust their faces right into the nuns' faces and shout, "You are a pig" or "You are a dog". They would put a pistol to a nun's head and pull the trigger, roaring with laughter when the gun turned out to be unloaded. One of them said to Mother Olga Sofia, "Do you love Chairman Mao?" She answered, "I am a Christian and I do love Chairman Mao. I love the Chinese people very much. In fact, I love you too." This discomfited the youth and he mumbled, "We don't love you. We hate you."

If there was one nun singled out for special persecution, it was Molly O'Sullivan. At 59 years old she was the youngest of the eight foreign nuns. As the years had rolled by, Molly had gained a lot of weight, yet she never let it dim her personality. She once wrote to her sister Pam, saying, "I am as fat as a fool." She had long ago adopted the motto, "Laugh and grow fat." It made her a natural target for the unsympathetic Red Guards. She was kicked and punched more than the other women, the guards perhaps thinking her larger frame would handle it easier than the others. "Fat Pig" became the normal way of addressing her. "Fat Pig, Fat Pig," they chanted at her for hours on end. They wrote "Fat Pig" on the walls of her room, and on her headdress.

Early one morning the women were told they were to be expelled from China, and were ordered to pack one suitcase of belongings each. Although they had all invested many years of their lives in China, it was an immense relief to know they would not be executed or imprisoned, but would soon be home with their families. That afternoon, the Red Guards picked on the nuns yet again. They were made to run up and down the stairs while their tormentors beat their feet and legs with bamboo canes. This continued until all the sisters collapsed from exhaustion.

The eight foreign nuns were taken to the Beijing train station, where people kicked and struck them as they made their way onto the crowded train. They faced a daunting 40-hour journey to the southern city of Guangzhou, followed by another three hours to the border town of Shenzhen, and hopefully, freedom across the Lowu bridge into Hong Kong. A large team of Red Guards accompanied them on the trip. They continued to mock and insult the elderly women, seeing it as their job to make the journey as unpleasant as possible. The sisters were not allowed to speak to each other, while at the many stops along the way mobs of Red Guards assembled on the platforms at the stations where the train stopped. They pressed their fierce faces up against the windows, shouting anti-imperialist slogans and making threatening gestures. For 1,500 miles the gentle Christian women were bombarded with these young faces distorted by hatred and young fists clenched in rage.

At the same time that Molly O'Sullivan and her colleagues were walking through their "valley of the shadow of death", some journalists picked up on the incident. As the train slowly made its way southward, the story of these eight nuns became front page news around the world, and was the lead item on radio broadcasts.

On the morning of 30 August 1966, Molly looked sickly pale. Her body and mind were broken from the lack of sleep and punishment of the previous week. The train arrived in Guangzhou at 2 p.m. on Tuesday. By the time they had to board the train to the border the next day, Molly had grown seriously ill, and had a fever of 40.5° C (105° F). As the train approached the railway bridge between Shenzhen and Hong

Kong she was barely conscious. The bridge at Lowu marked the boundary between Communist China and British Hong Kong. In later years this same place came to be well known to thousands of Christians from around the world as the main entry point for carrying Bibles into China. The bridge was about 200 metres long and was considered a "no man's land" between the two countries. The Chinese guards would never venture past their side of the bridge, and the British soldiers also never ventured too far, lest they be shot at.

On the Hong Kong side dozens of priests, nuns, policemen, medics, reporters and cameramen waited, having presumed correctly that the eight women would arrive on that particular train from Guangzhou. The train slowed down and stopped on the Chinese side of the bridge. After a pause, the onlookers on the Hong Kong side saw eight nuns get off the train. They were carrying suitcases in their hands. The Red Guards started chanting slogans and waving their fists at the sisters.

The nuns started to walk from the train but almost at once one of them collapsed and lay motionless on the ground. Some of the others tried to help her but were prevented by the Red Guards. They were forced to stand in line while the shouting and insults continued.

The sisters started to walk slowly towards the bridge. They tried to help the nun who had fallen but she appeared too heavy for the others to carry. The people on the Hong Kong side could only look on helplessly while the nuns appealed for someone to help. A few Chinese soldiers lifted the prostrate woman and threw her facedown into a baggage trolley. The other nuns managed to push the cart, with difficulty, across the bridge.

Cameras clicked and journalists called out questions, while fellow Christians welcomed the weary travellers to Hong Kong. An ambulance was called for and soon arrived,

Molly O'Sullivan being wheeled across the border
into Hong Kong on a baggage trolley.
She died a few hours later.

and Molly O'Sullivan was rushed off to St Teresa's Hospital. She was conscious, but gravely ill. Her condition seemed to stabilize and the doctors were not overly concerned, but during the night her temperature suddenly rose. Nothing the doctors did could lower her temperature. At 6:45 a.m. on 1 September 1966, Molly O'Sullivan passed into her eternal rest.

When news and photographs of Molly's death were published around the world there was anger and outrage. The reaction was particularly strong in Ireland. A special flight carrying the body of Molly O'Sullivan arrived at Cork Airport on 29 September. Her grieving 84-year-old mother was among the waiting throng. She had never imagined she would outlive her beloved daughter. The whole country seemed to stop in honour of this jovial, kind-hearted nun who had died for the cause of Christ in China. Hundreds of people lined the streets as the funeral procession made its way from Ballyphehane to the city hall.

Molly O'Sullivan's body lay in state that night at St Patrick's Cathedral, the church where she had been baptized many years before. She was finally buried at Loughglynn, where she had grown up. All along the 180-mile (290-kilometre) journey to County Cork people stood to honour the fallen sister.

It must have been a strange sight for Molly, looking down from heaven, as her home nation honoured her with an outpouring of emotion. Throughout her whole life she had been an unassuming, unpretentious woman who never sought attention for herself. Yet God had chosen to honour his maidservant in such a way. Perhaps Molly's familiar loud and joyful laugh rang out across heaven, for she was in a place prepared by Jesus, a place with no more pain, no more suffering, and no more insults.

Little is known about what happened to the dozens of Chinese nuns from the Sacred Heart school and convent who were arrested in 1966. Most of them were sentenced to 20 years in prison, but only one was ever located again. The rest simply disappeared. No doubt many of them joined Molly O'Sullivan as martyrs for Jesus Christ.

CHAPTER 50

WATCHMAN NEE

Watchman Nee

Thousands of Chinese Christians have been slain throughout the centuries, but perhaps none so well known as Watchman Nee (Ni Tuosheng in Chinese).

Watchman Nee was born in 1903 at Fuzhou, Fujian Province. His God-fearing Christian parents dedicated him as a baby boy for the glory of Jesus Christ and the advancement of the kingdom of God in China. As a youngster, Nee was extremely intelligent. At Bible school in Shanghai one of his teachers remarked that he never saw Nee take notes, because he was able to retain everything he read or heard. He was also known to read through the New Testament at least once a month. A visiting missionary commented, "Some of these dear brethren are very sincere and thirsting for truth. Watchman Nee is undoubtedly the outstanding man among them. He is far beyond all the rest. He has had a good education and is possessed of marked ability. He is a hard worker and reads much."

In 1922, at the age of 19, Nee started preaching in his home city. By 1928 he rented a property in Shanghai and held services there, having rejected standard missionary practices as unbiblical and ineffective. The congregation came to be known as The Little Flock. It grew into a nationwide movement, which by 1949 had over 70,000 members in 500 assemblies.

In June 1928 Nee completed the final chapters of *The Spiritual Man* – the only book he ever wrote. The rest of his many publications were transcriptions of his preaching and teaching. Watchman Nee's ministry was far from being smooth-sailing. He faced constant criticism from other church leaders over a number of controversial issues. One of them came from Nee's conviction that each locality should have only one church identity, and that numerous denominations and divisions were blights on the unity commanded by Christ. Existing church leaders and missionaries assumed Nee was arrogantly advocating The Little Flock churches as the only true congregations in each location.

Watchman Nee was ministering in Hong Kong when the

Communist threat overpowered China. The believers there encouraged him not to return to China, but to continue his ministry in Southeast Asia. After much thought and prayer, Nee decided to return to China and sacrifice everything for the Lord's work there. He explained, "If a mother discovered that her house was on fire, and she herself was outside the house doing the laundry, what would she do? Although she realized the danger, would she not rush into the house? Although I know that my return is fraught with dangers, I know that many brothers and sisters are still inside. How can I not return?"

The danger was not long in coming. In 1951 *Tianfeng* launched a sinister campaign against Watchman Nee and The Little Flock. Disgruntled former members were interviewed, and all kinds of accusations were levelled against Nee. *Tianfeng* was, and still is, the official mouthpiece of the Three-Self Patriotic Movement in China. Watchman Nee was one of the first in a long line of house church leaders slandered and attacked by the magazine. It was a sure sign that the authorities planned to arrest him. In 1952 newspapers published cartoons mocking and slandering Nee and depicting him as a devious, money-hungry pervert. His stubborn faith had infuriated the government, and it was obvious they would stop at nothing to silence him.

Watchman Nee was arrested in the northeast city of Harbin on 10 April 1952, and was charged as a "lawless capitalist tiger". He was handed a huge fine, which he couldn't pay. Nee was sent to prison and his Bible was confiscated. Little is known of his experiences in prison between 1952 and his trial in 1956. It is believed he was offered freedom on numerous occasions if he would agree to lead a government-sanctioned Three-Self church. He refused.

On 30 January 1956 a large crowd of 2,500 people attended an accusation meeting in Shanghai. All of the city's pastors were required to attend, and many of Nee's former church members were also present. Numerous false charges were laid against Nee. No doubt the ones that hurt the most were from former leaders of The Little Flock who had gone over to the Three-Self Church. In June 1956 Nee was formally excommunicated from his own church, which had by then been almost completely infiltrated by the Communists at the leadership level. He was found guilty of all charges and sentenced to fifteen years' imprisonment.

Watchman Nee

Watchman Nee was sent to Shanghai First Municipal Prison and placed in a tiny cell just longer than the length of his body. He was allowed to send and receive one letter per month. In 1957 his *Normal Christian Life* book was published, being a collection of sermons gathered over the years of his ministry. The book became a bestseller, blessing millions of Christians around the world. Unbeknown to Nee at the time, he had become like the apostle Paul, his message being widely read while he was behind bars. In total more than 50 books have been written about Watchman Nee. Two titles have sold more than a million copies each.

By 1962 other prisoners reported that Nee had become frail and weighed less than 45 kilograms (100 pounds). He was diagnosed with coronary ischaemia. In the summer of 1971, Nee's beloved wife Charity had a heavy fall, fracturing several ribs and suffering a slight stroke. Her condition quickly deteriorated and she died a few days later. Nee was calm when told the news. Charity had walked through many storms with her husband, and had been arrested and severely tortured in 1966.

Watchman Nee completed 20 years in prison on 12 April 1972. His release date passed, but China was in the throes of the Cultural Revolution and there was no way such a hated man as Watchman Nee would be allowed to re-enter society. Despite being in very poor health he was transferred to a dreaded prison labour camp in Anhui Province, which was to become his final home on this earth. Nee was suffering from angina pectora and was growing weaker by the day. He wrote to his sister in Beijing, explaining that even though his health was poor, "the inward joy surpasses everything". In another letter he wrote, "I deeply long to return to my own relatives and be with them, just as a falling leaf returns to its roots. I am seeing a final resting place."

A short time later, on 30 May, the man of God was granted his desire to be with Christ. Earlier that day the prison authorities finally realized Watchman Nee's heart condition was in urgent need of medical attention. He was placed on a tractor and taken to the prison hospital. The journey on the rough and bumpy mountain track was more than Nee's emaciated body could handle, and he died en route.

There was no official notification of Nee's death. The

prison authorities took his body and cremated it. Even in death the authorities attacked Nee. Rumours were circulated by the Chinese government and Three-Self Church, claiming that Watchman Nee had renounced his faith in prison. This lie was dispelled after his niece collected her uncle's few belongings after his death. She found a note under his pillow, which read: "Christ is the Son of God. He died as the Redeemer for the sins of humankind, and was raised up from the dead after three days. This is the most important fact in the world. I shall die believing in Christ. Watchman Nee."

CHAPTER 51 OLD TACTICS IN
NEW CHINA

House church Christians in Henan Province boldly preach the gospel
in the 1980s at a funeral of one of their members.

In the early 1980s a wave of serious crime swept across China. Rape, murder, kidnappings and extortion were among the many ills plaguing society. The government responded with a huge nationwide campaign to weed out "undesirable elements". In 1983 alone more than one million people were arrested and at least 10,000 executions took place throughout the country. Many Christians were caught up in the crackdown. Their refusal to register their congregations with the government-approved Three-Self Church resulted in their being considered criminals. Many house church Christians died in 1983, while thousands more managed to escape the persecution by hiding or fleeing to other parts of China.

Brother Hua of Hunan Province was a faithful servant of God who had established more than 50 house churches. His bold stand for Christ not only attracted the attention of the authorities but also the scorn of his own family members, who did not understand his zeal for the gospel. One night in late 1983, policemen arrived and took him away. Hua was brutally beaten to death inside the police cell. Several days later the police delivered a box of ashes to his family. It was all that remained of Hua.

Another house church pastor paid the ultimate price for his faith. He was caught by the police and tortured mercilessly in a bid to make him denounce his faith. When this failed the officers became so angry they brought in a coffin and placed the preacher inside it. They told him to either deny Christ or be buried alive. He replied, "I will never deny my Lord." They nailed the coffin shut and waited for a while, thinking the pastor would plead for his life. No sound was heard. After more threats went unanswered, the enraged men buried him alive.

Another story is told of a beloved Christian doctor who refused to say that "Chairman Mao is greater than Christ". He was beaten and left for dead on the hospital floor. A few days later the police returned to see if he had changed. The doctor declared, "My Christ is the Lord of Lords and King of Kings. He has been given a name above all names in heaven, on earth, and under the earth." The doctor's boldness infuriated his persecutors and they decided to settle the issue once and for all. They returned several days later, stripped him naked, and made him stand on a narrow bench less than six inches wide. They laughed at him but the good doctor stood still, focusing his thoughts on the Bible while quietly quoting passages of Scripture about those who had endured persecution for the faith. Hours passed, and the doctor remained in the same position without moving. After ten hours people started to realize something strange was taking place. It was a great testimony to the power of God. The Red Guards stormed out, threatening that the doctor's time would soon come. A week later they dragged him from his surgery and hanged him. As he died he told his persecutors, "My heart is melting for you."

Several well-known Catholic leaders were martyred during the 1983 crackdown. All of them had spent many years in prison for their faith. One of them was the 70-year-old Jesuit Francis Zhu Shude, who was first arrested in 1953. Five of his brothers, four of whom were Catholic priests, were also arrested. For seven years Zhu was held without trial or charge, until finally in March 1960 a formal sentence of 20 years' imprisonment was handed down, backdated to the time of his arrest. Zhu was completely baffled as to what crime he had committed. He was known as a man of iron will and unbending principle. Once, during his long prison sentence in Anhui Province, the authorities urged him to admit he had made mistakes and that he would reform himself. In response, Zhu assured his captors that he had nothing to be sorry for, and added that he would continue to baptize any prisoners who came to faith in Christ!

In 1973 his prison sentence concluded, but the authorities decided Francis Zhu Shude had not reformed, so even though he was technically free he was not allowed to return home, but was forced to remain working at the labour camp. Finally, in 1979, Zhu returned to Shanghai, where he spent most of his time writing spiritual articles for the edification of believers. An insight into Zhu's humble character can be gained from an account of the morning he returned to Shanghai after 26 years' imprisonment. His family were not notified of his release, so he made his own way home, arriving at five o'clock in the morning. Not wanting to wake his family, Francis squatted in the doorway, trying to keep warm in the

Francis Zhu Shude

chilly Shanghai winter. When one of his brothers opened the door on his way to work he found Francis still squatting on the ground. He went back and woke everybody up. Zhu's family said they would buy him a new overcoat, but he refused, saying he didn't want to be any trouble.

Seeing that the many years of incarceration had not dampened Zhu's religious fervour, the government again arrested him in November 1980 and sent the humble priest back to prison. Despite being in his late sixties, he was again subjected to much torture and mistreatment. In the summer of 1982 Zhu was formally sentenced to another twelve years in prison, which, if he had served them, would have meant almost 40 years of his life would have been spent in prison for the sake of the gospel. This never eventuated, however, as on 28 December 1983 Francis Zhu Shude passed from this life to the next, and into the sweet presence of the Lord whom he had steadfastly served his whole life.

The Youtong bloodbath

The tension and sharp division between Catholics belonging to state-sanctioned churches and the "underground" churches has occasionally spilled over into violence. One of the worst examples of this occurred in 1989 at Youtong village in Hebei Province. Youtong at the time had a population of 3,400, half of whom were Catholics. Of these, just 200 belonged to the Catholic Patriotic Association and the remaining 1,500 were underground believers. For some time the latter had pleaded with the government to let them build a church to worship in, but their request fell on deaf ears. They subsequently erected a large tent in the village and used it for their services. In the month before the bloodbath, Public Security officers came to Youtong and ordered the people to stop praying, and to dismantle the tent. The believers respectfully declined, citing the freedom of religion guaranteed in the Chinese constitution.

At about eight o'clock in the morning of 18 April the government launched a massive, unexpected attack on the Catholics of Youtong. Approximately 5,000 police and armed militia arrived in several hundred trucks and surrounded the entire village. They demolished the temporary church and began beating Christians with their batons. Several dozen women who were praying in the church were dragged out. Six elderly women were knocked unconscious.

Later in the day a large number of armed police wearing steel helmets and bulletproof vests arrived. They viciously attacked the believers with electric batons, clubs and bricks. Some Christians barricaded themselves inside a house. They were beaten until their whole bodies were covered with wounds. By the time the chaos subsided more than 100 people were injured, 60 of them severely. Twenty people lay unconscious. More than 30 believers were arrested and carried off for questioning and more brutal treatment.

The government originally tried to whitewash the incident, claiming nobody had been injured and that the police had operated lawfully against the "illegal occupation" of a school campus. It was later revealed that three Christians had been killed in the Youtong bloodbath, and more than 300 injured including a nun who had her eyes knocked out after being beaten in the face. Two of the martyrs were Pei Guoxin and Dong Zhouxiao, both of whom were beaten to death in detention.

The carnage continues

The 90-year-old Catholic priest Philip Wang Ziyang died on 31 January 1990 at a labour camp in Shandong Province. Wang had been in prison since the 1950s – almost 40 years in total. He had been offered a chance of release in 1978, but chose to remain in prison because he could not accept the terms the government offered in exchange for his freedom.

Extraordinarily, the Communist authorities did not confine their persecution of Christians just to unregistered believers. In September 1991 a massive persecution against a government-sanctioned Three-Self church in Datong, Shanxi Province, resulted in the death of a Christian woman. Approximately 300 police surrounded the church while a worship service was in progress. They ordered the Christians to leave, dragged out those who refused, and then levelled the building with bulldozers. One elderly woman was so frightened that she suffered a heart attack and died the following day.

In the early 1990s a number of long-suffering Christians died in prison. Among them was the underground Catholic bishop of Baoding, Paul Shi Chunjie, who had spent 28 of his last 34 years in prison. When Shi was last arrested in 1990 he was blind in both eyes. No news was heard about him until November 1991, when the police returned the bishop's bruised corpse and refused to reveal the cause of death. Catholics were sternly forbidden to attend his funeral, but more than 1,000 people turned up anyway to pay their respects.

Another bishop, Joseph Fan Xueyan, was a strong opponent of the government-sanctioned church from the time of its inception until the day he died. For his beliefs he spent 21 years in prison, being released in 1979. He immediately

Joseph Fan Xueyan

recommenced his work for God, which led to his re-arrest in 1982. This time he spent five years in prison, his sentenced shortened due to widespread diplomatic protest at his treatment, but he remained under house arrest. The police kept a close eye on all his visitors in an attempt to arrest other underground Catholic leaders. Fan was taken away by the police in 1990 and died in 1992 after a total of 34 years in prison or under house arrest. The government claimed the bishop had died from pneumonia, but wounds and scars were found on his face and body.

Fan's funeral was heavily guarded, but such was the impact of this man's life that 30,000 Catholics flocked to the service from many areas. Almost a decade after Joseph Fan Xueyan was placed in the grave his legacy was still upsetting the government. They dug up his remains and cleared the gravesite to prevent people visiting it. Fan had been a thorn in the side of the Communist authorities his whole life, and now even in death they had their hands full trying to prevent the impact of his life of courage, unbending principle and uncompromising faith.

In recent decades not all martyrdoms of house church Christians in China have been at the hands of the Communist authorities. Starting in the mid-1980s, the house churches from eastern and central parts of China have sent hundreds of evangelists to the far-flung minority areas of China, including the Islamic northwest and the Tibetan Plateau. There they have sometimes met with violent opposition from the people they have tried to reach with the gospel. At least five evangelists have been murdered by Tibetan Buddhist monks.

In 1999 one preacher experienced a remarkable escape after he was seized by Buddhist monks in Tibet, put inside the wet skin of a dead yak, and placed on a rock. The yak skin was then tightly stitched together, making escape impossible. As the moist yak skin contracts the victim trapped inside is literally squeezed to death. On this occasion however, vultures sensed the evangelist was about to perish and swooped down on the yak carcass. They pecked at it, trying to break the skin, but instead only succeeded in loosening the stitching, allowing the evangelist to escape unharmed!

CHAPTER 52

LILIES AMONG THORNS

House church Christians in Henan Province boldly commemorating the death of one of their members despite government warnings not to gather

An act of mercy ended up costing one Christian family dearly during the 1983 nationwide crackdown against crime and religion. The Shi family lived at Zunzhuang village in Henan Province. Shi Gushen and his wife Lishi had raised three sons and two daughters. A few relatives also lived in the Shi household, making eleven people in total. One of them was the Shis' daughter-in-law, Meiying.

Shi Lishi, the mother, fell seriously ill in 1976. The doctors were unable to treat her condition and discharged her as a hopeless case. Her elderly grandmother, who had followed the Lord for many years, told the Shi family they should believe in the Lord Jesus. They did, and Lishi was soon healed of her ailment. In time they established a house church in their village.

In the summer of 1983, Meichun (the older sister of Meiying) became very sick. Doctors diagnosed a terminal illness and said there was nothing they could do. They encouraged Meichun to go home, put her affairs in order, and prepare to die. Instead, she went to her sister Meiying's house and asked the Shi family to pray for her. Over the next several days Meichun's condition fluctuated between satisfactory and poor. Just as she prepared to return home she suddenly died. In China, when a person dies while they are guests in someone else's house, the host family is often considered legally responsible. Because they were widely known for operating an illegal house church, the Shi family were worried the authorities might use the death as an excuse to persecute them. The Shis' second son, Wuming, went to the local police station and reported the death. The other family members stayed at home and packed their bags in expectation of being arrested. They prayed fervently, committing their lives into the hands of God. Several Public Security Bureau officers came to the Shi home and arrested all except the youngest children.

The family of the dead woman filed an official charge in the court, listing Shi Lishi and her son, Shi Wuting, as co-murderers. A remarkable scene unfolded at the packed courtroom the next day. Shi Lishi was on trial first. She told the truth about the dead woman's terminal illness and how her family had only tried to pray for her. The incensed judge instructed the guards to kick Lishi to the ground. They then beat her with batons until she passed out. A bucket of cold water was thrown on Lishi to revive her, but she still refused to confess to a crime she hadn't committed. The infuriated judge sent her back to the prison cell. On the way, the bloodied and bruised woman passed some of her crying children. She whispered to them, "Children, remain strong. We are considered worthy to suffer reproach for the Lord."

Next it was Shi Wuting's turn to be interrogated, followed

by Wuming. The two brothers were severely beaten by the guards so that when they returned to the cell they were barely recognizable beneath a mass of bruises and bloody wounds. Then came the testimony of three of the children, but the judge was left dumbfounded and amazed as each member of the Shi family claimed responsibility for Meichun's death. He had never seen anything like it in his many years presiding over criminal cases. On all other occasions accused murderers would do everything they could to deny guilt, but here each witness had personally claimed responsibility. Such was the love this family had for God and for one another! They preferred to take the punishment upon themselves than to see another family member suffer for a crime they hadn't committed.

Finally 16-year-old Shi Xiaoxiu was brought in. The judge was sure he would be able to make this skinny girl reveal who had committed the murder, so he spoke to her in a nice manner. Xiaoxiu calmly denied any laws had been broken, and told the judge that if anyone was held responsible it should be herself and her little sister, for they had prayed for Meichun more than anyone else! The judge angrily struck the bench and shouted, "You have the nerve! You are so young and yet you dare to deceive the People's government. Little child, I promise you there is no heaven for you here. If you continue to be stubborn and resist I will sentence you to prison. Your future will be finished! Don't think this is a game."

Maintaining her composure, Xiaoxiu replied, "My future is not determined by this world but by heaven. Since I have fallen into your hands I have no plans to return home. My family is prepared to finish the course our Lord Jesus has determined for us."

The Shi family was held in prison while the judge pondered the verdict. Although she had done nothing wrong, some of the cruellest punishment was meted out to Shi

Meizhen, the 24-year-old daughter. She was engaged to a primary school teacher, but her fiancé called the wedding off after her arrest. The prison guards were especially pitiless to her, beating her continually in a bid to extract a false confession.

The public sentencing of the Shi family was set for the morning of 30 August 1983. A theatre was used for the spectacle. The whole community was present, and not a single seat was left empty. The assembled crowd gasped and shrieked as Shi Lishi (the mother) and Shi Wuting (the oldest son) were sentenced to death. Meiying, the sister of the deceased woman, was sentenced to life in prison for her part in the "murder", while the bold Meizhen received a sentence of fifteen years. The youngest son, Shi Wuhao, was given ten years, Shi Wuming four years, while the 16-year-old Xiaoxiu was sent to prison for two years, her only "crime" being to have the courage to tell the truth in court. The father of the family, Shi Gushen, and his brother Shi Guzhen were imprisoned for two months each.

All of a sudden a loud thud was heard as someone fell to the floor of the courtroom, followed by loud wailing. "Daughters, I have done you harm!" wailed Meiying's mother. The grieving mother of the deceased girl had intended to use her bitterness to wreak vengeance on the Shi family, but she had never imagined that her own daughter would be punished so severely, by being sentenced to life in prison. She knew she would never see her again.

When the condemned Shi Wuting passed his wife in the hallway of the prison, the handcuffed and bruised 35-year-old told her, "Meiying, my beloved wife, why are you crying? How can I not drink the cup that the Lord has given me? Don't you realize that we live for the Lord, and if we die, we die for the Lord? Therefore, whether we live or die we are the Lord's! Beloved Meiying, it is only that I will be one step ahead of you.

Before too long, we will be together again, never to be apart. Don't be sad. Be strong and courageous. Whatever happens, you must live fully for the Lord. Don't waste any time."

For the last two weeks of her life, Meiying shared the same cell as her mother-in-law. One night they both dreamed that they saw themselves dressed in white robes and flying through the clouds to heaven! Then they saw the Lord Jesus. His hands were stretched out to receive them. With great emotion they went towards him, and he stretched out scarred hands to wipe the tears from their eyes.

On 14 September 1983 Shi Lishi and Shi Wuting were taken to an execution ground at a place known as Frog Mountain. Wuting briefly saw his wife, and said, "Meiying, I will go first. I will wait for you in Father's house. Goodbye!" Both of the condemned Christians were perfectly calm and smiled to their friends and relatives. There was no fear. The house church historian Danyun recalled the moment when the mother and son left this world for their heavenly reward:

> Mrs. Shi turned towards the soldier at her side and smilingly asked him, "Can I be allowed to pray?" The soldier nodded his silent approval. Mother and son knelt down, lifted up their heads heavenwards and prayed to the Saviour who created heaven and earth: "We ask you to forgive our country and our people for the sin of persecuting us. Save our country and the people. Forgive the sins of those who harmed us. Lord, we ask you to receive our spirits."
>
> Bang! Bang!
>
> Blood spurted out of Mother's head and her soul entered Paradise. Wuting, however, was not yet dead. He turned to look at the soldiers behind him and saw they were so frozen with fear they could not fire a second time. But two other soldiers raised their pistols and fired at Wuting. He slumped over, his brains and blood splattered all over the ground. Suddenly, there was a heavy downpour, with thunder and lightning flashing. But all

the rain could not wash away the blood of the innocent that was
spilled there on the execution ground.

When the surviving family members collected the two martyrs' bodies for burial they found a note in Wuting's coat
pocket. It said: "It is now finished. Do not be sorrowful for me.
I am only going to that place before you. Love the Lord fervently and hold steadfast to his Word. Later, you will also go
to the Heavenly Father and meet me. He that endures to the
end shall be saved. For my funeral, make it very simple. Take
care of my two children and let them know that I died for the
Lord."

CHAPTER 53

HOUSE CHURCH MARTYRS OF THE 1990S

By the start of the 1990s China was changing at an astonishing rate, as the world's most populated nation opened up and embraced the rest of the world. Staggering economic growth brought financial relief to many, and a flood of overseas Christians entered China, sharing their faith in a myriad of ways. Many foreigners have proclaimed that China is now an open country with religious freedom, but this has not been the experience of the house churches in many parts of China, who continue to be persecuted, harassed and imprisoned for their belief that Jesus Christ, and not the Chinese government, is the Head of the church. Throughout the 1990s a number of house church Christians paid for their faith with the ultimate sacrifice – their lives.

Cui Chaoshu

Huize County is located in the mountainous Yunnan Province. When the government's religious policy appeared to relax, many Christians who had been worshipping secretly in house meetings decided to apply for registration so that they could worship legally. In 1992 an evangelist named Cui Chaoshu was involved with one such church in Huize. The local authorities, however, refused to consider the application.

In the previous decade more than 70 Christians in Huize had been fined and imprisoned by the corrupt local police. Despite the extreme provocations, believers continued to meet together, and with God's blessing their churches continued to grow. In April 1992 Cui Chaoshu was kidnapped during a meeting and pounded to death with a thick stick.

The brutal officials at Huize were not deterred by the murder of Cui. They posted notices around the countryside offering rewards for the capture, dead or alive, of two church leaders. For Pastor Wang Jiashui they announced: "Alive: 300 Yuan; Dead: 400 Yuan". And for evangelist He Chengzhou: "Alive: 150 Yuan; Dead: 200 Yuan".

Lai Manping

The bruised and battered body of Lai Manping, spitefully beaten to death by China's Public Security Bureau

Lai Manping was a 22-year-old farmer and house church Christian from southern Shaanxi Province. During a house church meeting on 27 March 1993, eight or nine Public Security officers appeared and started to beat the gathered Christians wildly with their batons. Five visiting evangelists, including Lai, were stripped naked from the waist down. The 26 other believers in the meeting were forced to beat these brethren 100 times with bamboo rods. Failure to comply resulted in a savage pounding from the officers. The preachers were beaten until they were totally covered with blood, with gaping wounds and injuries all over their bodies. They were then hung up and beaten further with rods on their backs until they were barely alive.

The women were also barbarously treated. Two were thrown over a stove, and 59-kilogram (130-pound) millstones were placed on their backs while they were beaten and bashed. Their trousers were ripped open in front of the male Christians in order to humiliate them and beat their private parts. A twelve-year-old boy was struck on the head until blood flowed. The wicked men then threw him across the room like a stone.

At daybreak the three men and two women who had been beaten the most were instructed to walk from the remote village to the Public Security office 18 miles (30 kilometres) away. They crawled along the paths, taking a day and a half to reach their destination. The five Christians collapsed in agony on the floor, more dead than alive. The worst affected was Lai Manping. One of the other detainees testified that "his face was totally black and clots of blood came out when he relieved himself. His breath smelled terrible and everyone in the room could smell it. He had sustained severe internal injuries as a result of the beatings".

The guards were concerned that Lai might die in custody, so they called a doctor to examine him. She was horrified at his condition and offered only some external medicine before leaving. The guards thought it best if Lai died outside their office, so they made him leave. Mustering all the energy he could, Lai attempted to crawl back home. His parents heard of his release and rushed to get him. After an exhaustive search they finally found their beloved son dead on the side of the road.

The authorities denied any responsibility, saying Lai had died because of a pre-existing heart condition. An official autopsy was carried out which revealed the young Christian's heart had turned totally black. In the corrupted minds of the local officials this finding only confirmed their story.

Zheng Musheng

On a cold evening in January 1994, evangelist Zheng Musheng participated in a house church meeting with 20 others believers at his home in Hunan Province. At about ten o'clock officers from the Public Security Bureau suddenly arrived and broke the meeting up before the participants could flee. The Christians were detained and questioned, and most were released after paying fines. Zheng, being the leader, was not afforded the same opportunity. The police handcuffed him and took him to the local station, where they severely beat the evangelist and accused him of raping 70 women. They also raided his home and stole all the possessions they could carry off. The next day Zheng was denied medical treatment and subsequently died. His body was sent to the morgue, the officials claiming that he had been beaten to death by other prisoners.

Zheng Musheng's family were not notified of his death until eight days had passed. When they went to see the body they found deep rope burns on his ankles, which indicated that he had been suspended in the air and beaten, a technique commonly employed by the police in extracting confessions. There were also deep rope burns on his neck, and the area around his kidneys had numerous stab wounds made by a knife. The rest of his body had been beaten so badly that it had turned dark and the flesh was putrefying.

The authorities offered Zheng's family a considerable amount of money if they would sign a document granting them permission to cremate the body. Zheng's wife rejected the offer, so the authorities simply signed it themselves and had the body cremated to destroy the evidence of their crimes. Overwhelmed with the evil perpetrated against her husband, Zheng's wife Yin Dongxiu suffered a nervous breakdown.

Little Wang

In 1994 a small group of Christian men on Hainan Island travelled to a town to conduct evangelism in an unreached area primarily occupied by members of the Li minority group. As they began to share the gospel, an angry mob of Li people gathered and told the evangelists, "The spirits of the mountains rule our land. You Chinese dogs have only been here 500 years and you know nothing. You have stolen our land and now you wish to steal our gods as well. You will pay for this!"

The mob attacked the Christians with sticks and farm implements. A particularly fierce young man continued to beat one of the evangelists, Little Wang. When the crowd dispersed, Little Wang didn't move. He had paid the ultimate price. He and his family had only been believers for five months. After returning home battered and bruised, the other preachers broke the news of Little Wang's martyrdom to his wife Liang.

The following Sunday the church decided to send two of their members, Old Wang and Cai Wen, back to the same hostile Li village to evangelize again. There were no churches in the entire county. Someone had to take the message of salvation to them. The church grew strangely silent when Liang, the widow of Little Wang, requested to go too. The Christians worshipped for hours that day, praying fervently for the salvation of the Li people. The other house churches in the county were also notified to pray and fast for three days.

When the trio arrived at the Li village it was evening, and they slept beside a pig pen. The next morning they went to the market. Soon word spread of their return and a mob quickly formed again and a few people began to yell threats. Old Wang felt fear sweep over him. Suddenly Liang stepped to the front and spoke up: "I am the widow of the man you killed less than three weeks ago. My husband is not dead, however, because God had given him eternal life. Now he is living in paradise with Jesus. My husband came here to tell you how you could have that same eternal life. If he were here he would forgive you for what you did. I forgive you as well. I can forgive you because God has forgiven me. If you would like to hear more about this God then meet us under the big tree outside of town this evening." The crowd grew quiet and gradually broke up.

That day Old Wang instructed Liang as to what she should say. In the evening most of the villagers gathered under the big tree to listen to her, and many decided to follow Christ. Old Wang stayed behind to baptize them and to teach them how to serve God while Cai Wen accompanied Liang back home. Two months later Old Wang returned home with three men from the new Li church. During the Sunday worship they brought their greetings and expressed their appreciation. Then one of the men said, "I am the man who murdered Little Wang. The Lord has graciously forgiven me and I ask for your forgiveness as well. I, and our entire church, owe an eternal debt of gratitude to Little Wang and Liang for bringing us the message of life."

Martyrs of the Eastern Lightning cult

In the mid-1990s a new kind of persecution came to the Christians in China – one not born of a totalitarian government or angry mobs, but a much more insidious threat, from a wicked and dangerous cult called the Eastern Lightning whose members seek to destroy God's children through infiltration, deception, entrapment and violence. Each year the list of Christians who have been killed after becoming entangled with this cult grows.

The Eastern Lightning believe in a female Messiah, who they claim returned to the earth in 1990 and lives in Henan Province. She is waiting for the appointed time to reveal her true identity to the world. Like all cults, they reject the authority of the Bible and attack it at every opportunity. Starting in the mid-1990s the Eastern Lightning launched a new, openly aggressive strategy against China's Christians – especially those belonging to Protestant house church groups. Thousands of Christians across China have been beaten, tortured or poisoned by the Eastern Lightning. Many have had ears or noses chopped off, legs broken, and a host of other cruel mutilations. Hundreds of believers are still missing. Although most of those missing may have ended up changing sides and joining the cult, there are dozens of known deaths caused by the cult's brutality.

The Eastern Lightning continues to operate throughout China today, wreaking havoc among Christians in many areas. In recent years even Western missionaries have been targeted by the cult, with attractive young women sent to sexually entice and blackmail male missionaries. Awareness of the cult was raised when they kidnapped 33 top leaders of the China Gospel Fellowship house church network in 2002. Although all of the captives were finally released after several weeks, they were in such dire physical, emotional and mental condition that it took months of prayer before they started to feel restored to normality.

Zhang Xiuju

House church Christians in China are regularly beaten and kicked when the police break up meetings. Often electric cattle prods are used to stun believers with high volts of electricity. While they are being detained, females are sometimes sexually abused and on occasion even gang-raped by these monsters, who see the degrading of Christians as their right as policemen. The believers invariably do not fight back, as they realize lodging a complaint with another government office is an exercise in futility. As one woman expressed,

"There is no point complaining to one wicked authority about another. Nothing will happen. All crows are black." Instead, the Christians retain a calm peace and consistent witness that infuriates their captors even more. The black hearts of many officials cause them to react violently against the shining good deeds of the Christians, whose light cannot be snuffed out.

A 36-year-old Christian woman, Zhang Xiuju, was dragged out of her home by police in Xihua County, Henan Province, in the middle of the night on 25 May 1996. She died after being continually beaten throughout the night. Two days later the authorities returned Zhang's body to her parents' home, claiming she died after jumping out of a car while in police custody. Local Christians dismissed the claims, pointing out that the scars and rope marks around her wrists were consistent with torture techniques commonly employed by the authorities.

Liu Rongyao

Liu Rongyao is remembered as a faithful believer and zealous soul-winner among the house churches in Anhui Province, a part of China that has experienced great revival. The government has conducted much spiteful persecution and oppression of the believers in Anhui, yet the more it attacks the church, the more it grows.

Liu and six other house church elders came together for prayer and fellowship in 1997. The meeting was raided by Public Security officers, and all seven Christians were arrested and sent to a prison coalmine labour camp for three years. The seven men were treated with brutal disdain by the guards. One had coal forced down his throat, so that the lumps of coal could clearly be seen pressing against the walls of his stomach. This didn't stop him from preaching the gospel, however, and many prisoners found Christ. The guards then smashed his legs so that he was unable to walk, but still he continued to preach to everyone he came into contact with.

Local gang members, who had been called into the prison by the guards to brutalize the Christians, smashed Liu's head with rocks. The prison authorities saw he was badly injured but refused to provide any medical treatment. When it became apparent that he would die, Liu Rongyao's relatives were told he had sustained his injuries from smashing his own head against a wall. He was taken to a hospital where doctors found fragments of embedded rock in his brain. Miraculously, Liu's condition improved and he was able to walk and talk, but about 18 months later he was diagnosed with brain cancer in the place where his skull had been smashed. Liu Rongyao died in 1999, leaving his wife and children behind.

CHAPTER 54   MARTYRS OF THE NEW MILLENNIUM

At the dawn of the 21st century religious persecution in China had become something of an enigma. Tourists and investors who flocked to China's major cities and were presented with a pristine façade created by a government eager to impress the world. The country has been rewarded with international recognition, the hosting of the Olympic Games, and admission to the World Trade Organization. Away from the glistening lights and karaoke bars in the large cities and towns, however, torture and hellish persecution of Christians continues. Thousands of house church believers every year are mercilessly targeted by the Chinese authorities, usually in rural locations away from the attention of the rest of the world.

The new millennium commenced with more bitter acrimony between the Chinese Communists and the Vatican. On 1 October 2000 Pope John Paul II announced the names of 120 Chinese martyrs who had been accepted for canonization as saints. China strongly condemned the Vatican for what they saw as interference in their internal affairs. China not only denounced the Vatican's 120 martyrs, but also proceeded to rewrite history for a number of them, producing new "evidence" accusing them of the most vile sins and crimes, including sexual deviancy.

In 2000 a Protestant church pastor in Fujian Province, Lin Mingying, was beaten to death by Chinese police because of his refusal to join the registered church. When his family were allowed to see his body they found Lin's head had been smashed open and his whole body was covered in deep bruises. Local officials, concerned that news of their murder would reach the outside world, offered Lin's wife 20,000 Yuan (approximately US$3,000) in an attempt to cover up their crimes.

Wang Zuomei was the leader of 52 house churches comprising approximately 4,000 believers in Inner Mongolia. All the churches had been established in the previous three years, after people in the region heard the gospel from house church evangelists who had travelled to Inner Mongolia from Heilongjiang Province. The new believers' lives were changed by the powerful preaching they heard. The growing size and influence of the house churches soon came to the notice of the authorities and Wang was taken into the police station. The believers were concerned, but thought he would just be questioned and released. When he didn't return that day their concerns deepened. A few days after the arrest, the Public Security Bureau claimed that Wang had committed suicide while in custody, but everyone knew he had been tortured to death. The martyrdom added impetus to the churches. By February 2001 – just seven months after Wang's death – the 52 house churches had grown to 130.

Twenty-one-year-old Liu Haitou was arrested in September 2000 at Xiayi County, Henan Province, when the police raided a house church meeting he was attending. After being interrogated and held in prison, Liu was charged with participating in illegal religious activities. Facing daily beatings from the guards and weakened by the prison's poor hygiene and barely edible food, Liu's condition quickly worsened. He developed a high fever and started vomiting, partly because of an existing kidney condition.

Liu's parents were first notified of their son's arrest on 28 September, three and a half weeks after he was taken into custody. They were told to come down to the local police station

Liu Haitou

and pay 5,000 Yuan (US$600) for his release. Being a poor farm-
ing family they had no way to raise this sum, which was more
than one year's income for most families in this part of China.
Liu Haitou was harshly beaten with different kinds of sticks
and tools. Because of the brutality, his kidney disease relapsed,
causing him to faint several times. Liu and the other Christians

who had been imprisoned pleaded with the authorities to give him medical treatment, but their requests were ignored.

When they realized that Liu was dying, the prison officials tried to distance themselves from responsibility and signed his release papers. That night Liu died in the arms of his loving mother. His face radiated the peace and joy of the Lord as he told her, "Mum, I am very happy. I am fine. Mum, just persist in our faith and follow the Lord to the end. I am going now, mum. Pray for me." As he reclined in his mother's arms, his final word as he departed this world was a weak but clear "Amen".

Liu Haitou had been a Christian for only 18 months, yet had gained a reputation as someone who served God with all his heart. In prison he shared his meagre food rations with his fellow inmates, hoping they might see the goodness of Jesus through his life. Liu's commitment is summarized by this excerpt from a letter he wrote:

> By His unlimited great love, the Lord saved me. He leads me to eternal life and entitles me to become a son of God. How can I ignore His salvation and freely accept His grace without doing something for Him in return? More than 90% of people in China don't know God. My heart is broken. If the Lord is going to use me, I am ready to give my life to Him and start the journey of serving Him.

Yu Zhongju, a 27-year-old female Christian, was beaten to death in Hubei Province, even though she had not been the main target of the police. Yu happened to drop by while they were arresting Sister Ma Yuqin on 27 May 2001, and was herself taken in for questioning.

Ma and Yu were two of 63 members of the South China Church arrested at this time. They were beaten with clubs, electrocuted with electric batons, and had their skin burned with cigarettes. Interrogators stomped on the fingers of the male prisoners while they stripped off the clothing and sexually abused the females. Yu Zhongju was tortured to death. She left behind a five-year-old daughter.

Although no one was held accountable for Yu's death, God has recorded her martyrdom, and has already welcomed her into his warm embrace. The remorseless crackdown on the South China Church continues, and with Gong Shengliang and other leaders currently serving life sentences in dire prison cells, there are likely to be more martyrdoms resulting from the persecution of this house church network.

Matthias Pei Shangde, an underground Catholic bishop, served the Lord Jesus Christ for the duration of his 74 years. He was sent to prison soon after the Communists came to power in 1950 and was not released until 1980. In 1989 Pei's faithfulness was rewarded by the Catholic Church when Pope John Paul II secretly appointed him the bishop of Beijing. Because his appointment was not ordained by the government-sanctioned Catholic church, Pei immediately became a target for arrest. Many times during the 1990s he was detained and questioned. In April 2001 he was again arrested, but because he was already in his eighties they sentenced him to house arrest instead of prison, hoping to prevent him from travelling and overseeing the underground church. A few months after his arrest Pei suffered kidney failure and was hospitalized at Shengxing Hospital in Zhangjiakou, Hebei Province. He died there on Christmas Eve, aged 83, still under arrest some 52 years after his first incarceration.

In June 2004 Jiang Zongxiu travelled to Tongzi in Guizhou Province, where she went to the marketplace with her mother-in-law, Tan Dewei. Both women had been active in house church work for more than a decade. At the market they distributed Bibles and gospel tracts to some of the stall owners and shoppers. Some were appreciative, while others

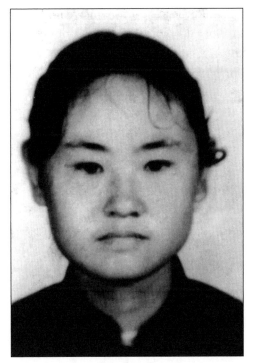

Jiang Zongxiu

reported their activities to the authorities. Public Security officers were dispatched to the market and arrested the Christian pair. They were handcuffed together and taken to the local detention centre for questioning.

Jiang and her mother-in-law were sentenced to fifteen days' imprisonment. The official police report listed the charge as "seriously disturbing the social order by distributing Christian literature to the masses in the market". Before they got the chance to commence their sentence, however, officers beat and kicked Jiang Zongxiu to death at around 2 p.m. on 18 June. The official reason for her death was given, ludicrously, as a "sudden disease". The authorities, no doubt afraid of the ramifications of murdering someone on such a minor charge, ordered Jiang's family to cremate the body immediately, and even sent an invoice demanding 100 Yuan (about US$12) per day for the preservation of the body at the funeral home.

CHAPTER 55   INTO THE FUTURE

Xu Shuangfu, the founder of the Three Grades of Servants Church,
was executed with two coworkers in November 2006

Almost from the first time the gospel reached China in 635, Christians have faced severe persecution and death as they have sought to lift up Jesus Christ in the world's most populous nation. Throughout the last thirteen centuries, countless thousands of followers of Christ have been massacred. Numerous times the church in China has proven the veracity of Jesus' warning to his disciples, "No servant is greater than his master. If they persecuted me, they will persecute you also" (John 15:20).

As long as Satan remains active on the earth the Bride of Christ will be buffeted and attacked by the devil and his agents. The style of persecution may change, but nothing is more certain than the fact that Christians in China will continue to lay down their lives as martyrs until the Lord Jesus returns.

Starting in the mid-1990s the Chinese government, concerned with creating a positive image around the world, adopted a new strategy for persecuting Christians. Realizing the international community would never tolerate open religious persecution, they have cunningly launched a new tactic of persecuting believers by claiming they belong to "evil cults" which break the law. Many of the house churches in China have subsequently been labelled "evil cults" by the government simply because of their refusal to register with the authorities. These include almost all the large house church networks based in Henan and Anhui provinces. To complicate matters, some of the groups the government has labelled "evil cults" are, in fact, cults and sects that deny the essential doctrines of biblical Christianity.

By classifying a church group as a cult, the government insidiously opened up a way to prosecute Christians for "breaking the law", rather than appearing to do so for strictly religious reasons. Western governments and human rights organizations are therefore largely silenced in their outcry against incidents of persecution, as often when they ask about

Gong Shengliang, the leader of the South China Church,
who is currently serving a life sentence in prison, and co-workers

a certain pastor who has been arrested they are told he was detained because he broke the law, and not because of his faith. This subtle manoeuvre has resulted in much confusion within the Chinese church and outside China, as believers disagree on which groups deserve to be outlawed as cults, and which are genuine followers of Christ who have been targeted by a hostile government bent on their destruction.

The Chinese government has also launched a concerted propaganda campaign, smilingly assuring the world that religious persecution is a thing of the past in China. They have managed to deceive many Western church leaders and high-profile Christian media figures. This glorious new "religious freedom" means little to the hundreds of Protestant and Catholic believers currently languishing in prisons throughout the country.

At the present time the leader of the South China Church, Gong Shengliang, rots in prison in Hubei Province, serving a life sentence for crimes he never committed. More than 700 members of his house church movement have been arrested and subjected to torture and abuse during the past several years. The Chinese authorities labelled the South China Church an "evil cult" before launching their vicious persecution. Some Chinese believers who investigated the church's doctrine and practices, however, have found its adherents to be orthodox Bible-believing Christians.

Another example is the *San Ban Puren*, or "Three Grades of Servants Church", established by Xu Shuangfu and believed to number between 500,000 and one million adherents nationwide. Xu was born in Henan Province in 1945. Having devoted his life to evangelism at the age of twelve, Xu was arrested on numerous occasions and spent three years in prison on six different occasions – a combined 18 years behind bars for his faith.

In June 2006, house church leaders Xu Shuangfu, Li Maoxing and Wang Jun were found guilty of involvement in the murders of 20 members of the Eastern Lightning cult and were sentenced to death. Three more, Zhang Min, Zhu Lixin and Ben Zhongjia were given suspended death sentences. Eleven more Christians received three- to fifteen-year prison sentences.

The police claimed Xu Shuangfu had admitted involvement in the crimes, but Xu's lawyers claimed he had been so brutally tortured while in custody that he had signed a confession under extreme duress in order to save his life. Xu testified in court that his interrogators had tied his fingers, toes and genitals with wire and then connected the wire to electricity. Xu told the court he was innocent of all charges and exhorted the people in attendance to follow Jesus Christ. Li Maoxing showed his wounded fingers to the court and said that the torturers had made him hang in the air wrapped in a wet blanket and then electrocuted him.

Just prior to this book going to press, the three leaders, Xu, Li, and Wang, were secretly executed in Heilongjiang Province on 24 November 2006. The first anyone knew about it was on November 28 when Li Maoxing's wife was asked to collect her husband's ashes at the court as soon as possible. Neither the families or the attorneys of the three martyrs were informed of the execution in advance.

It is apparent that after eight decades of bitter persecution, the Communists are still fearful of the role that Christians continue to have in Chinese society. Not only have they been unable to eradicate faith in Jesus as they believed they would, but the Church in China has grown at least twentyfold since 1949. Only heaven will tell the full extent of suffering and martyrdom that China's Christians have endured under the terror of Communist rule. All across China, the Communists' plans to destroy God's church have usually resulted in the opposite effect. An expert on the China church, the late Jonathan Chao, wrote,

> The Church in China has been transformed from a timid, "foreign-coloured", institutionalized church into a bold, indigenous, institutionless church, and it has been changed from a dependent "mission church" into an independent "missionary church". It is a Church that has gone through the "steps of the Cross", following the footsteps of her Lord: betrayal, trial, humiliation, abandonment, suffering, death, burial, resurrection and the gift of the Spirit of Pentecost.

Incredibly, in a way that only God can orchestrate, the decades of brutal persecution suffered by the Body of Christ in China has resulted in one of the most far-reaching and sustained revivals in the history of Christianity. Tens of millions of people have been swept into the kingdom of God since the 1970s.

The Chinese church has discovered that the road of the cross leads to the place of resurrection power.

*   *   *

Approximately 1,800 years ago the early church leader Tertullian boldly declared,

> Our sect will never die. The more it is smitten the more it grows, for every one who is moved by our patience to enquiry straightway becomes our follower. The more you mow us down, the more quickly we grow; the blood of Christians is seed. The blood of the martyrs is the seed of the church. Dying we conquer. The moment we are crushed, that moment we go forth victorious.

Satan, with the help of wicked and ignorant men, has tried repeatedly to destroy the advance of the gospel in China. But his efforts have only provided fuel to the flame of revival that has burned ever more brightly down through the centuries. The same thing has happened to God's people in China as happened to the children of Israel in Egypt. The Bible records, "The more they were oppressed, the more they multiplied and spread; so the Egyptians came to dread the Israelites" (Exodus 1:12).

Satan has never understood that persecuting God's people only results in the growth of the church. To kill the church is to give it new life, for the church is a living organism that *has* eternal life and can never be snuffed out. Indeed, this is the very same miscalculation the devil made by killing Jesus Christ. The Bible says, "None of the rulers of this age understood it, for if they had, they would not have crucified the Lord of glory" (1 Corinthians 2:8).

Today there are approximately 80 to 100 million Christians of all kinds in China. Many fellow believers around the world have wondered why the gospel has advanced so powerfully in China. Many wish to somehow duplicate the results without wanting to pay the same cost that the Chinese have paid. Resurrection is impossible unless there has first been a death. Jesus said, "I tell you the truth, unless a kernel of wheat falls to the ground and dies, it remains only a single seed. But if it dies, it produces many seeds. The man who loves his life will lose it, while the man who hates his life in this world will keep it for eternal life" (John 12:24–25).

In many areas of the world, Christians hear stories about persecution in countries like China and consider it abnormal. Could it be that according to Scripture, the Chinese experience is "normal", and our Christianity is abnormal? The Chinese believers have much in common with the New Testament church, of which it is written:

> Some faced jeers and flogging, while still others were chained and put in prison. They were stoned; they were sawn in two; they were put to death by the sword. They went about in sheepskins and goatskins, destitute, persecuted and mistreated – the world was not worthy of them. They wandered in deserts and mountains, and in caves and holes in the ground (Hebrews 11:36-38).

A major component in China's revival has undoubtedly been the persecution, hardship and cruel martyrdom that followers of Christ have been called to endure for many centuries. They have truly learned to die to self and to this world, and in so doing, Christ's resurrection power has touched and empowered them to see tremendous results for God's kingdom.

I hope you have been inspired in your walk with Jesus and empowered for action by the testimonies in this book. The blood of the martyrs has truly been the seed of the church in the world's most populated nation.

One day, at a time known only to the Father in Heaven, His children's suffering will come to an end and all wrongs will be avenged. Until that day, heaven's book of martyrs will continue to be written, and the list containing the names of tens of thousands of faithful followers of Christ who have sealed their commitment by laying down their lives in China will continue to grow.

"When he opened the fifth seal, I saw under the altar the souls of those who had been slain because of the word of God and the testimony they had maintained. They called out in a loud voice, 'How long, Sovereign Lord, holy and true, until you judge the inhabitants of the earth and avenge our blood?' Then each of them was given a white robe, and they were told to wait a little longer, until the number of their fellow servants and brothers who were to be killed as they had been was completed" (Revelation 6:9-11).

The author would like to thank the following individuals and organizations who kindly gave permission for us to use their images in this book.

Chinese Regional Bishops' Conference
65, 67, 69, 72, 92, 94, 95, 97, 173, 174, 175, 177, 179, 180, 186, 267, 270, 346

China Insight
101

Julian Hawken
117, 118, 122

David V. Plymire
336

The Voice of the Martyrs
402, 489

Asian Report
425

Revival Chinese Ministries International
456, 465

China Aid Association
485, 487

Paul Hattaway is a New Zealand-born missionary who has authored many books about the Church in Asia, including the best-selling The Heavenly Man, Back to Jerusalem, and Operation China. He is married to Joy, and they have two sons, Dalen and Taine. Hattaway is also director of Asia Harvest, an inter-denominational ministry which serves the Church in China and around Asia through various strategic initiatives, including Bible printing in China, and supporting the families of persecuted believers. To purchase more of Paul Hattaway's books or to receive the free Asia Harvest newsletter, go to www.asiaharvest.org, or write to the address below nearest you:

Asia Harvest
1903 60th Place, Suite M1204
Bradenton, FL 34203
UNITED STATES

Asia Harvest
c/o SALZ
Postfach 1144
D-72206 Altensteig
GERMANY

Asia Harvest
2 Kingswood Close
Lytham, FY8 4RE
ENGLAND

Asia Harvest
Clementi Central PO Box 119
SINGAPORE 911204

Asia Harvest
36 Nelson Street
Stepney, SA 5069
AUSTRALIA

Asia Harvest
PO Box 8036
Pejabat Pos Kelana Jaya
46780 Petaling Jaya
Selangor
MALAYSIA

Asia Harvest
PO Box 181
Te Anau 9640
NEW ZEALAND